Caring for Children in School-Age Programs

Volume II
A Competency-Based
Training Program

Derry G. Koralek
Roberta L. Newman
Laura J. Colker

TEACHING STRATEGIES INC.

Washington, DC

Updates to Module 1 (Safe), Module 2 (Healthy), and Bibliography © 1999

Updates to Bibliography, learning activities, and Module 13 (Professionalism) © 2000
Printed and bound in the United States.

Editor: Diane Trister Dodge
Layout Design: John Fay
Illustrations: Jennifer Barrett O'Connell
Cover Design: Margaret C. Pallas
Production: Chris Redwood

Published by:
Teaching Strategies, Inc.
P.O. Box 42243
Washington, DC 20015

4th Printing: 2000

Two Volume Set, ISBN: 1-879537-13-3
Volume II ISBN: 1-879537-15-X

Library of Congress Catalog Card Number: 95-060465

ACKNOWLEDGMENTS

Caring for Children in School-Age Programs is based on a set of training materials originally developed for the U.S. Army Child and Youth Services. It is the last in Teaching Strategies' series of competency-based training programs that includes: *Caring for Infants and Toddlers, Caring for Preschool Children,* and *Caring for Children in Family Child Care.* All of these materials are organized into 13 modules that address the competencies required to provide a quality program.

Many individuals contributed to the development of these training materials. M.-A. Lucas, Chief of Army Child and Youth Services, recognized the important role school-age programs play in the lives of children and initiated the development of this training. Dr. Victoria Moss, Program Manager, Supplemental Programs and Services, Department of Army, guided the development of the training modules and provided us with constructive and helpful suggestions that greatly improved the program. We are grateful to P. K. Tomlinson and Linda Harwanko, Education Program Specialists, Department of Army, who reviewed and gave extensive feedback on the modules. The following Service representatives also reviewed and provided input that enriched these training materials: Keith Painter, Recreation Specialist, Department of Army; Carolee Van Horn, Community Recreation Specialist, Department of Navy; Madeline Wagner, Communication Recreation Specialist, The Marine Corps; and Maryalice Howe, Child Development and Youth Specialist, Department of Air Force. Dr. Charles H. Flatter, Professor, Institute for Child Study, University of Maryland, provided us with initial guidance on the development of the modules.

Caring for Children in School-Age Programs was reviewed by Ellen Gannett, Associate Director, and Susan O'Connor, Research Associate, School-Age Child Care Project at the Center for Research on Women at Wellesley College. Their critique of each module and suggestions for enhancing the content were invaluable. Ellen and Susan also verified the linkages between this training program and the criteria outlined in *Advancing School-Age Child Care Quality.* We are indebted to each of them for taking a strong interest in this project and sharing their expertise so generously.

In 1999, we updated Modules 1 (Safe) and 2 (Healthy) to reflect current guidelines. We thank Karen Sokal-Gutierrez, M.D. for reviewing and revising these modules. We thank Caitlin Pike for updating the resources and she and Toni Bickart for editing the 1999 reprint.

In 2000, we again updated resource information, including web sites, and revised learning activities to incorporate the *National School-Age Care Alliance (NSACA) Standards for Quality School-Age Care.*

It is our hope that as school-age staff undertake this training program they will gain knowledge and develop new skills that will allow them to offer the highest quality of programming. We also hope this training will lead to greater understanding of how school-age programs encourage and support children's development, allow them to explore and build on their interests, and help them grow into competent, independent, and productive citizens.

Module 7:
CREATIVE

OVERVIEW

PROMOTING SCHOOL-AGE CHILDREN'S CREATIVITY INVOLVES:

- providing a rich and varied environment that invites exploration and experimentation;

- offering a variety of activities and experiences that promote self-expression; and

- interacting with children in ways that encourage and respect original ideas, thoughts, and expressions.

Children who are creative are willing to try new ways of doing things. They see more than one possibility in how to play a game or use an art material. They are curious about how things work and why things happen as they do. They are willing to take risks. When they try something new and it doesn't work, they learn from their mistakes, and try another approach.

The definitions of creativity are many and varied. Some say it is the process of creating, others say it is the product of creative efforts. According to Teresa Amabile, a social psychologist who has studied children's creativity, anything a child does or says can be considered creative if it meets two criteria. The first is **novelty**: it must be substantially different from—rather than an imitation or repetition of—something the child has seen or heard before. The second is **appropriateness**: it should be correct, useful toward achieving a goal, appealing, or meaningful to the child in some way.[1] Thus, the cook who follows a recipe exactly is not using creativity; the cook who experiments by adding new ingredients is.

There are many ways to define creativity.

In attempting to define creativity, it might be helpful to first consider what it is not, rather than what it is. Creativity is not the same as high intelligence. Many people of average intelligence are highly creative. Creativity is not the same as talent. Many talented people are skilled performers; however, they are not all creative. Creativity is not the same as being eccentric. Creative people often do things in different ways; however, this does not mean they are unbalanced or suffer from mental illness. People often equate creativity with high intelligence, talent, and eccentricity. Some creative people have these characteristics; however, many do not.

---

[1] Teresa Amabile, *Recognizing Children's Creativity* (NY: Crown Publishers, Inc., 1989), p. 25.

Children maintain creative behaviors when their creativity is supported and valued by adults.

Everyone is born with the ability to be creative. Some children are more creative than others and children use and express their creativity in different ways. When they enter the school-age years, most children are eager learners, naturally imaginative and creative. They learn by doing as they interact with people and things in their environment. Whether they maintain this ability depends, in part, on whether their creative behaviors are valued and encouraged by parents, teachers, and others. Some children remain highly creative even when their behavior is not reinforced. Their drive to be creative is far greater than their drive to conform to accepted norms.

School-age children use their skills and talents in creative ways.

School-age children can use all their skills—cognitive, language, physical, socio-emotional—in creative pursuits. In fact, almost everything they do involves creativity: they make up jokes, work on open-ended craft projects, plan and carry out their ideas for drawings, design and conduct experiments, and make up new rules for traditional games. They can be excellent problem solvers and often resolve their own disagreements. In addition, children in this age group may have special talents and interests they want to explore in creative ways.

The relationships between children and staff are the foundation for nurturing creativity. When children feel secure, they are likely to explore and express themselves. Staff support children's creativity by including a variety of interesting materials in the environment that encourage children to explore and experiment. They plan activities that provide opportunities for self-expression and support children's interest and involvement in activities they plan themselves. Finally, they demonstrate respect for children's original ideas, thoughts, and expressions.

Listed on the next page are examples of how school-age staff demonstrate their competence in promoting children's creativity.

Providing a Rich and Varied Environment That Invites Exploration and Experimentation

Provide open-ended materials with which children can do many things. "Francie, we've had these styrofoam squiggles all year, but you're the first one to think of using them to make jewelry."

Arrange the environment so children can spread out, explore, and be messy. "Kyle and Tim, your paper maché mountain is enormous. Would you like me to help you move it to the hobby area? There's plenty of room there for you to work."

Provide sufficient storage space for projects and creations that cannot be completed in one day. "Your display of rocks and shells is impressive. You can store it on the hobby shelf overnight; tomorrow, you can work on it again."

Allow creations to stay in place for several days so children can continue using them and possibly expand them. "We'll save the store you and André made so you can play in it tomorrow."

Provide sufficient time in the daily schedule for children to make plans and carry them out. "Carol and Mia spent every afternoon this week planning and rehearsing their gymnastics show."

Follow a daily schedule that includes long blocks of time when children are free to organize their own games and activities without adult involvement. "Ms. Harper, have you noticed the children playing 'space travelers?' Every day they gather props, head for the playground, and use the climber as a space ship."

Surround children with examples of creative work—reproductions of paintings and sculptures, award-winning children's literature, photographs of architectural treasures, biographies of inventors and scientists, a wide variety of music on tapes and CDs. "We just got a new biography of Buckminster Fuller, the man who invented the geodesic dome. He began his work in kindergarten when he made triangular structures using toothpicks and peas!"

Store materials and equipment where children can easily select, replace, and care for them without adult assistance. "There are lots of materials in the board and games area you can use to make up games. They're in the tote box on the shelf."

Offer materials that allow children to explore subjects and interests introduced at school or through experiences such as field trips. "Seth, you seemed to enjoy the presentation on meteorology. Would you like to do some research and find out how you can track rainfall here?"

Encourage children to express their ideas and feelings. "Thanks for your suggestion, Paula. I agree, it would be easier to keep the guinea pig cage clean if we had a screen bottom. Does anyone have an idea about how we could make one?"

Offer activities that introduce new ideas and allow children to develop and carry out their own plans. "Now that I've told you about Rube Goldberg, does anyone want to make their own labor-saving invention? There's a box of recycled 'junk' in the science and nature area you can use for your creations."

Offering a Variety of Activities and Experiences That Promote Self-Expression

Extend younger children's dramatic play. "I could really use a shave and a haircut. Do I need an appointment or is this a 'walk-in' hair salon?"

Introduce children to brainstorming so they can use it as a problem-solving tool. "Brainstorming is a way to think of new ideas. Each pair will have five minutes to write down all the possible uses for a paper towel they can think of. All ideas will be accepted—none are right or wrong. Tomorrow, we'll use brainstorming to think of a way to make space for our new aquarium."

Plan a variety of activities that introduce children to drama, dance, music, art, literature, film, and the many forms of visual art—for example, painting, drawing, sculpture. "Haiku is a form of Japanese poetry. Today we're going to read some examples. Maybe some of you will want to write your own haiku."

Help children develop specific skills they can use in their creative work. "Now that you've mastered the techniques for doing cross stitch, would you like to learn to design your own patterns?"

Respond to children's ideas for projects and activities. "That's a great idea! What materials will you need to turn the loft into a two-story restaurant?"

Avoid using coloring books, pre-packaged craft projects, and dittos. "The art shelf has lots of supplies—papers, markers, pens, crayons, paste, yarn, string, scissors, and collage items."

Interacting With Children in Ways That Encourage and Respect Original Ideas, Thoughts, and Expressions

Value the characteristics that make each child a unique individual. "Steven, I'm always interested in hearing your ideas. You have a special way of looking at things and lots of times your unusual solutions are the ones that work best."

Help children understand it takes hard work and practice to develop their talents. "Thank you for sharing your science fiction story with me. I enjoyed reading it. If you're interested, I have a few suggestions for expanding the plot."

Encourage children to take risks, learn from their mistakes, and try again. "Hannah took pictures of her friends from lots of different angles. Some of her pictures came out and some didn't. Next time she's going to experiment with different exposures."

Invite children to display or share the products of their creative work. "Camille, we've been admiring the weavings you made from vines and dried grass. Would you like to choose one we can hang on the wall?"

Call attention to sensory experiences. "How does it feel when the clay moves under your hands as the pottery wheel spins round and round? Is it a different feeling when you press down with your thumbs?"

Ask a variety of questions that encourage children to think about things in new ways. "What might life be like if we could fly?" "If you had a time machine would you go back in time or forward?"

Accept and value each child's unique creative expression. "Jamal, you've invented a lot of knots for your tie-dye project. I can't wait to see the designs they make on your shirt."

Model creativity by sharing your interests, taking risks, and solving problems. "I've been teaching myself carpentry. These are some pictures of a table I made."

Promoting School-Age Children's Creativity

In the following situations, school-age staff are promoting children's creativity. As you read, think about what the staff are doing and why. Then answer the questions that follow.

Providing a Rich and Varied Environment That Invites Exploration and Experimentation

Jessica and Cassandra are telling Ms. Andrews about some abandoned birds' nests they found on a recent hiking trip. They are impressed with how the birds made their nests by combining vines, twigs, and grasses with "manmade" items such as paper and bits of cloth. Ms. Andrews asks, "Would you like to weave like the birds?" Cassandra says, "That would be fun. Let's make something. I know where I can get some twigs and other stuff." Jessica replies, "I'll help, too. Where can we store our materials and work on our projects?" Ms. Andrews suggests the arts and crafts area. Several children overhear and ask if they can weave too. "Sure," says Jessica. "Let's make a list of the things we need."

During the next week the children collect items from nature—branches, seed pods, vines, dried weeds, and flowers—and a variety of scrap materials—string, buttons, plastic-covered wire, and yarn. By the end of the week, the collection is taking over the arts and crafts area. They decide they have enough!

Next, they sort the items using separate dishpans for each type of material. They place the dishpans on the shelves, display samples of the materials on the bulletin board, and set aside a table for weaving projects. Ms. Andrews suggests keeping "works in progress" on a shelf out of the way of the younger children who use the room during the school day. Over the next week, children explore and experiment as they weave baskets, wall hangings, jewelry, and even miniature hammocks.

1 . **How did Ms. Andrews involve the children in creating a rich and varied environment?**

_____

_____

_____

2 . **How do open-ended materials promote creativity?**

_____

_____

_____

Offering a Variety of Activities and Experiences That Promote Self-Expression

Last week Ms. Ramos overheard two sixth graders, Alex and Brianna, continuing a discussion begun in school about whether there could be life on other planets. Their conversation reminded her of a project from her own sixth grade science class—learning about conditions on other planets and making a "being" that could possibly live on one. She explained the project to Alex and Brianna and asked if they would like to help her plan a similar activity. Both children said, "Yes!"

Today, Ms. Ramos introduces the activity at a group meeting. She asks Alex and Brianna to share what they know about life on other planets. Next, the children look at books about other planets in our solar system. They ask lots of questions and share with each other what they find out through their explorations. Ms. Ramos brings out a box of recycled items and arts and crafts supplies. She suggests the children work in pairs or threes to create a being that could live on one of the planets they've learned about.

As the children work, Ms. Ramos asks thought-provoking questions. "Would a being from another planet need eyes and ears like humans do? Would it be a he, a she, or an it? Would it have legs? Would it move at all?" Denise responds, "Our being just looks like a weird human. We're going to start over." Some children finish their beings that afternoon, others want to continue working on them. Ms. Ramos shows them a place on the shelf where they can store their projects.

1. Why did Ms. Ramos plan this activity?

_____

_____

_____

2. What did Ms. Ramos do to encourage the children's creativity?

_____

_____

_____

Interacting With Children in Ways That Encourage and Respect Original Ideas, Thoughts, and Expressions

Mr. Ryan announces there will be a dodge ball game outdoors today. In the program, they use a Nerf ball to make the game safe. He overhears Ginny say to her friend Renée, "I hate that game. Once you're out there's nothing to do." Renée responds, "I hate it, too. I'm always out first." Mr. Ryan approaches the girls and asks them to tell him more about why they don't like dodge ball. After listening to their concerns he says, "Well, you have some good points. It's hard to get better at playing dodge ball if you have to leave the game as soon as you are hit. Do you have any ideas for making up a new kind of dodge ball that would be more fun to play?" Ginny quickly answers, "I do. We could play that you're only out until someone else gets 'Nerfed.' Then that person would come out and you'd get to go back in." Renée adds, "So you'd never be out of the game for more than a minute or two." Mr. Ryan compliments the girls on their new kind of dodge ball. He says, "Let's talk to the rest of the group about your idea."

1 . **How did Mr. Ryan interact with the children to encourage creative thinking?**

_____

_____

_____

2 . **How did Mr. Ryan demonstrate respect for the children's ideas?**

_____

_____

_____

Compare your answers with those on the answer sheet at the end of this module. If your answers are different, discuss them with your trainer. There can be more than one good answer.

Your Own Creativity

As adults, we sometimes confuse creativity with talent. Creative people are innovative and resourceful. They can take an idea, a plan, or an object and adapt it to make something new. Although some people are more creative than others, everyone has creative abilities they use on the job and at home. Artists, musicians, architects, and writers are all creative people—but so are cooks, secretaries, lawyers, plumbers, and school-age staff. You don't have to be able to paint a picture or write a book to be creative. Thinking of new ways to help children learn to negotiate, making up a song to sing on a field trip, or rearranging your space to create a cozy reading area are all examples of creativity.

We sometimes confuse creativity with talent.

Understanding your own creativity and how you approach problems and new situations will help you become sensitive to creativity in children. Recognizing how you feel when you are being creative will help you support children as they try out new ideas.

Think about the satisfaction you feel when you solve a problem while cooking, gardening, reading, talking with a friend, or planning new activities. That feeling is similar to the pride children feel when they have figured something out for themselves.

Here are some exercises you can do to help stimulate your own creative thinking.

How do you get to work each day? Can you think of an alternative route or mode of transportation to get to work?

_____

_____

_____

_____

Think of some unusual ways to use a common object—for example, an egg carton, a newspaper, a pencil, or a suitcase.

_____

_____

_____

_____

Think of three ways to make a sandwich without using bread.

_____

_____

_____

_____

Describe something you did with children that was very creative.

_____

_____

_____

_____

Describe something creative you did last week at home, in a relationship, at work, or anywhere else.

_____

_____

_____

_____

These questions or similar ones can help you think of new ways to approach a problem. They can also be useful in helping children develop their creativity. Supporting children's creativity is one of your major tasks—and one that gives much satisfaction in return, as you watch children gain in self-confidence and enthusiastically move out into the world.

When you have finished this overview section, you should complete the pre-training assessment. Refer to the glossary at the end of the module if you need definitions of the terms used.

PRE-TRAINING ASSESSMENT

Listed below are the skills school-age staff use to promote children's creativity. Think about whether you do these things regularly, sometimes, or not enough. Place a check in one of the boxes on the right for each skill listed. Then discuss your answers with your trainer.

Providing a Rich and Varied Environment That Invites Exploration and Experimentation	I Do This		
	Regularly	Sometimes	Not Enough
1. Providing open-ended materials with which children can do many things.	☐	☐	☐
2. Arranging the environment so children can spread out, explore, and be messy.	☐	☐	☐
3. Providing sufficient storage space for projects and creations that cannot be completed in one day.	☐	☐	☐
4. Allowing creations to remain in place for several days so children can continue using them and perhaps expand them.	☐	☐	☐
5. Following a daily schedule that includes long blocks of time when children are free to organize their own games and activities without adult involvement.	☐	☐	☐
6. Providing sufficient time in the daily schedule for children to make plans and carry them out.	☐	☐	☐
7. Surrounding children with examples of creative work.	☐	☐	☐
8. Storing materials and equipment where children can easily select, replace, and care for them without adult assistance.	☐	☐	☐
9. Offering materials that allow children to explore subjects and interests introduced at school or through experiences such as field trips.	☐	☐	☐

Offering a Variety of Activities and Experiences That Promote Self-Expression	I Do This		
	Regularly	Sometimes	Not Enough
10. Encouraging children to express their ideas and feelings.	☐	☐	☐
11. Offering activities that allow children to develop and carry out their own plans.	☐	☐	☐
12. Extending younger children's dramatic play.	☐	☐	☐
13. Introducing children to brainstorming so they can use it as a problem-solving tool.	☐	☐	☐
14. Planning a variety of activities that introduce children to the visual and expressive arts.	☐	☐	☐
15. Helping children develop specific skills they can use in their creative work.	☐	☐	☐
16. Responding to children's ideas for projects and activities.	☐	☐	☐
17. Avoiding the use of coloring books, prepackaged craft projects, and dittos.	☐	☐	☐

Interacting With Children in Ways That Encourage and Respect Original Thoughts, Ideas, and Expression

	Regularly	Sometimes	Not Enough
18. Valuing the characteristics that make each child a unique individual.	☐	☐	☐
19. Helping children understand it takes hard work and practice to develop their talents.	☐	☐	☐
20. Encouraging children to take risks, learn from their mistakes, and try again.	☐	☐	☐
21. Inviting children to display or share the results of their creative work.	☐	☐	☐

**Interacting With Children in Ways
That Encourage and Respect Original
Thoughts, Ideas, and Expression** (continued)

I Do This

	Regularly	Sometimes	Not Enough
22. Calling attention to sensory experiences.	☐	☐	☐
23. Asking a variety of questions that encourage children to think about things in new ways.	☐	☐	☐
24. Accepting and valuing each child's unique creative expression.	☐	☐	☐
25. Modeling creativity by sharing your own interests, taking risks, and solving problems.	☐	☐	☐

Review your responses, then list three to five skills you would like to improve or topics you would like to learn more about. When you finish this module, you can list examples of your new or improved knowledge and skills.

_____

_____

_____

_____

_____

_____

_____

Begin the learning activities for Module 7, Creative.

LEARNING ACTIVITIES

Learning Activity I.
Using Your Knowledge of Child Development to Encourage Creativity

---

IN THIS ACTIVITY YOU WILL LEARN TO:

- recognize some typical behaviors of school-age children; and

- use what you know about children to encourage their creativity.

Many experts on creativity believe children are most creative during the preschool years. Preschoolers have vivid imaginations. They tend to be very curious and adept at solving problems that arise from their curiosity. Frequently their parents and teachers value and encourage these skills.

When children reach kindergarten, however, they face new challenges such as learning to pay attention at appropriate times. This is an important skill; however, children also need to continue using their creativity. School-age programs can give children many opportunities to explore their interests, investigate their world, and make discoveries. The environment you establish and the ways in which you interact with and respond to children can let them know you value creativity. What you say, how you ask and answer questions, and the ways in which you encourage exploration all nurture children's creativity. Careful listening to what a child has to say and recognizing each child as an individual are crucial. Your enthusiasm for children's efforts and successes will greatly support their creativity. Children will learn that creativity is an important part of life.

5- to 7-Year-Old Children

Children 5- to 7-years old ask a lot of questions and really want to know the answers. They are learning to read, write, and understand beginning concepts used in arithmetic and science. They use these skills in their creative work—writing and illustrating stories, weighing or measuring objects, then making a display of their results, doing simple experiments to test their predictions or to answer their own questions. Children this age are acquiring the ability to work through problems in their minds.

During these years, children double their vocabularies and can express their thoughts and feelings—often using great and vivid detail. They enjoy learning new words and use them in creative—but not always accurate—ways. Staff can introduce metaphors and analogies as they describe their own experiences and feelings. "When everyone rushes at once to get out to the playground, I feel like I'm in a huge, confusing traffic jam. How does it make you feel?" Word association games are another way to introduce new words. "When I say 'freeze,' what other words come to mind?" "Can anyone make up a sentence using all of these words—sugar, computer, and rain?"

Many 5- to 7-year-olds have active imaginations. They express their creative ideas through dramatic play, making good use of costumes and props to invent games and scenarios that last for several days. Prop boxes that reflect children's interests and/or give them a chance to further explore an experience are popular with this age group. For example, after the bus breaks down on the way from school, children might use a mechanic prop box to reenact and build on the experience. Staff can extend children's play by assuming roles and joining in "pretend" conversations.

Most children in this age group love to paint, draw, glue things together, or manipulate a lump of clay. These are relaxing activities that stimulate all the senses and allow children to use their imaginations as they create something of their own. They explore fresh ways of using familiar art materials—paints, playdough and clay, crayons, and markers—and they use new materials such as Plaster of Paris and colored chalk. Children enjoy arts and crafts experiences because these are relaxed, comfortable times when they can move at their own pace.

Like preschoolers, young school-age children enjoy the process of creating—making up a dance, inventing characters for a story, hammering nails into a wooden board. They are, however, becoming increasingly interested in the products that result from their creative efforts. They take great pleasure in making things that can actually be used (a potholder), displayed (a weaving), read (a poem), taught to someone else (a part in a play), or performed (a dance routine).

8- to 10-Year-Old Children

By this age children have developed many skills they can use in creative efforts. For example, their increased fine motor skills allow them to do more complex arts and crafts activities; they have the social skills needed to work with others; they understand how some concepts relate to one another; and they can apply their reading, writing, and arithmetic skills as they make step-by-step plans and carry them out.

Children this age may become intensely interested and involved in a specific activity or topic. They often pursue these "passions" on their own and through special interest clubs. For example, Daniel is fascinated by building things, spending every afternoon for three weeks creating a city of the future. Miguel loves to draw cartoon figures and spends every afternoon perfecting his version of a cartoon character. In a month's time these children may drop their city of the future and cartoon projects and throw themselves into new endeavors. Staff need to observe children to know when it's time to provide for their changing interests.

As they become increasingly independent of adults, 8- to 10-year-olds enjoy being with friends and participating in group activities. Spontaneous dramatic play activities may become planned skits and plays. Such activities can build children's confidence and help them feel comfortable expressing themselves.

Some children in this age group are extremely self-critical and look to others for encouragement and approval. At times, even the approval of others will not convince them of the value of their creations, and they may destroy them or throw them away. In these instances, staff can urge them to start again. These "perfectionists" may need help learning to enjoy and value the process of creating. Staff can let them know it's okay to take risks—taking risks is how people learn. These children may also need help establishing realistic goals. "Walter, painting a mural by yourself is a big job. Perhaps you might ask some of your friends to work with you."

Children's increased small muscle coordination and control allow them to explore a wide variety of art media and learn the skills and techniques used in calligraphy, macramé, silk screening, wood block printing, rug hooking, or mask making. This age group focuses on both the process and the products of their creative efforts. As they get older, children want to develop skills and competencies that lead to real accomplishments. The "products"—drawings, weavings, macramé plant hangers—provide children with "evidence" of their competence. Children like making objects that can be displayed simply because they are beautiful, interesting, or unusual and making items that are both attractive and practical—crocheted or woven clothing, tie-dye shirts, leather-tooled belts, or clay vases.

11- to 12-Year-Old Children

Some of the behaviors that characterize children in this age group can both contribute to and detract from their creativity. Their desires to be independent from adults and their rapidly expanding academic skills and knowledge can introduce them to new interests, stimulate curiosity, and encourage experimentation and discovery. Conversely, their strong attachment to and identification with their peer group, can lead them to conform with the behaviors and activities the group deems appropriate.

School-age staff can promote creativity by letting children know it is all right to be different, to explore their own interests, and to define themselves as individuals as well as group members. They can harness the power of the peer group by encouraging children to get involved in creative group efforts such as producing skits, plays, and videos. These activities allow children to apply their unique talents within the group. Individual children can contribute by writing scripts, designing and making costumes, directing the "actors," building stage sets, or making posters to advertise the production.

Many children in this age group show proficiency in particular areas and want to further develop their skills and talents. The program can provide time, space, and resources so children can fully develop their talents. It may be possible to arrange for dance, theater, and music specialists to "teach" classes at the program. Or, program staff might coordinate with parents so children can attend classes in the community.

These "almost teenagers" experience strong feelings such as sadness and joy in a deep way, much as adults do. They may express their feelings through many forms of media: art, music, drama, dance, writing, and photography.

Some children in this age group define themselves through popular culture—magazines, music, dancing, television, movies. It is important for staff to understand and accept that this age group's interest in popular culture is related to their need to be independent and in touch with their peers. They need time and space to pursue these interests without adult interference. Staff can expose children to a wide range of cultural offerings so they will be aware of the many different ways people express their creativity.

This age group is particularly interested in popular music and may bring their own tapes and CDs to the program. The lyrics to some songs are controversial and might be considered offensive and inappropriate. It's important to work with parents and children to set standards and guidelines related to the music children bring to the program.

Many 11- to 12-year-olds are eager to assume leadership roles and responsibility. School-age programs can address this need by asking children to apply their creativity to program planning and operations. Staff can encourage children's creative thinking by asking: "What activities would you plan if you were in charge of the program for a day?" "Is there another way to do this?" "How can we find out what children really want to do at the program?"

Like 8- to 10-year-olds, this age group continues to focus on both the process and products of creative work. They want the outcomes of their work to be viewed as "good" and may spend a lot of time planning, creating, practicing, evaluating, and revising, before performing or displaying their products. Being able to work hard on a task is a valuable skill; however, some children are too anxious to create products that conform to external standards. They are so worried about making something "good" that they aren't able to fully enjoy the creative process. It is important to regularly assess the program's atmosphere to make sure it is not overly competitive and to help children relax and enjoy the creative process.

Applying Your Knowledge

In this learning activity you keep a log for three days noting all the times you encourage children's creativity. Focus on the small things you do each day to help children solve problems, express their feelings, use materials in new ways, try new ideas, and explore their environment. Record examples for children ages 5 to 7, 8 to 10, and 11 to 12. Review the example that follows. Then use the blank form to record your words and actions.

Encouraging Children's Creativity

(Example)

Dates: _October 3–5_

What You Did	How This Encouraged Creativity
Max (11 years) tied a mobile to a hook in the ceiling. He stood back and asked me to look at the mobile too. He asked, "Do you think I should move the pebble to the other side so the mobile balances?" I agreed this would help and said, "Even if the mobile doesn't balance precisely, it is still very beautiful."	Max was very proud of his mobile—he had worked on it for a long time. I let him know his creation did not have to be "perfect" to be of value.
Oscar (6 years) and Tina (7 years) were having an argument. Tina wanted to be the doctor, but Oscar said he had never seen a doctor who was a lady, so there must not be any. Tina said her doctor is a lady. Oscar looked surprised and said maybe ladies could be doctors. He agreed to let Tina be the doctor today if he could be the doctor tomorrow. I said, "I liked the way you talked to each other about your disagreement. You found a way for both of you to have a chance to be the doctor."	I let Oscar and Tina work out their disagreement by themselves and let them know they had done a good job solving their problem.
Kent (9 years) put the hamster back in its cage and couldn't get the latch to close. He was getting frustrated. I said, "Kent, I've been having trouble getting the cage door to latch, too. Do you know what's wrong with the door? Maybe we could fix it together."	I let Kent know it wasn't his fault the cage door wouldn't shut. I asked for his ideas on how to solve the problem and gave him a chance to help fix the door.

Encouraging Children's Creativity*

Dates: _____

What You Did	How This Encouraged Creativity

Discuss this activity with your trainer and plan ways to continue encouraging children's creativity.

* Make additional copies of this form if you need more space.

Learning Activity II.
Motivating Children to Be Creative

IN THIS ACTIVITY YOU WILL LEARN TO:

- recognize the elements of children's creativity; and

- provide an environment and interactions that motivate children to be creative.

Domain skills grow from an individual's talents, education, and experience.

Teresa Amabile, a social psychologist who has studied creativity, describes three characteristics of creative people: domain skills, creative thinking and working skills, and intrinsic motivation.[2] **Domain skills** are the talent, education, and experience an individual has in a specific area, for example, natural science, cooking, or creative writing. To some extent, we are born with talents; however, education and experience can help us develop them to the maximum. For example:

> Kinya loves to read and enjoys writing stories. Much of her writing mimics her favorite authors. After taking a creative writing course sponsored by the program, she learns to make up interesting characters, develop a plot, and write in her own style—one that reflects her unique experiences and personality.

Creative thinking and working skills allow children to concentrate on their projects.

Creative thinking and working skills allow children and adults to stick with a task until they have completed it to their own satisfaction. These skills are the positive work habits that enable children to concentrate on their projects for long periods of time, change course if their ideas are not working, accept and overcome temporary failures, and feel a great sense of pride in both their efforts and their accomplishments. For example:

> As Kinya further develops her writing abilities she spends many hours at the computer—writing, revising, revising again, and sometimes deleting an entire story because she doesn't think it is a high quality piece. When she does finish a story she is immensely pleased with herself and the result of her hard work.

---

[2] Teresa Amabile, *Recognizing Children's Creativity* (NY: Crown Publishers, Inc., 1989), p. 25.

Intrinsic motivation is the desire to do something just because it is interesting, challenging, or satisfying—not because it is required. Like talent, it is somewhat inborn; however, parents, teachers, and others who influence children can encourage the development of intrinsic motivation. For example:

> The school-age program Kinya attends provides materials, time, and support so she can master her creative writing skills and explore other topics of interest. In addition, she is allowed to choose what she wants to do, which reinforces her self-determination.

Children with intrinsic motivation do things because they find them interesting, challenging, or satisfying.

Children and adults are most creative in the areas where their domain skills, creative thinking and working skills, and intrinsic motivation overlap. For example:

> In addition to creative writing Kinya has other talents—strong science and math skills. She enjoys using these skills in school work and other projects; however, she is not as driven to use them as she is to write. She does not have the intrinsic motivation to be creative in these areas. Kinya is most creative when writing stories. She has domain skills (talent and experience as a writer), working skills (she keeps trying even when her writing isn't as "good" as she would like it to be), and intrinsic motivation (she loves writing because it makes her feel competent and successful). Although only 10 years old, Kinya has already discovered where her overlap lies.

A well-designed school-age program, stocked with open-ended materials and resources, and staffed with skilled individuals who engage in thoughtful, positive interactions with children can motivate children to be creative. Some examples of the characteristics of such a program and its staff follow:

A well-designed school-age program can motivate children to be creative.

- The daily schedule provides large blocks of time during which children can choose what they want to do and with whom they would like to be. They are free to pursue their own interests, be with their friends, and initiate their own games and activities.

- Most planned activities are voluntary. Children can choose to participate or not. They can decide when they are ready to move on to something else.

- There are a wide variety of materials, activities, and interest areas to meet the varied interests of children and to accommodate a wide age range.

- Children are exposed to the arts and aesthetic experiences. Examples of creative "products" are included in the environment—music, paintings, scientific discoveries, inventions, photographs, recipes, dance, sculpture.

- The program invites art, music, dance, drama, and other specialists to offer classes on site for interested children or works with parents to make sure children have access to similar classes in the community.

- Staff serve as facilitators rather than directors. They create an environment, plan and introduce activities, provide opportunities for children to learn new skills, explain the rules in games, ask stimulating questions, and guide children's participation.

- Staff allow children to make messes and mistakes. They avoid telling children the "best" way to do things, instead, they let children make and carry out their own ideas and plans.

- Children's differences are valued. Staff help children appreciate their own uniqueness and that of others. They let children know each individual makes important contributions to the group.

- Staff identify sources of stress and change the program's schedule, environment, activities, and interactions to reduce stress and anxiety. They involve children in planning ways to make the program a pleasant and supportive place to spend time each day.

Applying Your Knowledge

In this learning activity you review some characteristics of a school-age program and assess how your program's environment and human interactions motivate and support children's creativity. For each characteristic, provide an example of why your program does or does not match the given description. Next, share the assessment results with your colleagues and plan ways to improve the program's "creative climate."

Assessing the Program's Creative Climate

As you read the following characteristics of a school-age program, think about whether your program includes **similar** characteristics regularly, sometimes, or not enough. Place a mark in one of the columns on the right for each characteristic listed and give a brief explanation for your "rating." An example is provided for the first one.

We Do This

Environment	Regularly	Sometimes	Not Enough
1. During a 60-minute free choice time block, children can choose what they want to do, and with whom.	X	☐	☐
We have two, 45-minute free choice periods. Children can select a new activity after the first period, continue the first one, or make up their own activities.			
2. Every day there are simultaneous activities, indoors and outdoors, ranging from quiet to active.	☐	☐	☐
3. Snack is a relaxed time. Children choose what they want to eat, and when.	☐	☐	☐
4. The interest areas respond to children's skill levels and current "passions."	☐	☐	☐
5. The interest areas have a wide variety of open-ended materials children can use in many ways.	☐	☐	☐
6. The environment is rearranged when children want to perform a play or dance.	☐	☐	☐

Environment	We Do This		
	Regularly	Sometimes	Not Enough
7. Works-in progress are stored on top of cabinets or in the craft area.	☐	☐	☐
8. There are several long-term projects underway. They are at different stages of completion.	☐	☐	☐
9. There is room to spread out and be messy. Cleaning supplies are stored at children's level.	☐	☐	☐
10. A display of children's arts and crafts or photographs greets visitors to the program.	☐	☐	☐
11. The music area has a wide variety of CDs and tapes—classical, jazz, popular, instruments, and materials for writing music.	☐	☐	☐
12. There are materials for all the visual arts.	☐	☐	☐

Human Interactions	We Do This		
	Regularly	Sometimes	Not Enough
13. Staff remind children it takes hard work and practice to develop their talents.	☐	☐	☐
14. Staff congratulate children who take risks and help them accept their mistakes as a natural part of life.	☐	☐	☐
15. Staff ask open-ended questions to help children think, develop solutions, or evaluate ideas and products.	☐	☐	☐
16. Staff participate in creative activities alongside children.	☐	☐	☐
17. Children are regularly involved in planning activities and sharing their ideas for improving the program.	☐	☐	☐
18. Both children and adults value each person's uniqueness—it's okay to do things in new ways.	☐	☐	☐
19. Staff spend most of their time as facilitators. They make it possible for children to be creative.	☐	☐	☐

Meet with your colleagues to share and discuss your assessment results. Use the space below to record any changes you would like to make.

Environment

_____
_____
_____
_____
_____
_____

Human Interactions

_____
_____
_____
_____
_____
_____

Discuss this activity with your trainer.

Learning Activity III:
Supporting Children's Long-Term Projects

IN THIS ACTIVITY YOU WILL LEARN TO:

- encourage children's creativity by introducing and supporting long-term projects;

- help children maintain and expand their interests in ongoing projects; and

- provide different kinds and levels of support as children pass through the steps in the creative process.

Whether initiated by children or staff, some projects are so engaging they go on for several weeks at a time. Such long-term projects provide many opportunities for children to exercise their creativity.

Graham Wallas, an early creativity theorist, defined the four steps in the creative process: preparation, incubation, illumination, and verification. As children become fully immersed in their projects they pass through these four steps. The process begins after a "problem" or challenge arises. The problem may be an assignment (explain the life cycle of a frog), or a personal decision to focus on solving a particular problem (how to keep the squirrels out of the bird feeders) or the decision to do or make something (make a hat). During the creative process children and adults may move back and forth between and among the steps rather than going from beginning to end. Understanding these steps can help you support children by providing space, time, and materials, and by offering suggestions and encouragement.

Each of the steps in the creative process[3] is described below with an example of how a group of children passed through the steps as they used a variety of objects to create a musical environment.

In the first step, **preparation** or **brainstorming**, we use our skills, knowledge, and understanding to experiment, explore, and play with ideas or objects. We study the problem, think, conduct research, seek information from others, and gather resources.

Steps in the Creative Process

We use *preparation* or *brain-storming* to study and think about the task.

---

[3] Based in part on the work of Graham Wallas (1926) and Teresa Amabile (1989).

Mr. Kelly, an amateur percussionist, brings to the program a sample of "found sounds" (objects that are not musical instruments but can be used to make interesting sounds). He displays the objects at a group meeting, demonstrates how to use them, and invites interested children to join him in the large-group area after the meeting to explore the found sounds.

Mr. Kelly encourages children to play with the objects and find out how to use them to make sounds. Jeremy suggests expanding the collection: everyone can bring objects from home or look for them in the program—indoors and outdoors. Mr. Kelly is pleased with Jeremy's suggestion. If Jeremy hadn't made it, he would have suggested it himself.

During the next week the children collect "found sounds" from home and go on a sound hunt at the program. Mr. Kelly puts a box in the large-group area so children can store their objects. Here are some examples of what they collect:

- garbage can lids;
- auto parts;
- bottles and cans (different sizes and shapes);
- spoons, ladles, and other household utensils;
- pots, pans, and lids;
- combs;
- sandpaper;
- rubber bands (different sizes);
- plastic and cardboard food containers (different sizes);
- pencils with rubber erasers; and
- dried gourds or seed pods.

During *incubation*, we generate many solutions and ideas.

In the second step, **incubation**, we make lists, draw sketches, or plan ways to combine ingredients and materials. Many different solutions and ideas are generated. We may even decide to put the task or problem aside for a while. During incubation our minds continue to work on the problem through both conscious and unconscious thinking.

When the box is more than full, Mr. Kelly gathers the children to discuss what they want to do next. Mary says the objects remind her of a one-man band she saw on television. Nat pipes in, "I've seen those too, and my dad has a record of jug band music. Jug bands use all sorts of objects to make music. Maybe we could do that too." The children are excited about the possibility of creating a band. Mr. Kelly listens to the suggestions, then repeats them for the children. He says, "You have a lot of good ideas. Perhaps you could think about them for a few days. Next week the talent show performers need to practice in this area. I know some of you are in the performance. Let's come back to this activity after the talent show is over." The children agree. They will think about what they want to do with their "found sounds" and meet again in a week or so.

During the next week the children participate in other activities; they also think about what to do next with their objects. Several children draw sketches of jug band instruments. Others continue to bring in objects.

During the third step, **illumination**, we review our ideas, keep some, and reject others. Some ideas may just "pop" into our heads. A famous example of illumination is when Archimedes jumped out of his bathtub shouting "Eureka! I have it." When he saw the change in the height of the water after he entered the bathtub, he suddenly understood the theory of the displacement of water.

We review and evaluate our ideas during *illumination*.

When they meet again, the children share and discuss their ideas. Britt says, "I think we have more stuff than we need for a band. Maybe we could create a whole orchestra." Jeremy suggests hanging some objects from the ceiling and placing others in designated places on the floor. He says they would be like large instruments in an orchestra—a piano or a kettle drum—that stay in one place. The others like his idea.

Mr. Kelly shows the children some new objects he brought from home—the back of an old dryer (it makes a great gong!) and a washtub. Britt wonders out loud, "What sound would the washtub make if we filled it with water?" Mr. Kelly gives her the go-ahead to try her idea. With the help of several children he checks the program's supplies for different lengths and thicknesses of aluminum and plastic tubing, metal and plastic-coated chains, and wooden doweling. They find some aluminum tubing that makes a beautiful chime-like sound when they let it swing freely. Nat puts some tubing on a piece of foam padding, "It will absorb the loud sound and make it soft and tinkly," he says.

In the *verification* stage, we evaluate our ideas and products and make changes if necessary.

In the fourth stage, **verification** or **communication**, we consider whether our creative ideas or products are useful, complete, or correct. We might seek the opinion of others. We change and fine tune our creations.

In the verification stage, we may decide to: stop working because the task is finished successfully; try again because the outcome is not successful; or set aside the task because the approach is just not working. When the outcome is successful, we often want to share the idea or product with others.

> After working for a week to create their musical environment the children tell Mr. Kelly they are ready to "use it." He suggests having two children experiment with making sounds while the others watch, listen, and make suggestions. This will be less disturbing to others, and it will be easier to hear the unique sounds made by each object. Two children are picked to be the first "musicians," while the others make suggestions. After a while they reverse roles until everyone has a chance to "play" the environment. The musicians use the following techniques:
>
> - Shaking, striking, blowing on, and plucking objects.
>
> - Playing the objects in different ways—rapidly, slowly, softly, loudly, strongly, and gently—as if they were musical instruments.
>
> - Using the sounds in different combinations to create musical texture.
>
> - Using selected sounds to "talk" to each other (as jazz musicians might do).
>
> - Playing objects like an orchestra—they choose one or two "instruments" to play; another child conducts—directing when to play and when to be silent, how loudly or softly, and how rapidly or slowly.
>
> - Using the sounds to create a special mood or feeling, and asking others to guess what mood they are trying to express.
>
> Experimenting with ways to "play" the environment continues for another week. Britt, who is in the school band, suggests creating a musical performance for the whole program. Preparing for the concert goes on for another week.
>
> Jeremy suggests taping the concert so Mr. Kelly helps him set up the tape player. They play the tape at pick-up time so parents can hear it.

Britt borrows the tape to take to school She asks her band teacher to help her compare the sounds made by the objects in the musical environment with sounds made by instruments. The children decide to use the found objects to create sounds to match those made by playing instruments.

Before introducing the project described above, Mr. Kelly developed a general plan. To fully support children's creativity; however, he remained flexible and responded to their ideas and interests. He recognized and understood the steps in the creative process so he was able to provide an environment and interactions that supported children's creativity and helped them get fully involved in their long-term project.

Some examples of ways school-age staff can support children's long-term projects follow:

- Help children understand there is no hurry for them to complete their projects. Unlike school, where deadlines may be necessary, the school-age program does not ask children to complete their work according to a precise schedule. Help them value the process of creating. Work begun today can continue tomorrow, and longer if appropriate.

- Participate with children from time to time so you are available to encourage and offer assistance when asked. Children won't have to leave their work to ask your opinion or to share their ideas.

- Encourage children to take time to think about what they want to do and to develop plans. Suggest trying unique and different techniques. Listen to their ideas and ask questions to encourage them to think of a variety of options: "How do you want the audience to feel about your character?"

- Allow works-in-progress to stay in place until the creators are ready to work on them again. Provide paper files or floppy disks for unfinished plays and stories; cardboard boxes to store a child's unfinished project and the materials he or she plans to use; space for ongoing experiments.

- Let children know you are available to help them critically evaluate their ideas and products. At the same time, remind them that taking risks, experiencing success and failure, and learning from mistakes are all part of the creative process.

Supporting Children's Long-Term Projects

Try these suggestions.

- Provide space and opportunities for interested children to share the results of their creative work. Offer bulletin boards, the opportunity to make a proposal during group meeting, time in the schedule to perform a play or piece of music, and a column or featured story in the weekly newsletter.

- Praise children for their hard work and perseverance. Let them know you value their willingness to take chances, try new ideas, and accept challenges.

Applying Your Knowledge

In this learning activity you keep a journal noting the different ways you support children as they carry out a long-term project. The project might be one you introduce or one suggested by the children. Once you get started on this activity, it may take several weeks to complete. This will depend on the level and length of the children's interest and involvement. You can start the activity when the children's project begins and make journal entries as you provide support. At the same time, continue with the other learning activities in this module. By the time you complete them, you should have enough journal recordings about the children's project. Begin by reviewing the example that follows.

Supporting Children's Long-Term Projects
(Example)

Children/Ages: _Annika, Mauricio, Thomas, Caroline, Wendy, Inez (10 to 11 years)_

Dates: _April 10-23_   **Setting:** _Outdoors_

Activity: _Building a clubhouse_

Briefly describe how and why the activity began:

These children are fifth-graders. Their parents want them to attend the program next year. I heard Annika tell Thomas she is too old for the program. He agreed and complained there are too many little kids and the big kids have no privacy. We live in a warm climate, so we use the outdoors almost all year round. I asked Annika and Thomas if they would like to build an outdoor clubhouse for the older children to use this year and next. They said yes, and gathered the others at a planning session.

Journal Entries

Date: _April 10_

I sat in on the planning session and made a few suggestions: decide where to build, get permission, make a list of supplies and tools needed. Then I left the children to conduct their own meeting.

Annika and Thomas gave me a list of supplies and tools they will need. They said they would like to build a two-story clubhouse in the oak tree. I said I would ask the director if this would be okay. I explained it might take a few days to get an answer.

Date: _April 14_

I gathered the group to let them know the director's response. She said they could build the clubhouse in the oak tree, however, they would need to make sure it is safe. Inez said her dad helped her uncle build a beach house, so she would ask him to help them design a safe clubhouse. At the end of the day I reminded her to ask her dad. He was excited about helping.

Date: _April 23_

Inez's dad gave us a list of supplies needed after meeting with the children and drawing up plans. To raise money to buy the supplies, the children decided to have a bake sale. (It will probably take several bake sales, but they are very excited).

Supporting Children's Long-Term Projects

Children/Ages: _____

Dates: _____ **Setting:** _____

Activity: _____

Briefly describe how and why the activity began:

_____
_____
_____
_____
_____
_____

Journal Entries (Record your entries below or in a notebook if you prefer.)

Date: _____

_____
_____
_____
_____
_____
_____

Date: _____

_____
_____
_____
_____
_____
_____

Journal Entries (continued)*

Date: _____

_____

_____

_____

_____

_____

Date: _____

_____

_____

_____

_____

_____

Date: _____

_____

_____

_____

_____

_____

Date: _____

_____

_____

_____

_____

_____

Review your journal entries, then discuss the children's project and how you provided support with your trainer.

* Make additional copies of this form if needed.

Learning Activity IV.
Planning and Conducting Activities That Encourage Creativity

IN THIS ACTIVITY YOU WILL LEARN TO:

- plan activities designed to encourage children's participation and creativity; and

- encourage children to fully explore and try out their ideas.

School-age programs typically offer children a wide variety of activity choices. Children can play group games, care for pets, listen to music, make a collage, or just explore the materials in a favorite interest area. In addition, staff may plan and carry out special activities that respond to children's interests, allow them to develop or use specific skills, and/or encourage their creativity.

School-age staff are facilitators—they encourage, question, guide, and assist children.

When planning and leading creative activities, your role is that of a facilitator. This role does not involve judging or telling children exactly what to do. Instead, you encourage, question, guide, and assist children as they explore materials or try new ways to express themselves. Creative activities can include making paper maché vegetables, baking bread, playing dramatic games, taking photographs, writing and illustrating haiku, or developing hypotheses and conducting experiments. Even outdoor games and sports can be creative activities. Children can make up new rules for a game, turn hopscotch squares into circles, rearrange an obstacle course to make it more challenging, or find out what happens when the tail on a kite is longer or shorter.

Some creative activities involve specific techniques or processes, for example, baking bread. These activities are considered "creative" because they offer opportunities for children to explore the properties of materials, invent variations on basic techniques, or alter the ingredients or steps in a recipe. For example, after learning the basics of bread baking, children might decide to add juice instead of water, let the bread rise for a longer time, or sculpt the bread dough into interesting shapes.

Planning creative activities is no different than planning in general. It begins by finding out what children would like to do. You can collect this information through surveys, by listening to conversations, and by conducting regular observations. Sometimes, children will ask you to help them plan and carry out a specific activity. Sometimes, you will plan activities you think children will find fun or interesting, or that will help children learn a specific skill.

Planning creative activities begins by finding out about children's interests.

Before offering an activity, it is a good idea to try it yourself. For example, before introducing children to tie-dying, you might want to create your own T-shirt. You could experiment with different knots and colors and wear your finished shirt the day before the activity to inspire interest.

Steps to take when planning creative activities follow.

Try these suggestions for planning activities.

- **Set some goals** for the activity. What do you hope children will learn? What opportunities for creative expression will you offer?

- **Collect the materials and equipment** you will need. Some may be on hand at the program (dyes), some might come from the children (white T-shirts), some could be gathered from home or the program office (string or rubber bands), and some may need to be retrieved from a storage closet (plastic or aluminum tubs).

- **Review the instructions**—usually included in activity books, magazines, or your own "idea" file. Ask several children to help you make numbered "recipe cards" to illustrate how to do the activity. Use a different card for each step and draw pictures so children with beginning reading skills can follow along. Cover these with clear Contact paper so they can be saved and reused.

- **Anticipate the kinds of questions** children might ask. Also, think of questions you can ask to encourage children's creative thinking, risk taking, and experimentation.

- **Make the activity open-ended**. For example, in the tie-dying activity, children will learn the techniques used to tie knots that create specific patterns. However, children will also make their own creative choices. They can choose where to place the knots, what size to make them, what colors to use, what fabric or article of clothing to dye. Thus, there are many open-ended aspects of the activity.

- **"Advertise" the activity**. Describe it during a group meeting, set up an example to encourage children's curiosity, ask for volunteers to help gather materials or set up the activity.

43

- **Adapt the activity** to address the needs and interests of children you expect will participate. For example, how can you structure the activity so Denise, a highly distractible child, will enjoy herself? You might help Denise break the activity into smaller tasks—reviewing design patterns, making the knots, dying the T-shirt. Or, what can you do to help Carl carry out the interesting ideas for new colors he is likely to have? You might provide some small basins so Carl and other interested children could experiment with mixing new colors.

Try these suggestions for setting up activities.

Some strategies for setting up creative activities follow.

- **Set up the activity near the resources** children will use. Exactly how you set up will depend on the activity. For example, for arts and crafts activities such as tie-dying, place the materials where children can easily see and reach them and where it is all right to make a "mess." To set up for drama or music activities you might only need to clear an open area, put a tape in the boom box, and get out the props.

- **Prepare in advance**, or with children's help. If children are involved in setting up, use this time to explain what you will be doing during the activity.

- **Organize the activity so children can complete one step at a time.** For example, children can explore designs at one end of the table; tie knots at the other end; dye T-shirts in tubs full of dye on the counter next to the sink; and hang shirts to dry on the drying rack (place newspapers or a piece of plastic underneath to catch the drips).

Try these suggestions for conducting the activities.

Here are some ideas for conducting creative activities.

- **Gather the children** who are interested in the activity. If space is limited, explain you will offer the activity again—later in the day or on another day. Ask for volunteers to wait until later to participate. Children will not be able to fully explore their ideas if they are cramped and have to worry about getting into each other's space.

- **Give a brief overview of the steps** involved in the activity; then go back to the first step and explain it in detail. Children will be eager to get started so they will not want to hear lengthy explanations of the whole activity. As children finish each step, you can give instructions on what each child needs to do next.

- **Allow plenty of time** for children to make their own plans and explore the materials and equipment. Encourage them to fully enjoy this part of the creative process. Children are often so eager to make a finished product they miss out on the pleasure that comes from considering many different ways to carry out their ideas.

- **Observe children's involvement**. Look for cues to see if children find the activity interesting and if it matches their skills. For example, can the children follow the directions? Do they seem actively involved? Do they need a lot of help from you?

- **Allow children to participate in activities in their own way.** For example, Lance might prefer to use one color rather than several for his tie-dye shirt. Perhaps he is more interested in experimenting with the knots than with colors.

- **Talk to children** about what they are doing. Ask questions to stimulate their creativity. "What would happen if you tied your knots with string instead of rubber bands?" "If the purple dye is too dark, how can you make it more violet?" Draw attention to a child's creative approach. "Tony, tell us how you made the patterns on the shoulders of your T-shirt. They look like fringe."

- **Give plenty of notice** before clean-up time so children can finish what they are doing or reach an appropriate stopping point. Some activities are completed in a day, others carry over to the next or last even longer.

- **Leave the materials in place** so children can use them on their own, without adult direction. This will allow children to continue exploring the materials and using their creativity.

One final point to remember when planning and leading "creative" activities is to remain flexible and open to changing your plans. Children may think of different ways to use craft materials, move to music, or carry out an experiment. This is not only "okay," it is to be encouraged. Some children are always eager to apply their own creativity to a situation and others may catch their enthusiasm. For these children, the planned activity serves as a stimulus, suggesting many more options than you had envisioned. If the result of your planned activity is to spark creativity, then it is a success.

It is important to remain flexible and open to change.

Some suggestions for activities that can promote creativity follow:

Try these suggestions.

Make up a new ending. Read a story out loud; stop at an exciting moment. Children can work alone, in pairs, or in small groups to make up their own ending to the story. Children can read or perform the new endings, then read the author's.

Paper bag plays. Place a variety of props in several large paper bags. Each bag should have at least as many props as there are children in a group. Give each group a bag. Ask the children to make up a play using the props. Have children perform their plays the same day. The "actors" tend to lose their spontaneity if they have to wait until the next day to perform.

Make African thumb pianos. Have children place different lengths of tongue depressors between a piece of wood and the edge of a table. The weight of the wood will keep the tongue depressors in place. Shorter segments will make higher sounds when stroked with the thumb; longer segments will produce lower sounds. Children can experiment with different lengths to tune the instrument to play different songs.

Tell me about yourself. Put out a box of photographs of people—old family photos from a second-hand shop, photos from magazines, photos taken by staff or children. Ask children to work in pairs. Each pair selects a photo; one child pretends to be the person in the photo while the other acts as an interviewer. The pairs can write or tape record the "autobiography." "I was born in Topeka in 1945. My parents ran a small grocery store. I had six brothers, four sisters and…"

Count to a million (or as close as you can get). Ask pairs or small groups to think of something—indoors or outdoors—which is made up of a million different parts. For example, children might estimate there are a million grains of sand in the sandbox, a million blades of grass, a million leaves on a tree, or a million floor tiles. Next, ask children to prove their estimate is reasonable. For example, to prove there are a million blades of grass on the field, they might measure the area of the whole field, count the blades of grass in a one square foot area, and use these two measurements to estimate how many blades of grass are on the field.

Plaster masks. Gather headbands or barrettes, petroleum jelly, Plaster of Paris strips (cut into pieces two to three inches long), and a shallow container of water. Explain the procedure and ask for a volunteer to be a "model." Have the volunteer fasten his or her hair away from the forehead using head bands or barrettes, then cover his or her face with petroleum jelly. Place the plaster strips in water; run two fingers between them to remove excess water. Gently place a strip on the child's face, then make it smooth. Continue placing wet strips on the face, overlapping so no skin shows. Leave holes for the eyes and mouth. Allow the mask to dry for about 20 minutes. (Play soft music to relax the volunteer.) Carefully lift the mask off the child's face and put it in a safe place to dry overnight. After the demonstration, children work in pairs to create their own masks. The next day they can paint and decorate them.

Mirror images. Have each child work face to face with a partner as if looking into a mirror. One child acts as the leader, moving arms, legs, fingers, or head in slow motion. The partner imitates the motions as if he or she was the leader's mirror image. Children can switch partners or do mirror images to music. Older children can choreograph mirror images and perform them for others.

Let me tell you about life on earth. Ask children to use whatever creative medium they prefer to tell a visitor from another planet what daily life is like on earth. Cultural practices they might want to explain include: transportation, sleeping habits, clothes, food (home-cooked and restaurants), toys and games, houses and other buildings, sports, leisure activities, and any others the children think of. Creative media might include drawing, painting, making a video, storytelling, creating a photo mural (using original photos or pictures cut from magazines), songwriting, or any others the children think of.

Make up new rules for a familiar game. When children seem bored with games and sports, involve them in making up new rules and new ways to play. For example, they might play a variation of baseball by using different equipment—street hockey sticks (instead of bats) and small rubber balls (instead of softballs). Players could run around the bases and score runs, as in baseball; however, children might want to change the rules in other ways to make the game new and different.

Applying Your Knowledge

In this learning activity, you plan and conduct an activity that provides opportunities for children to use their creativity. Begin by thinking about what the children might enjoy. Your cues will come from reviewing the ideas in this learning activity, reading your observation notes, listening to children's conversations, talking to other staff, and consulting activity books. Develop a plan, set up, and conduct the activity. Think about what happened as you answer the questions that follow. Begin by reviewing the example.

Planning and Conducting Activities That Encourage Creativity
(Example)

Children/Ages: _Teresa, Justin, Hannah, Monica, Ricardo (5 to 7 years); Dina, Rita (11 years)_

Date: _November 11_   **Setting:** _Large-group activity area_

Activity: _Creative music and movement, using props and instruments, listening to music_

Planning and Setting Up

Why do you want to offer this activity?

I've seen several younger children watching the older ones listening to music and teaching each other new dance steps. They seem to want to join in, but most of the older children tell them to go away because they want to spend time alone. I think the younger ones would enjoy dancing and moving in their own way.

Which children do you think will participate?

Teresa, Justin, Hannah, and Ricardo are likely participants. Once we get started some of the older children—Dina and Rita might join us. They tend to enjoy leading the younger children in activities.

How could children use their creativity?

They could make up their own movements, take turns making music, select and use props such as scarves and streamers to enhance their movements, and "choreograph" a dance.

What materials and equipment are needed?

Props: streamers, lightweight fabric, sheets, scarves, feathers, balloons, capes, ribbons, hula hoops.

Rhythm instruments: drums, xylophones, bells, clackers, maracas, cymbals, tambourines, wood blocks.

Tape player and assortment of tapes.

How will you "advertise" the activity? Where and how will you set up?

I will mention it to the children I think might be interested and announce it at group meeting. Then I will spread out the materials in the large-group area for children to explore. While they are exploring I will describe what we can do with the props and instruments.

Conducting the Activity

How did you begin the activity?

When several children had gathered to explore the materials I put in a tape—Ravel's Bolero. I asked the children if they would like to use the props and instruments to move and play along with the music. I demonstrated with a scarf and a maraca.

What did the children do?

Hannah and Monica picked up a scarf and each held an end while they swayed to the music. Soon they began moving as they swayed.

Ricardo asked for my maraca and picked up the other one so he had a pair. He stood in place and shook the maracas while moving his body from one side to the other.

Justin jumped in and out of the hula hoop. He didn't seem to pay attention to the music.

The children continued using the props and instruments for about ten minutes. Then Dina and Rita joined them and began making suggestions of how to use the materials in different ways. Dina asked if there were other tapes, looked through them, then selected another one—Rock and Roll Oldies.

Teresa asked Justin to dance with her. He said no, so she danced with Rita. Justin stood and watched for a while, then danced alone.

What did you do and say to encourage children's creativity?

I offered Justin the drum and asked if he might like to listen for the beat in the music, then play along.

I suggested changing the tape when the children seemed to be tiring of it.

I suggested to Hannah and Monica they could each hold a side of the hula hoop, dance with it, and perhaps take turns stepping in and out of it.

When children seemed ready to do something different, I suggested making up a dance together.

After the Activity

How did the children continue enjoying this activity on their own?

Dina and Rita continued their leadership and led the others in making up a dance.

All the children continued using and exploring the props and instruments.

Justin continued to be more interested in playing the instruments than moving with the props. He explored each instrument and asked if he could make some new ones.

How did you provide support?

I helped Dina and Rita plan a simple dance the younger children could learn.

I asked the children if they needed more props and instruments for their dance.

I showed Justin a book on making musical instruments and told him to pick some to make and to let me know what materials were needed. When Daniel also showed interest in making instruments, I suggested he and Justin work together.

Planning and Conducting Activities That Encourage Creativity

Children/Ages: _____

Date: _____ **Setting:** _____

Activity: _____

Planning and Setting Up

Why do you want to offer this activity?

_____

_____

_____

_____

Which children do you think will participate?

_____

_____

How could children use their creativity?

_____

_____

_____

_____

What materials and equipment are needed?

_____

_____

How will you "advertise" the activity? Where and how will you set up?

_____

_____

_____

_____

Conducting the Activity

How did you begin the activity?

_____
_____
_____
_____

What did the children do?

_____
_____
_____
_____
_____

What did you do and say to encourage children's creativity?

_____
_____
_____
_____
_____

After the Activity

How did the children continue enjoying this activity on their own?

_____
_____
_____

How did you provide support?

_____
_____
_____
_____

Discuss the activity with your trainer.

Learning Activity V.
Filling the Environment with Open-Ended Materials That Promote Creativity

---

IN THIS ACTIVITY YOU WILL LEARN TO:

- select open-ended materials that promote creativity; and

- ensure all interest areas contain items children can use in creative work.

One of the easiest ways to promote children's creativity is to fill the environment with open-ended materials—items children can use in a variety of ways. They are ideal for school-age programs because they are interesting to children of different ages and stages of development and trigger their imaginations. For example, given a box of recycled materials children might do the following:

Open-ended materials can be used in many different ways.

- make collages;

- sort and classify the items;

- make mobiles;

- decorate masks;

- use them in experiments;

- use them for inventions; and

- use them as props for skits and plays.

Children get involved in many kinds of creative work at the school-age program, therefore, it is important to include open-ended materials that invite discovery in all interest areas. Here are some examples of children engaged in creative work in different areas.

Include open-ended materials in all interest areas.

Eduardo uses the T-square and ruler in the *math area* to draw a layout of his room at home. He plans to design a built-in platform bed, loft, and desk.

Wanda is in the *large group area*. She ties several streamers across a hula hoop, then weaves more streamers across the hoop until it is filled with color. She uses the hoop as she choreographs a dance.

Rhonda and Janine are in the *science area* taking apart a broken remote control unit to see how it is made. They want to rewire it so it can be used to control the program's tape player.

Brianna and Abdullah are in the *board and table games area* using Legos to build a multi-level space station.

J. J. is working on the computer in the *quiet area*. He is rewriting the dialogue for one of the characters in his play.

Carley, Nikki, and Shoshana are *outdoors* jumping rope. Nikki makes up a jump rope rhyme and teaches it to the others.

Module 3, Program Environment, includes a checklist for indoor interest areas and for the outdoor area. Refer to these checklists for more examples of open-ended materials.

Coloring books, dittos, and craft kits do not encourage creativity.[4]

Many school-age staff wonder if it is a good idea to offer coloring books, dittos, or craft kits as part of their creative activities. The answer is simple. No, it is not a good idea.

For one thing, it is difficult for some younger children to stay in the lines of a ditto or coloring book figure. This sets up children for failure. Materials such as craft kits may help children learn to read and follow directions and develop specific skills; however, children are more likely to use their imaginations, experiment, and express their individuality when they plan and carry out their own projects using a variety of open-ended materials.

What should you do if parents want their children to use these materials, as they do in school? Explain that teachers may want to reinforce the concepts and information covered in their lessons. For example, they might provide dittos so children can practice doing arithmetic problems. When teachers want to encourage creativity, they offer open-ended materials and activities similar to those at the school-age program.

Most parents who look forward to seeing colored dittos and professional-looking art are really looking for signs that their children are doing well at the program. What they want to see is evidence of their child's progress. Completed craft projects that look just like everyone else's seem to be proof that their child is accomplishing something at the program.

---

[4] Adapted with permission from Diane Trister Dodge and Laura J. Colker, *The Creative Curriculum® for Family Child Care* (Washington, DC: Teaching Strategies, 1991), p. 139.

By sharing your approach to encouraging creativity with the children's parents, you can help them understand that, even without dittos, coloring books, and craft kits, their children are doing important things during their time at the program. It doesn't take long to convince parents that making a slightly crooked box in the woodworking center provides a more valuable experience than making a construction from a kit.

Applying Your Knowledge

In this learning activity you focus on promoting children's creativity in all interest areas and outdoors. The chart that follows lists typical interest areas in school-age programs. For each one, list three open-ended materials found in your program and how these encourage children to use their creativity. Two examples are provided for each area to get you started.

Filling the Environment With Open-Ended Materials

Quiet Area

Material	How It Encourages Creativity
Puppets, flannel board, props	Children can use for storytelling
Book-binding supplies such as a paper punch, thick yarn and needles, cardboard, glue, stapler	Children can publish their stories and poems

House Corner/Dramatic Play Area

Material	How It Encourages Creativity
Paper and writing materials	Children can write skits and plays
Dress-up clothes (male and female)	Children can explore different roles and perform skits and plays

Art and Crafts Area

Material	How It Encourages Creativity
Painting "tools" such as paint rollers, sponges, cotton swabs, eye droppers, string, and twigs	*Children can explore painting techniques*
Scissors that children who are right- or left-handed can use	*Children can cut paper and other materials to the sizes they want to use in projects*

Sand and Water Area

Material	How It Encourages Creativity
Many different kinds of props	*Children can use props to pour, spray, measure, squeeze, sift, and mold*
Waterproof aprons or smocks and clean-up supplies (sponges, mops, brooms)	*Children know it's okay to make a mess and that they can clean up after themselves*

Science and Nature Area

Material	How It Encourages Creativity
Posters and charts showing how children use the scientific method to conduct experiments	*Children can learn from and be inspired by each other's explorations*
Oil, colorings, powders, gelatin, soap suds	*Children can use in experiments with water*

Woodworking Area

Material	How It Encourages Creativity
Assorted objects—bottle caps, wheels, fishing line, rubber bands, tongue depressors, pie pans, sandpaper	*Children can use to make simple instruments*
Soft wood (pine and balsa) and carving tools	*Children can make wood carvings*

Music Area

Material	How It Encourages Creativity
Tape player and blank tapes	*Children can record their own music and songs*
Scarves, streamers, and props	*Children can use in spontaneous or choreographed dances*

Blocks and Construction Area

Material	How It Encourages Creativity
Crates, cardboard boxes, or appliance cartons	*Children can make hideaways or clubhouses*
Complete set of wooden unit blocks	*Children can plan and build roads and structures*

Board and Table Games Area

Material	How It Encourages Creativity
Cardboard, markers, scissors and tape	Children can make up board games and puzzles
Games such as Scrabble and chess	Children can think creatively to consider ways to make words and the impact of their moves

Math Area

Material	How It Encourages Creativity
Graph paper, pencils, rulers, and calculators	Children can design buildings or create room layouts
Parquetry blocks	Children can make designs

Outdoors

Material	How It Encourages Creativity
Colored chalk	*Children can create sidewalk art and design new ways to play hopscotch*
Balls and rackets	*Children can invent new games*

Are there materials in all the interest areas and outdoors to encourage children's creativity? If not, what can your program do to provide additional stimulating materials? Discuss this activity with your colleagues and your trainer.

SUMMARIZING YOUR PROGRESS

You have now completed all the learning activities for this module. Whether you are an experienced school-age staff member or a new one, this module has probably helped you develop new skills for promoting children's creativity. Before you go on, take a few minutes to review your responses to the pre-training assessment for this module. Summarize what you learned, and list the skills you developed or improved.

If there are topics you would like to know more about, you will find recommended readings listed in the Orientation in Volume I.

Your final step in this module is to complete the knowledge and competency assessments. Let your trainer know when you are ready to schedule the assessments. After you have successfully completed them, you will be ready to start a new module. Congratulations on your progress so far, and good luck with your next module.

ANSWER SHEETS

Promoting Children's Creativity

1. How did Ms. Andrews involve the children in creating a rich and varied environment?

a. She responded to the children's interest in how birds weave their nests.

b. She supported the children's interest in weaving by providing space in the art area for meetings and storage of materials.

c. She suggested they set aside a shelf to keep "works in progress" out of the way of the younger children who use the room during the day.

2. How do open-ended materials promote creativity?

a. There is no right or wrong way to use the materials.

b. They invite children to explore and experiment without any rules about what to do.

c. They allow children to use their imaginations and to make choices and decisions about how to use the materials.

Providing a Rich and Varied Environment That Invites Exploration and Experimentation

1. Why did Ms. Ramos plan this activity?

a. She overheard Alex and Brianna discussing whether there could be life on other planets.

b. She remembered she enjoyed a similar activity when she was their age.

c. An activity such as this one could build on the children's school experiences.

Offering a Variety of Activities and Experiences That Promote Self-Expression

2. **What did Ms. Ramos do to encourage the children's creativity?**

   a. She raised children's awareness by talking about conditions on other planets.

   b. She provided books about the planets so children could explore them and ask questions.

   c. She provided materials for making the "beings."

   d. She asked thought-provoking questions while children were making their beings.

   e. She showed the children where they could store their unfinished projects.

Interacting With Children in Ways That Encourage and Respect Original Thoughts, Ideas, and Expression

1. **How did Mr. Ryan interact with the children to encourage creative thinking?**

   a. He approached the girls to ask them to tell him more about their concerns.

   b. He listened to the girls before making any comments.

   c. He asked for their ideas for making up a new kind of dodge ball.

   d. He complimented them on their idea.

2. **How did Mr. Ryan demonstrate respect for the children's ideas?**

   a. He let the girls know that their concerns were important to him.

   b. He asked for their ideas for a new kind of dodge ball.

   c. He encouraged them to share their ideas with the other children.

GLOSSARY

Creativity	The ability to develop something new—an idea or product—that is substantially different from anything the person has seen or heard before and is correct, useful toward achieving a goal, appealing, or meaningful to the person in some way.
Creative process	The four steps an individual moves through while creating an idea or product.
Creative thinking and working skills	Positive work habits that allow an individual to concentrate and complete a task.
Domain skills	Talent, education, and experience in a given area.
Illumination	The third step in the creative process during which people review their ideas, keep some, and reject others. Ideas may "pop" into their heads.
Incubation	The second step in the creative process during which people generate many different solutions and ideas.
Intrinsic motivation	The desire to do something because it is interesting, challenging, or satisfying.
Open-ended materials	Materials that can be used in many different ways.
Open-ended question	A question that can be answered in a number of ways.
Preparation	Also known as brainstorming, this is the first step in the creative process. People use their skills, knowledge, and understanding to experiment, explore, and play with ideas or objects.
Problem solving	The process of thinking through a problem and coming up with one or several possible solutions.
Self-esteem	A sense of worth; a good feeling about oneself and one's abilities. Someone with strong self-esteem feels respected, valued, and able to do things successfully and independently.
Verification	Also known as communication, this is the fourth step in the creative process. People evaluate their creative ideas or products, share them with others, and fine tune them.

Module 8:
SELF

OVERVIEW

FOSTERING SCHOOL-AGE CHILDREN'S SELF-ESTEEM INVOLVES:

- developing a positive and supportive relationship with each child;

- helping children accept and appreciate themselves and others; and

- providing children with opportunities to be successful and feel competent.

This module is about two interrelated topics—how children gain a sense of self and how this self-knowledge can lead to self-esteem. A sense of self is an awareness of your identity: who you are. Your identity is made up of many variables: physical characteristics, likes and dislikes, strengths, interests, language, the foods you do or don't eat, experiences in your family, at school, and in the community, your expectations and values, what is expected of you, and whether you feel valued by others. Our identity and sense of self develops and changes throughout our lives. Our physical appearance changes, we develop new skills and interests, we experience and learn from our successes and failures, and we establish relationships with new people.

Self-esteem evolves from a sense of self.

Self-esteem grows out of a sense of identity. Some people have negative feelings about themselves. They might dislike the way they look, feel they have nothing in common with other family members, reject their ethnicity and culture, or think they are not capable of succeeding. Other people are comfortable with their sense of self. They may still want to improve some aspect of their lives, for example, by beginning an exercise program or being more attentive to their families, but, overall they accept who they are and feel valued by others.

Your self-esteem develops when others accept you and you have successful experiences. People with self-esteem have the confidence to tackle problems, attempt new challenges, offer support to others, recover from setbacks, and learn from their mistakes. They have personal standards for their own behavior that are based on the values held by their families, culture, society, and other groups to which they belong.

Self-esteem develops when you feel valued and experience success.

There has been much discussion among teachers, administrators, school-age staff, and others who work with children concerning the importance of self-esteem and what adults can do to foster children's positive feelings about themselves. Some popular practices designed to promote self-esteem may lead instead to over-indulgent self-love that is based solely on trivial things. For example, when children are asked to draw a picture of something that makes them special, they may focus on relatively insignificant personal characteristics such as their long hair or new shoes. As a result, they may begin to believe that superficial traits are what make them special. The strategies recommended in this module provide opportunities for children to experience the deep satisfaction that comes from accepting oneself, mastering a difficult skill, helping a family member, and contributing to the success of a group project. Children's self-esteem grows when they learn to accept and appreciate other people, as well as themselves.

During the school-age years, children seek challenges and thrive on real work. Their sense of self grows as they learn what they can do and receive praise for meaningful efforts and accomplishments.[1] They become more aware of how their family and cultural lifestyles, economic levels, expectations, and values are alike and different from those of other families and cultures. Working and playing with peers, understanding the need for rules and limits, and contributing to the community help children see themselves in relation to others. This is an essential component of gaining a sense of self and developing self-esteem.

School-age staff can help children develop a positive sense of self.

School-age staff play an important role in helping children develop a sense of identify and self-esteem. By demonstrating respect—for each child as an individual, for the needs of the group, and for yourself and your colleagues—you convey the message that each person is valued.

When adults who interact with children are proud of who they are and what they can do, children have a model for self-esteem. If they support children's efforts and provide constructive feedback, children are likely to be willing to take risks and not give up when they encounter difficulties.

That's why you are such an important person to the children in your program. In the course of daily life at the program—as you help a child carry out an experiment, listen and respond to how they are feeling, involve children in planning activities, or encourage a child to solve a problem—you are giving them realistic opportunities for success. Each day the children in your program learn about themselves—their strengths, interests, skills, views about the world around them, and how they are viewed and accepted by others. Through your relationships with these children, you can help them learn to value themselves and others.

[1] Based on Willam Damon, *Greater Expectations* (New York, NY: The Free Press, 1995).

Your support and encouragement help children develop confidence in their own abilities which will motivate them to continue learning throughout their lives.

Listed below are examples of how school-age staff demonstrate their competence in fostering children's sense of self.

Developing a Positive and Supportive Relationship with Each Child

Observe children to identify what makes them unique—personality, learning styles, temperament, skills, talents, interests, and needs—and let them know you value their individuality. "Each of you has a different writing style. Roxanne, you think and organize what you're going to write before you sit at the computer. Jeremy, you think and write at the same time."

Show children you enjoy being with them. "Carlos, you tell such funny stories. I look forward to Mondays when I can hear about your latest weekend escapade."

Listen to children as they express their feelings and take their concerns seriously. "When Dana came back from kindergarten today, she told me she's worried about growing up because her clothes won't fit her. I reminded her she gets new clothes as she outgrows the old ones. She may have mixed feelings about becoming more independent."

Learn and use words in the home language of children whose first language is not English. "Silvia, ¿puedes ayudárme buscar estós libros por favor?" (Can you help me look for those books?)

Know what each child is able to do and show you value each child's unique skills and characteristics. "James, the gerbil ran behind the shelves. You're good at getting him back in his cage. Could you help us?"

Identify children's interests through observation, surveys, and conversations; use this information to plan activities and provide materials. "Lori told me she wants to learn how to do origami. I can get a book from the library and help her follow the instructions."

Work with parents and colleagues to make sure each child receives the individual attention he or she needs. "Mr. Trent, Gerald just slammed the dictionary down on the table. I think he needs some help learning to use it. Can you please help him while I finish up this club meeting?"

Show children you have a positive relationship with their parents and that their family's involvement is valued and appreciated.

"Ms. Cane, I was pleased to get your recipe for flat bread. The children had a great time making it. If you have other recipes that we could use, we'd appreciate it if you would send them with Kyra."

Offer gentle physical or nonverbal contact—a hug, a touch, a smile—to show you care.

Helping Children Accept and Appreciate Themselves and Others

Provide a wide variety of activities and materials that do not limit children's options because of individual differences. Avoid making biased remarks concerning gender, disabilities, culture, ethnic background, or any other differences. "Danielle and Bradley make a good team. She's a great pitcher and he's a great catcher."

Offer sports and games that help children learn to value fairness, cooperation, and personal growth. "When we form teams for softball and soccer, we try to make them balanced so one team doesn't have an unfair advantage over the other."

Acknowledge children's efforts and accomplishments. "Leila, I enjoyed the play you wrote for the Drama Club. The characters seem so real."

Reinforce children's behavior when they cooperate with others, help someone achieve a goal, or show that they value each other's accomplishments. "Sofia, you spent a lot of time coaching Krystina so she could learn to do a handstand with straight legs. I noticed you clapping louder than anyone else when Krystina performed in the gymnastics show."

Make sure the program's environment and activities reflect the cultures of all children who attend and help children learn about and appreciate a wide variety of cultures and ethnic groups. "Teresa, you're right, Mardi Gras masks are very similar to the masks people from other countries wear in their celebrations."

Encourage children to take pride when they solve a difficult problem, learn something new, or improve their own performance. "Petra, it wasn't easy to learn how to play checkers. You must feel proud of yourself for sticking with it."

Provide opportunities for children to develop leadership skills. "Rion wants to start a Skating Club. Anyone who is interested can come to the first meeting on Tuesday afternoon."

Help children deal with setbacks by accepting their feelings about failures and responding respectfully. "I know you were disappointed when your mug blew up in the kiln. You were experimenting with a new way to attach the handle. Now you know it has to be attached more securely."

Plan activities and select materials that can be enjoyed by children with different abilities and skill levels. "Charmaine and Renée have sketched the outline for the outer space mural. Now they need someone to paint planets, stars, and spaceships and someone to paint the sky in the background."

Allow children to choose what they want to do and to choose not to participate in an activity. "Alex and Kyle prefer to work on their invention today rather than play soccer with the group."

Help children gain the skills they need to overcome fear of failure. "Whenever I had to prepare for an oral report in school, it helped to put my key points on note cards. There are some cards on the shelf in the quiet area."

Provide children with the time and resources they need to pursue their interests or master a skill. "Drew, one of the parents donated an old tape deck. You and Tinh might want to take it apart."

Encourage children to solve their own problems; intervene only when children seem to be unable to solve the problem or when someone might get hurt. "I know you two can work out a way to take turns with the puppets. You don't need my help to solve this problem."

Help children to learn through trial and error. "Marjorie has been experimenting with different designs for kites. Some of her kites stayed up; some didn't. She can tell you what she learned from her experiences."

Allow children to exercise their growing independence in safe and age-appropriate ways. "Kristi, your mom and I agree you can walk to your dance class. She's given us written permission to let you leave the program on your own."

Involve children in the daily operations of the program and in completing weekly chores. Rotate assignments so children can try a variety of tasks such as watering the plants, changing the pictures on the bulletin board, and checking which books are overdue.

Providing Children with Opportunities to Be Successful and Feel Competent

Fostering Children's Self-Esteem

In the following situations, school-age staff are fostering children's self-esteem. As you read them, think about what the staff are doing and why. Then answer the questions that follow.

Developing a Positive and Supportive Relationship with Each Child

Mr. Denton is outside helping the children organize a volleyball game. Several other children are using the playground equipment, two are painting at easels, and another is sitting under a tree reading. Once the game gets started, Mr. Denton walks over to the playground where five-year-old Peter is climbing higher and higher. "Peter, I don't think I've ever seen you climb so high," he says. Looking down from his perch, Peter says, "Yeah, this is the highest I've ever been. I'm taller than everyone." "You sure are," says Mr. Denton. He walks over to the painters, Jaimie and Bradley. He stops to look at Jaimie's picture and says, "It looks like you're almost finished with your painting. Would you like some help hanging it up?" "In a minute," says Jaimie. "I'm not through with the sky. Look at Bradley's fish." Mr. Denton walks to the other side of the easel. "Hi, Bradley," he says. "Those are some fancy fish. I like the one with the face like a lion." "I'm ready," says Jaimie. Mr. Denton helps hang the painting, then goes to see Diego who is sitting nearby reading. "Can I interrupt?" he asks. Diego looks up and nods. "I just wondered what you're reading." Diego holds up his book—*Charley Skedaddle,* by Patricia Beatty. "Can you tell me about it?" asks Mr. Denton. Diego looks pleased to be asked. "Sure," he says. "It's about a kid my age who's a drummer boy in the Union Army during the Civil War. He runs away during a battle." They discuss the book for a while, then Mr. Denton returns to the volleyball game. He notices one team has more older children, so he asks if he can play on the other side. Several children answer at once, "Yes. We need you." Nobody on the other side objects, so Mr. Denton joins the game.

1. How did Mr. Denton build a positive and supportive relationship with each child?

_____

_____

_____

2. How did Mr. Denton's interactions with the children show respect or recognize real accomplishment?

_____

_____

_____

Kandace and Quintan are sharing the results of their opinion survey of children. For the past week they carried clipboards and pencils, recording children's views on many topics. Quintan and Kandace hold a large poster board between them showing the survey results. Kandace points to the first bar graph. "We asked, 'Should recycling be required?' 65% of you said yes and 35% said no. Then we asked 'Do you recycle now?' 40% said yes and 55% said no and 5% said they didn't know." Next, Quintan has a turn. "We asked, 'What's your favorite movie?' and got 25 different answers. We have lots of favorite movies!" "We also asked, 'Should children watch TV on school nights?' 54% said yes, if you've done your homework. 30% said children would get better grades if they didn't watch TV. Others were undecided." When some of the younger children begin to squirm, Ms. Kettler steps in. "You collected some interesting information. May we hang up these charts so your parents and other children can look at them later?" "Sure," says Kandace. "We made lots of charts and graphs. I did some on my computer." "Thanks for your hard work," says Ms. Kettler. After the meeting she asks Quintan, "What's the most interesting thing you learned in your survey?" "That's easy," he says. "We talked about it a lot. Everyone is different and everyone is the same!" "That's a good description of people everywhere," says Ms. Kettler.

Helping Children Accept and Appreciate Themselves and Others

1. **How did this activity help children accept and appreciate themselves and others?**

   _____

   _____

   _____

2. **What did Ms. Kettler say and do to encourage children to accept and appreciate themselves and others?**

   _____

   _____

   _____

Providing Children with Opportunities to Be Successful and Feel Competent

Ashleigh comes running into the school-age program. She pulls off her coat and stuffs it and her backpack in her cubby. "Ginny," she shouts as she hurries across the room. I need to talk to you." Ms. Lamont looks up from her game of pick-up sticks and says, "Hi Ashleigh. What's up?" Ashleigh talks so quickly her words run together. "This weekend I saw my cousin and she has a doll house and it has six rooms, three up and three down, and lots of furniture and wallpaper and dolls and I'm going to make one just like it. I'm going to start this afternoon." "It sounds like you were very impressed with this doll house," says Ms. Lamont. "Yeah," says Ashleigh. "And my cousin made lots of the stuff inside the house so I know I could do it too. I've drawn some designs and started collecting stuff I can use. I have wooden spools to use as tables and fabric scraps for curtains and bedspreads." Ms. Lamont asks her, "Building and decorating a doll house is a big job. Is this something you will do at home or at the program?" "Well," says Ashleigh, "I was thinking we could build a big doll house in the woodworking area, or maybe use some boxes taped together. And I could organize a club for making the furniture and dolls and decorating the house." "That's a great idea. If more children are involved the job won't seem so big," replies Ms. Lamont. "You can discuss your idea with the other kids." "Okay," says Ashleigh. "There's Darlene and Scott. I want to tell them about the doll house. See you later."

1. Why did Ms. Lamont ask if Ashleigh was planning to build the doll house at home or at the program?

   _____

   _____

   _____

2. How did Ms. Lamont help Ashleigh to feel competent?

   _____

   _____

   _____

Compare your answers with those on the answer sheet at the end of this module. If your answers are different, discuss them with your trainer. There can be more than one good answer.

Your Own Sense of Self

The more you know about yourself (likes, dislikes, learning style, opinions, feelings) and your background (culture, home life, school experiences, successes, failures), the more sensitive and supportive you can be of children from different backgrounds. How you interact and respond to children conveys your respect and acceptance of them. And that is what most children, and most people, ultimately want from others.

Before you can help children to value themselves and others, appreciate differences, and feel free to bring their culture and all the aspects that make up their lives into the program, it is important for you as a program staff member to take a look at yourself. How did you come to be who you are today? Our past experiences unconsciously guide us in forming our personalities, attitudes, feelings toward ourselves and others, and our reactions to others.

With greater personal awareness, you will be able to help children appreciate their own differences as individuals. You can help them feel that they do not have to be like everyone else, or to ignore how they do things at home. There is a place for everyone in the program and we are all alike and different in many ways.

Listed below are questions to help you consider how experiences in your childhood might influence your views of others today.[2]

Examining your own personal experiences and preferences will help you understand how they affect your interactions.

How did your childhood influence your opinions and expectations   Yes   No

- Was it okay to be noisy and physically active in your home/community?   ☐   ☐

- Was it okay for boys to cry?   ☐   ☐

- Were girls allowed to play "rough"—climb trees, get dirty?   ☐   ☐

- Was it rude to look adults directly in the eye when they were talking to you?   ☐   ☐

How was your racial/ethnic identify described to you? Were there any characteristics of your group that were described as special? What about other ethnic groups?

_____

_____

_____

[2]Adapted with permission from Toni S. Bickart, Judy R. Jablon, and Diane Trister Dodge, *Building the Primary Classroom* (Washington, DC: Teaching Strategies, Inc., and Portsmouth, NH: Heinemann, 1999), pp. 223-224.

How has the media's labeling of different groups influenced you at different times during your life?

_____

_____

_____

What messages did you receive about your family's socio-economic position?

_____

_____

_____

What types of exposure did you have to people with mental or physical disabilities?

_____

_____

_____

What messages did you receive about "being smart?" Were boys treated differently from girls?

_____

_____

_____

How important was the ability to express yourself verbally? Was it acceptable to speak when others were speaking (did everyone talk at the same time)?

_____

_____

_____

Were some children always teased or avoided by others? Why weren't these children accepted?

_____

_____

_____

We can keep, change, or do away with our beliefs.

As you recall your experiences growing up and what was valued in your home and your community, you will probably come to realize that you no longer value the same things as you did as a child. You'll probably be able to make a connection, as well, to how your experiences (or lack of experiences) with people of different backgrounds has helped to shape how you interact with people today. With this awareness of your beliefs, attitudes, and assumptions, you can decide which ones you want to keep, change, or do away with altogether.

We are all influenced by our past. We make decisions and respond to others based on our prior experiences, what we've been taught, what has been successful and what has not. As professionals, we can use our experiences to help us understand children and to become aware of the influences children may have in their lives that affect who they are and their sense of identity.

Question and challenge your attitudes and beliefs. Ask yourself: "Why do I have trouble working with Casey?" "Why am I uncomfortable around disabled people? Have I ever really interacted with anyone who had a disability?"

Reflect on and check your reactions to situations that occur on a regular basis (especially if you have strong reactions to something). "It really make me angry when Maya won't look at me when I talk to her. It seems like bad upbringing to me. Could there be a cultural difference that I'm not aware of?" It's a good idea to become your own personal gauge. The more you do this, the better you'll become at detecting invalid messages that may be influencing you.

Talk with other staff members as a way to get a fresh look at things. "Frank, I'm having a lot of difficulty this past week with L'nora. Will you observe me this week to see if you can help me see why we're having such a personality clash?"

Your notion of who you are and how you'd like to be identified affects all aspects of your life. If you have a strong sense of yourself—your interests, strengths, weaknesses, attitudes, learning styles—and have been accepted and responded to positively because of who you are, you will likely feel good about who you are and what you do. By knowing yourself, you can help children by modeling a positive sense of self and guide them in developing their individual skills and abilities to feel competent and good about themselves.

Self-awareness of is key to helping children feel capable.

When you have finished this overview section, you should complete the pre-training assessment. Refer to the glossary at the end of the module if you need definitions of the terms used.

PRE-TRAINING ASSESSMENT

Listed below are the skills school-age staff use to build children's sense of self. Think about whether you do these things regularly, sometimes, or not enough. Place a check in one of the boxes on the right for each skill listed. Then discuss your answers with your trainer.

Developing a Positive and Supportive Relationship with Each Child

	I Do This		
	Regularly	Sometimes	Not Enough
1. Observing children to identify what makes them unique—personality, learning styles, temperament, strengths, interests, and needs—and letting them know you value their individuality.	☐	☐	☐
2. Listening carefully to children and taking their concerns seriously without interrupting, judging, or giving unasked-for advice.	☐	☐	☐
3. Showing children in many ways that they are enjoyable to be with.	☐	☐	☐
4. Knowing what each child is able to do and showing you value each child's unique skills and characteristics.	☐	☐	☐
5. Learning words in the native language of children whose first language is not English.	☐	☐	☐
6. Working with parents and colleagues to make sure each child receives the individual attention he or she needs.	☐	☐	☐
7. Showing children you have a positive relationship with their parents and that their family's involvement is both valued and appreciated.	☐	☐	☐
8. Letting children know they are cared for by offering gentle physical or nonverbal contact—a hug, a touch, a smile.	☐	☐	☐
9. Identifying children's interests through observation, surveys, and conversations; using this information to plan activities and provide materials.	☐	☐	☐

Helping Children Accept and Appreciate Themselves and Others

	I Do This		
	Regularly	Sometimes	Not Enough

10. Offering a wide variety of activities that do not limit children's options because of individual differences; avoiding biased remarks regarding gender, disabilities, culture, ethnic background, or any other differences. ☐ ☐ ☐

11. Making sure the program's environment and activities help children learn about and appreciate a variety of cultures and ethnic groups. ☐ ☐ ☐

12. Acknowledging children's efforts and accomplishments. ☐ ☐ ☐

13. Encouraging children to take pride in their efforts and accomplishments. ☐ ☐ ☐

14. Reinforcing children's behavior when they cooperate with others, help someone achieve a goal, or show that they value each other's accomplishments. ☐ ☐ ☐

15. Offering sports and games that help children learn to value fairness, cooperation, and personal growth. ☐ ☐ ☐

Providing Children With Opportunities to Be Successful and Feel Competent

16. Providing opportunities for children to develop leadership skills. ☐ ☐ ☐

17. Helping children deal with setbacks by accepting their feelings about failures and responding respectfully. ☐ ☐ ☐

18. Encouraging children to solve their own problems, intervening only when they seem unable to find a solution or when someone might get hurt. ☐ ☐ ☐

19. Encouraging children to learn through trial and error. ☐ ☐ ☐

Providing Children With Opportunities to Be Successful and Feel Competent (continued)

I Do This

	Regularly	Sometimes	Not Enough
20. Involving children in the daily operations of the program and in completing weekly chores.	☐	☐	☐
21. Providing a wide variety of materials, equipment, and activities to meet a wide range of abilities.	☐	☐	☐
22. Allowing children to exercise their growing independence in safe and age-appropriate ways.	☐	☐	☐
23. Providing children with time and resources needed to pursue their interests or master a skill.	☐	☐	☐
24. Allowing children to choose what they want to do and to choose not to participate in an activity.	☐	☐	☐
25. Helping children gain the skills they need to complete a task so they can overcome fear of failure.	☐	☐	☐

Review your responses, then list three to five skills you would like to improve or topics you would like to learn more about. When you finish this module, you can list examples of your new or improved knowledge and skills.

_____

_____

_____

_____

_____

_____

_____

_____

_____

_____

_____

_____

Begin the learning activities for Module 8, Self.

LEARNING ACTIVITIES

Learning Activity I.
Using Your Knowledge of Child Development to Foster Self-Esteem

---

IN THIS ACTIVITY YOU WILL LEARN TO:

- identify the stages of socio-emotional development of school-age children; and

- use what you know about children to promote a positive sense of self.

Psychologist Erik Erikson has outlined eight stages of socio-emotional development from infancy to old age. Children (and adults) must deal with the challenges of each stage before they pass to the next one. If these challenges are handled successfully, children's socio-emotional development is enhanced. Socio-emotional development is the foundation for self-esteem.

Erikson's first stage of development is **trust**. Infants develop a sense of trust when the adults who care for them respond quickly to their basic needs. Responsive adults help infants to trust their world and feel safe. They begin to explore the environment, try new activities, develop new skills, and learn how to interact with others. Establishing a sense of trust is essential to the development of autonomy, which generally occurs during the toddler years.

Autonomy is about being independent, doing things for oneself, making decisions, and exploring the world. One reason toddlers like to say "no" and insist on doing everything themselves is to assert their growing independence. Autonomy is essential to the development of initiative, which generally occurs during the preschool years.

Initiative describes the active, talkative, and creative life of preschoolers. They demonstrate their growing initiative as they use their new social, physical, and cognitive skills to build, draw, mold, paint, climb, and swing.

When children enter school, Erikson says they begin the stage of **industry**. During this period (approximately 5 to 12 years of age) children focus on developing the physical, cognitive, and social skills they need for their work in school and life. They acquire a realistic self-image, discovering what they can and cannot do. They come to understand who they are in relation to

Erikson's Stages of Socio-Emotional Development

others. You can support children's sense of industry by encouraging them to pursue their interests and learn to work with others.

Erikson's last three stages cover adolescence through old age. They focus on intimacy, the ability to reach out to others, and a reflection on one's life. Erikson's message is that socio-emotional development continues throughout our lives.

Helping School-Age Children Develop Self-Esteem[3]

Most school-age children care about how well they perform a skill or complete a task. As preschoolers they might have been content to experiment with all the different colors at the easel; now they want to make something "good." At this age, children begin to evaluate their performance against accepted standards, and compare themselves to their peers. These comparisons can lower self-esteem: "Marta was moved to a higher reading group, but I wasn't, so I must be stupid."

Children typically view themselves in terms of extremes—smart or stupid, good or bad. You can help them understand that each child follows his or her own pattern and timetable for growth; one is not better than another. Reassure them that over time they will develop and increase their skills in many areas—reading, bike riding, or painting. Help them understand that because each person is unique, they are likely to be better at some things than others.

Younger school-age children tend to think they can do something well if they try harder. They may feel very disappointed when their efforts do not always result in success. As children get older, they begin to see ability as something a person either has or does not have. They view another child's seemingly effortless accomplishments as signs of great ability. To develop a realistic sense of their own skills, children may need adult guidance and support to stick with a project. You can help children recognize their many strengths and understand that, while it is nice to have a special skill or talent, how one uses the talent is very important.

For school-age children, acceptance by friends is critically important. The ability to make and keep friends has a great impact on the development of self-esteem. Some children don't know how to make friends or join a group. The harder they try, the

[3] Based with permission on Nancy E. Curry and Carl N. Johnson, *Beyond Self-Esteem: Developing a Genuine Sense of Human Value* (Washington, DC: National Association for the Education of Young Children, 1990), pp. 67-87 and 129-148.

more they are rejected. If a child in your program has trouble making friends, you can help that child learn more effective approaches. By observing the child's interactions with peers, you can figure out what is needed and be a coach. Social skills are important in childhood and throughout life. (This topic is also addressed in Module 9, Social.)

School-age children can use words instead of their fists when they are angry. But their words can be painful. The angry language may be directed against the child ("I hate you") rather than the goal ("I want a turn on the swings"). Most children understand and accept each other's bad behavior as a normal part of friendship; however, such personal attacks can be quite painful for children who are not able to take them in stride. They may need adult assistance to understand how a friend can be nice one minute and hurtful the next. (It may help to remind the child of a time when he or she said or did something that hurt a friend, even though it was unintentional.)

There are many ways you can help children develop self-esteem. Some suggestions follow:

Try these suggestions.

Encourage children as they tackle a difficult task. When a child is completing a homework assignment, writing a story, or building an obstacle course, provide information and encouragement that will help him or her be successful.

Plan activities that allow children to be totally involved over a long period of time. Allow children to determine when they are finished, rather than setting a predetermined time limit.

Help children set reasonable goals and break those goals down into manageable tasks. "Writing and illustrating a book is a big job, Corinna. Can you think of some ways to break the job down into smaller tasks? For example, you might want to start with an outline."

Help children think about the consequences of their actions. "How do you think Albert felt when you made fun of his new haircut? Is there something you can do so you can be friends again?"

Applying Your Knowledge

Each of the charts that follow give one example of behaviors typical of children at ages 5 to 7, 8 to 10, and 11 to 12, and how staff might respond to foster children's self-esteem. In the blank spaces following each example, add a typical behavior of a child in your program and how you responded to promote the child's self-esteem.

As you complete the charts that follow, keep in mind that many of the examples of children's behavior and staff responses apply to more than one age group. Developmentally appropriate programs are based on a knowledge of child development and are responsive to children's individual strengths, needs, and interests. Therefore, it is important to observe children regularly, and to use what you learn to individualize the program.

Responding to Children in Ways
that Foster Self-Esteem

Typical Behavior of a 5- to 7-Year-Old Child	Staff Response
Gillian is drawing a picture. She erases her work several times and she makes holes in the paper. Unhappy about the way it looks, she tears up the picture.	*Let Gillian know you understand that it is important to her to draw a picture that meets her own standards for being "right" or "good." Show her where to find some thicker paper that is less likely to rip and some soft erasers that make it easier to erase.*

Typical Behavior of an 8- to 10-Year-Old Child	Staff Response
Trey is having trouble learning his multiplication tables. This is the first time he has been asked to memorize something. He feels frustrated and says he is too stupid to learn multiplication.	*Explain that many people have trouble memorizing. Let Trey know that people use a variety of strategies to memorize information such as the following: using flash cards, playing games that involve multiplication, visualizing the correct answer, posting math facts at home on the bathroom mirror or on the refrigerator, working with another child who is also learning the tables. Offer to help figure out which strategies might work best for him. Follow up on the offer if he seems interested.*

Typical Behavior of an 11- to 12-Year-Old Child	Staff Response
Stacy thinks she is too old for the school-age program. She says the activities are boring and the younger children are "babies."	*Involve Stacy in planning activities and selecting materials. Give her a blank schedule and ask her to fill it out for an ideal day at the program. Ask for her ideas on how to make the program more interesting for her age group. Suggest she talk with her friends to find out what they would like to do at the program. Implement some of the suggested activities, then meet with the older children to evaluate the effectiveness of the activities.*

Discuss with your trainer how your responses were appropriate for each child and how they helped him or her develop self-esteem.

Learning Activity II.
Observing Individual Children

IN THIS ACTIVITY YOU WILL LEARN TO:

- observe children carefully and regularly to get to know what makes each one unique; and

- use this information to help each child develop a sense of identify and self-esteem.

Use observation to learn about individual children.

Because every child is different, how you promote a positive sense of self will depend on what you know about each child. One of the best ways to learn about a child is to observe and write down what that child does over a short period of time. You will be surprised how much you can learn just by watching and noting everything you see and hear. For example, during an observation you may notice that Sarah, who usually forgets to wash her hands before snack, finally remembers. You can tell her later you noticed she remembered to wash her hands—and thus let her know that you noticed and valued her positive behavior.

To complete a careful five-minute observation of a child, arrange a time when you will have no other responsibilities. Pick a time when the child will be actively involved with others. This will give you the most useful information. Use index cards or a notebook to jot down everything you see, including:

- where the child is in the room;
- what the child does;
- what materials the child uses;
- who the child interacts with; and
- what the child says.

Work with your colleagues to apply information gained through observation.

Later, review your notes and share the information with your colleagues. Together, you can discuss what you learned about the child and plan ways to respond to his or her skills, interests, and needs. You can also establish a system for conducting regular observations of each child.

Applying Your Knowledge

In this learning activity you complete a five- to ten-minute observation of a child. (You might want to review Module 12, Program Management, Learning Activity I: Using a Systematic Approach to Observing and Recording.) Begin by reading the example below. Then choose a child to observe either indoors or outdoors. During the observation, make quick notes about what the child does and says, who the child interacts with, and his or her facial expressions.

After the observation, spend a few minutes adding any details you left out. Review your notes and think about what you learned about the child. Then answer the questions on the blank form that follows.

Observing a Child
(Example)

Child: _Brett_   **Age:** _10 years_   **Date:** _January 10_
Setting: _Breakfast_   **Time:** _7:45 A.M._

Observation Notes

Brett sits next to Victor. Both are laughing. Brett asks Victor to pass juice. Victor passes pitcher. Brett pours some in glass. Spills some on table. Drinks juice, puts cup down. Asks Victor if he's done. Victor says, "Almost." Brett stands up, clears dishes. Gets sponge. Wipes spilled juice. Asks Victor if he's ready. Victor says, "Yes. Do you want to play chess?" Brett looks at clock. "Not enough time. How about Connect Four?" "Okay. I want to be red." Brett smiles. Boys walk to shelves. Brett gets out game. Sets it up. Victor takes red checkers. Brett takes black. Victor makes a move. Brett has serious look on his face.

Review your notes, think about what you learned about the child, and answer these questions.

What do you think the child was feeling? Describe any behavior that tells you how the child was feeling.

Brett seemed to enjoy being with Victor. They get along well. Brett laughed and smiled. He waited for Victor. He smiled when Victor said he wanted to be red. He had a serious look on his face as the game began. He seems to take games seriously.

What did you learn about this child that might affect his or her sense of self?

Brett seems responsible. He wiped the spilled juice. He seems to be good at negotiating. He showed respect for Victor by suggesting a game when he saw there was not enough time for chess. He let Victor use the red checkers.

How can you use this information to foster self-esteem?

I can provide opportunities for Brett to use his leadership skills—for example, he might want to help a younger child learn to play a game. When other children are having trouble working out a problem I can ask Brett if he would be willing to help them negotiate a solution. When I see him showing initiative—such as when he wiped the table—I can offer genuine praise and appreciation.

Observing a Child

Child: _____   **Age:** _____   **Date:** _____

Setting: _____   **Time:** _____

Observation Notes

_____

_____

_____

_____

_____

_____

_____

_____

Review your notes, think about what you learned about the child, and answer these questions.

What do you think the child was feeling? Describe any behavior that tells you how the child was feeling.

_____

_____

_____

What did you learn about this child that might affect his or her sense of self?

_____

_____

_____

How can you use this information to foster self-esteem?

_____

_____

_____

It would be helpful to repeat this activity for another five- to ten-minute period with the same child to collect more information. Plan to observe and get to know other children in the program over the next few weeks. Discuss your observations and how you plan to use the information you collected with a colleague and with your trainer.

Learning Activity III.
Responding to Each Child as an Individual

IN THIS ACTIVITY YOU WILL LEARN TO:

- respect and appreciate the characteristics that make each child unique; and

- use what you learn to respond in ways that build a positive sense of self.

Each child in your program is a unique human being. By the time children begin school, they have developed the personality traits that are likely to continue throughout childhood and into their adult years. As stated in the overview, there are many factors that affect how a child develops a sense of self. School-age children have many influences in their lives—parents, siblings, and other family members; neighbors; teachers and friends at school; and school-age staff. In addition, children's development is affected by their culture, ethnicity, place of worship, and involvement in community activities such as organized sports and scouts. It is important to learn about each child and the context (home, school, and community) in which he or she is growing up. By getting to know each child, you demonstrate respect and appreciation for his or her unique characteristics. When children know they are respected and appreciated, they learn to value themselves and others. This is the essence of self-esteem.

Each child is unique.

Although most children pass through the same stages of development in the same order, each child develops according to an individual timeline which can be faster or slower than the "norm" for a specific age group. In addition, children's development is uneven—a child may be more advanced than her age-mates in one area (for example, riding a two-wheeler before her friends have mastered this physical skill) and less advanced in another (for example, learning to do long division after most of her peers). It is important to use the stages of development as guidelines while remembering that within any age group there can be great variation.

Your own experiences as a child, as a school-age staff member, and perhaps as a parent affect your expectations of children's behavior. For example, you may have strong memories of your own school days and how you and your friends felt and behaved in different situations. A child in the school-age program may

Your experiences can influence how you view children in the program.

95

remind you of nieces or nephews, children you worked with in another job, or one of your siblings. In addition, if you are a person who prefers quiet activities you may find it hard to understand a child who is happiest when fully involved—physically, cognitively, and emotionally—in routines and activities. You will need to spend more time getting to know the child so you can respond in ways that support the child's needs and interests. Your experiences and memories influence how you view the children in your program.

Many factors affect a child's temperament.

Other factors that affect a child's "uniqueness" are the inborn characteristics that determine his or her temperament. Beginning in infancy, a child's temperament affects how he or she responds to people and environments. For example, some infants are sensitive to light, sound, texture, and temperature; they might become upset when changes in the environment startle them. Other infants seem less aware of what's going on around them and need human interaction to become engaged. Children's temperament can cause them to vary in the following ways:

- **Activity level.** Some children are always on the move; others are content to sit and read or work on a puzzle for long periods of time. It is important to accept and plan for a wide range of activity levels.

- **Regularity of body rhythms.** Some children have highly regular body rhythms; they function most effectively when routines—meals, snacks, resting after kindergarten—occur at the same time each day. Children who have less predictable body rhythms may need flexible schedules for routines.

- **Adaptability.** Some children find it easy to get used to new situations and people. Others need extra time to adapt to changes and to get to know new people.

- **Intensity.** Some children are very intense; they experience emotions at extreme levels and get very excited, angry, happy, or fearful. Children who tend to be less intense have "low-key" responses to people and situations.

- **Distractibility.** Some children can focus on what they are doing without being distracted by other activities, for example, other children's games. Highly distractible children, however, may have trouble sticking with an activity. For these children, staff can repeat directions and help them stay with a topic in conversations.

- **Persistence.** Some children are very persistent; they can entertain themselves, work at learning the rules to a new game, and read or do homework for extended periods of time. Other children may need encouragement to stick with a difficult task or frequent breaks while working on a homework assignment.

The temperamental extremes described above are neither good nor bad traits. They describe the different ways children (and adults) may respond to people and experiences in their lives. As you get to know each child, keep these characteristics in mind. You can use information about each child's temperament as you plan and implement the program.

There may be children in your program who have been professionally diagnosed with learning disabilities. (Many experts view them as "differences" rather than disabilities.) One example is Attention Deficit Disorder (ADD). Children with ADD have difficulty receiving, understanding, or expressing language. In recent years, great progress has been made in identifying these conditions and understanding how they affect children's self-esteem, social skills, and physical and cognitive abilities. As a result, many more children are diagnosed than in the past—a conservative estimate is that 5% of the population has ADD.[4] Often children with learning differences have creative abilities and strengths that are not tapped in a typical school environment. Their difficulty in performing required school tasks can cause lowered self-esteem and social problems. It is important for school-age staff to recognize how learning differences affect a child's participation in the program. Some examples of typical behaviors of children with ADD follow:

There may be children in your program with diagnosed learning disabilities.

- During club meetings Deon taps his fingers and fidgets. Once the hands-on activities begin he is very focused and has many creative ideas.

- Gina frequently leaves her homework papers at the program. She puts them in the wrong cubby, leaves them in the quiet area, or fails to notice them falling out of her notebook. She gets in trouble at school and has to stay in from recess to redo her work.

- Yolanda is usually eager to try new games and activities. On a trip to the museum she asked the tour guide more questions than anyone else.

- Marcus often has hurt feelings. He doesn't pick up on social cues and messages and tends to take words very literally. When Charles tells him, "You can't be my friend," he doesn't understand that Charles is venting frustration and doesn't mean to end their friendship forever.

As you can see from these examples, conditions such as ADD can have both positive and negative consequences. Deon's fidgeting gives way to great creativity and Yolanda's eagerness exposes her

School-age staff can assist children with ADD.

[4]Edward M. Hallowell, M.D. and John J. Ratley, M.D., *Driven to Distraction, Recognizing and Coping with Attention Deficit Disorder from Childhood through Adulthood* (New York, NY: Pantheon Books, 1994), p. 41.

to new experiences and information. On the other hand, Gina's forgetfulness leads to staying in from recess—an essential physical outlet for many children with ADD. School-age staff can help her develop a system for remembering her homework. Marcus also needs some assistance. Staff can help him to recognize nonverbal cues and understand that people don't always mean what they say in anger and frustration.

Talk with parents frequently about their child's learning disability.

When you know a child has a diagnosed learning disability (difference), you should talk with parents frequently to share information and successful approaches. Parents may hear many complaints about their child's behavior, so it is particularly important to share your positive observations—"Wendell came up with a great way to make his mobile balance," or "Sabrina spent the whole afternoon writing and illustrating a story." You can also contact one of the following organizations to learn more about supporting children with learning differences.

Children and Adults With Attention Deficit Disorders (CHADD)
8181 Professional Place, Suite 201
Landover, MD 20785
301-306-7070
www.chadd.org

LD ONLine
The Learning Project at WETA
2775 South Quincy Street
Arlington, VA 22206
703-998-2600
www.ldonline.org

Try these suggestions.

Here are several suggestions to help you get to know and respond to individual children.

Accept and respect individual differences without trying to change children. Children need to know that other people accept them in order to learn to value themselves. Feelings of self-worth enable children to accept and respect others.

Encourage children to express their ideas and opinions without judging whether they are "good" or bad." Children learn to think and solve problems when they know their ideas will not be ridiculed or censored.

Be aware of your own style. Are you a person who likes a lot of physical contact? Do you prefer quiet times, or enjoy excitement? Do you get angry easily? Are your feelings hurt easily? How does your own style affect your interactions with children?

Observe children frequently, especially those with whom you find it hard to work or to understand. Record their behavior for five minutes, several times a day for a week. Ask yourself what these children seem to be feeling and thinking. Look for patterns to give you insight into their behavior.

Ask a colleague, your supervisor, or your trainer to observe a child whose behavior you feel you do not understand or whose behavior you are having trouble handling. Compare notes. Often a fresh perspective gives insight.

Remember some children will be harder for you to understand than others. Building relationships with all children in the program is part of being a professional. Although it's easy to spend lots of time with the children who are your favorites, make a point of spending individual time with every child each day or week (depending on the size of your program). Chances are as you get to know each child, you will discover something interesting or appealing about the child you didn't see at first.

Applying Your Knowledge

In this learning activity you focus on a child in the program whose behavior you feel you don't understand or with whom you find it hard to work. First, answer the questions about that child's behavior. Then plan three strategies for getting to know this child. Try your strategies for a week and see what you've learned about the child that will help you support his or her sense of self. Begin by reading the examples that follow.

Responding to Each Child as an Individual
(Example)

Child: _Wendy_   **Age:** _10-1/2 years_   **Dates:** _March 3-7_

What is it about this child that makes it hard for you to understand or work with him or her?

> _Wendy is very bossy. She tends to take over any activity she gets involved in. She makes fun of the younger children when they make mistakes._

Think about yourself. Is there something about you that might make it hard for you to understand or work with this child?

> _I'm the youngest of three girls in my family. My older sisters often bossed me around and teased me until I cried. I may overreact when I see older children taking over and making the younger ones feel bad about themselves._

List three strategies to help you get to know and work with this child. Use each strategy over the next week and record brief observations of what happens.

Strategy	What Happened
I will spend time with her.	_I talked with Wendy about her ideas for the next issue of the newspaper. She had a lot of good ideas and wants to try as many as possible. I helped her make a list of the ideas she was most interested in pursuing._ _I observed Wendy leading the meeting. She seemed to want the newspaper to be perfect. When a younger child made a mistake she made fun of him. After the meeting I talked with her about how things went. I asked her to think about how her comments made the younger club members feel. She said her older sister makes fun of her all the time and it's no big deal._
I will observe her.	_Wendy was working on her math homework. She spent a long time on one problem. She erased her answer twice. When she finished the problem she looked satisfied._
I will read about young adolescents—what they're like and what they need from adults.	_I learned this is typical behavior for young adolescents. Maybe Wendy is still defining who she is. She may be unsure of her own abilities, which leads her to make fun of the younger children._

Summarize what you learned about this child:

Wendy has a lot of good ideas—too many for her to carry out by herself. She is not a "natural born" leader. It is difficult for her to accept the work of other children that is not "perfect" and does not meet her standards.

Wendy is open to learning new skills—she was willing to learn how to set priorities.

Wendy has an older sister who is a model for the behavior Wendy uses with the younger children—making fun of them when they make mistakes. Wendy can handle her sister's comments (or at least says she can).

Wendy shows a lot of persistence when doing a difficult task.

How will you use what you learned to help the child gain a sense of self and develop self-esteem?

I will help Wendy learn skills, such as listening and communicating, used by effective leaders.

I will help her understand that her personal standards are just that—personal—and she will continue to be disappointed if she expects other children to perform exactly as she would.

I will help her understand that everyone should be allowed to participate in writing the newspaper at his or her own level.

I will suggest pursuing an interest by herself—for example, she might want to write and illustrate a short story.

I will offer Wendy genuine praise for her strengths—such as her persistence—and suggest activities that are appropriate for a child who enjoys getting very involved in difficult tasks.

Responding to Each Child as an Individual

Child: _____ Age: _____ Dates: _____

What is it about this child that makes it hard for you to understand or work with him or her?

_____

_____

_____

_____

_____

Think about yourself. Is there something about you that might make it hard for you to understand or work with this child?

_____

_____

_____

_____

_____

List three strategies to help you get to know and work with this child. Use each strategy over the next week and record brief observations of what happens.

Strategy	What Happened

Summarize what you learned about this child:

_____

_____

_____

_____

_____

_____

_____

_____

How will you use what you learned to help this child gain a sense of self and develop self-esteem?

_____

_____

_____

_____

_____

_____

_____

_____

Discuss your strategies and plans for continuing to respond to this child with your colleagues and your trainer.

Learning Activity IV.
Talking to Children in Ways That Show Respect

IN THIS ACTIVITY YOU WILL LEARN TO:

- talk to children in ways that let them know they are respected and understood; and

- help children learn to accept themselves and others.

Your words can show respect and understanding.

Some children have highly developed verbal skills and find it easy to express themselves; however, many children need help identifying and communicating their feelings and ideas. As a school-age staff member, you model appropriate ways of using language. When those words are respectful and supportive, children will want to listen and use the information. For example, you might say to seven-year-old Monique, "Try putting less paint on your brush, then it is less likely to spill." Monique will appreciate your concern and positive suggestion. She will feel that she is a competent person who can learn the skills she needs to carry out her plans and ideas.

Sometimes adults lose control, take out their anger on children, or fail to pay attention to what a child needs. These behaviors can make children question their own worth. They may think our words carry more meaning than we intend. When a child hears an angry or thoughtless statement, "Can't you sit still and listen? Have you got ants in your pants?" he or she may translate the words into a negative self-image. "I am a bad person because I can't sit still." Words that demonstrate respect and caring help build a child's self-esteem. "I can see you are having trouble sitting for so long. Would you like to take a break and come back to this later?"

Give your full attention to children and listen carefully.

Whether delivering praise, a reprimand, or instructions for an activity, it is important to talk to children using the same courteous voice you use with your friends and family. Begin by giving the child your full attention. Stand near the child and establish eye contact. Listen carefully so you can determine what he or she is really saying and feeling. As you look and listen, think about your own experiences. This can help you understand what the child is feeling. Your response should show you understand and respect the child. An example follows.

Ms. Grimaldi watches and listens to Jake, who recently joined the program. He stands near some children who are weaving on a large loom. Jake watches them for several minutes. "That's an ugly thing they're making. It looks really stupid," he says to nobody in particular. Ms. Grimaldi walks over and says, "Jake, we have a lot of different weaving materials and looms. Children here can plan and make anything they like. They decide how they want to use the materials. When they're finished they can hang up their weavings or take them home. If children need help getting started, I can show them how to set up the loom and suggest some materials to weave with."

Ms. Grimaldi could tell by the way Jake was watching the other children that he was interested in learning to weave. She thought he called their weaving ugly because he was worried about how his weaving would turn out. In this situation Ms. Grimaldi listened carefully to what Jake said and figured out what he was feeling. She responded to him in a way that showed she understood he was feeling worried and she respected his concerns.

A person less skilled in listening and talking with children might have said, "The weaving isn't ugly. It isn't nice to say that about other children's work. How would you like it if someone told you your work was ugly?" This statement would make Jake feel bad. It would also leave him still worried about his own ability to try something new.

Talking to children in respectful ways takes some practice. It may be a while before new ways of listening and talking to children feel natural. There are many opportunities throughout the day to talk with children in ways that communicate acceptance and respect.

Applying Your Knowledge

In this learning activity you read several examples of how to talk with children in different situations. Then you write down what you might say in typical situations to show respect for children. If possible, tape record or videotape yourself talking with children to learn more about how your interactions affect a child's sense of self.

Showing Respect When Talking to Children
(Example)

Margo says to Shawn, "You're taking up too much room. Get your fat butt off the couch." What would you say to Margo?

"Margo, if you need more room on the couch, you can ask Shawn to please move over. In this program we all try hard to talk to each other in ways that do not hurt feelings."

Trish sits at the table drinking juice. When Lionel bumps into her chair, she spills juice on her shirt. Trish hits Lionel. What would you say to Trish?

"Trish, it's okay to be angry with people, but it's not okay to hit them. You can tell him how you feel. Say, 'I'm angry with you, Lionel. You made me spill juice on my shirt. I think you should be more careful.'"

Gail interrupts your conversation with another child because she wants you to hear her poem. What would you say to Gail?

"Gail, I know you want me to listen to your new poem, but right now I am talking to Justin. I will look for you when we're finished. That will be in about 10 minutes."

Showing Respect When Talking to Children

Michael strikes out in the softball game. He refuses to leave home plate, saying, "It's not fair. That was a lousy pitch. I should get another." What would you say to Michael?

_____

_____

_____

_____

Ramona is the last child to be picked up. She is sitting by the window staring at the parking lot. What would you say to Ramona?

_____

_____

_____

Todd tells you he plans to be an astronaut. What would you say to Todd?

_____

_____

_____

Alamin gets teased by the other children because she is Muslim and doesn't participate in the holidays. What would you say to the other children?

_____

_____

_____

Lori sees some friends from school hanging out on the fields used by the program and walks over to them. You notice Lori's friends are smoking cigarettes. What would you say to Lori?

_____

_____

_____

Discuss your responses with your trainer.

See and Hear Your Interactions

If you were able to tape record or videotape yourself talking with children, listen to or view the recording to determine what you did well and what you would like to improve. You might want to review the tape with your trainer and discuss the children's verbal and nonverbal reactions to your communication.

Learning Activity V.
Promoting Children's Sense of Competence

IN THIS ACTIVITY YOU WILL LEARN TO:

- provide the right level of support to individual children;

- create an environment that helps children achieve competence; and

- plan for a wide range of abilities and interests.

As children gain new skills they develop a sense of competence.

School-age children are developing the physical, cognitive, and social skills they will use throughout their lives. As children acquire new skills, they develop a sense of their own competence that contributes to self-esteem.

The development of competence can also be tied to four conditions that lead to self-esteem. People with self-esteem:[5]

- **feel connected** to their own bodies, friends, families, colleagues, classmates, clubs, teams, ethnic or cultural groups;

- **have a sense of being unique** because they can identify their personal qualities and attributes and know these are respected and valued by others;

- **feel powerful** because they can use their skills, make choices and decisions, solve problems, and do things on our own; and

- **have models on which to base their behavior**; their personal standards and values evolve from their experiences and their understanding of family, group, cultural, and societal expectations.

An example follows:

> Ten-year-old Carmelita feels **connected**. She attends a bilingual school where her family's native language is used in many classes; belongs to a gymnastics club; attends her church Sunday school; enjoys spending time with her cousins; and decorates her room with pennants from her favorite baseball

---

[5] Based on Harris Clemes and Reynold Bean, *How to Raise Children's Self-Esteem* (Los Angeles, CA: Price, Stern, Sloan Publishers, Inc., 1978), p. 16.

herself through writing and painting, and knowing that her parents and coach value her talents and enjoy being with her. She feels **powerful** because she has opportunities to make decisions and solve problems at school, at home, and at the school-age program. She has clear values and personal standards for behavior because she has **models**. She understands the expectations of her family, church, culture, school, coach, and of society in general. In addition to these external sources of expectations, she has her own goals—to master a new routine on the balance beam, to be nicer to her younger brother, to stop biting her fingernails.

The adults in Carmelita's life—parents, other family members, teachers, school-age staff, her coach—have helped her develop a sense of competence. They provided the resources, encouragement, praise, and respect that allowed her to develop and use a variety of skills and to experience pride in her accomplishments.

You can play an important role in helping children develop a sense of competence. By providing the right level of support to individual children, creating an appropriate environment, and planning for a wide range of abilities and interests you help children feel capable, learn to interact positively with others, learn to respect rules and authority, and develop a sense of responsibility.[6] In the program's safe and accepting environment, children can practice skills they already have, and learn new ones.

Providing the Right Level of Support

Every child has his or her own learning style and capacity to learn. As a school-age staff member, you use your knowledge of individual capabilities and limitations to provide the right kind of support and guidance as children approach new tasks. One of the hardest things to know is when to offer help to a child attempting something new, and when to withdraw this support gradually so the child can manage on his or her own. Observe children closely so you will know who needs support throughout the learning process, who needs words of encouragement, and who simply needs you to wave or smile at them as they try a new activity.

[6] Based on William Damon, *Greater Expectations* (New York, NY: The Free Press, 1995), p. 78.

For example, when Zoe and Rosa announce that they are going to write a play, Ms. Alexander knows they will ask for her help if they need it. On the other hand, when she sees Joe and Alec take out a new board game, she keeps her eyes and ears open. She knows they may have difficulty reading and understanding the rules for the game and are likely to ask for assistance. If you are careful to intervene only when necessary, you can help children acquire new skills in a way that builds their sense of competence.

Creating an Environment That Builds a Sense of Competence

The program's indoor and outdoor environment—its space, furniture, equipment, interest areas, materials, daily schedule, and the staff and children—can help children feel competent. The furniture and equipment must be the right size, sturdy, safe, and age-appropriate. If the materials are broken, have missing pieces, or are too simple to be of interest, the children will become frustrated or bored, and they are likely to misuse them. If the playground equipment is too small for school-age children to use, you will constantly have to remind them to keep off. Children will not be challenged to learn new skills.

Materials and equipment should be stored where children can reach them and return them when done. When children have access to the things they need—games, sports equipment, art materials—they feel independent because they don't have to rely on adults. The more they can explore the interest areas, make and carry out plans, and use their growing skills on their own, the more pride they will have in themselves. Their sense of competence grows with their increasing responsibility.

The daily schedule, including how routines are handled, can also contribute to promoting a sense of competence. A schedule with many opportunities for free choice lets children make decisions. Offering a self-service snack allows children to decide for themselves when and how much they would like to eat.

Group meetings are a time to promote feelings of connectedness. Cecily can announce she is forming an Inventor's Club; you can ask the children for ideas for next month's family evening; the children can discuss how to solve a problem (for example, the younger children are getting knocked over when the older ones rush to get on the bus in the morning).

You and the other school-age staff members are the most important factors in the environment. Your knowledge of each child allows you to plan activities and provide materials that are at the right level—challenging but not overwhelming. The children who grow to trust you will be free to explore and learn from their environment—and to trust themselves as well.

Planning for a Wide Range of Abilities and Interests

Children from 5- to 12-years-old have a wide range of interests and abilities. It is important to provide materials, equipment, and activities that represent this range. For example, the choices in the arts and crafts area might range from poster paints to water colors, wide brushes to calligraphy pens, and newsprint to rice paper. Puzzles and games go from the simple to the complex. Computer games can be played at different levels. When playing softball children can hit a ball thrown by the pitcher or a ball perched on a "tee." Providing these choices allows each child to determine the skill level and challenge most appropriate for him or her.

It is also important to provide equipment and materials that respond to children's individual interests. Toby tells a staff member he would really like to learn to tie dye. The next week the program has a tie dye activity. Toby experiences his own competence as he ties the knots and dies his own T-shirt. He feels important because someone listened to him and responded to his interest. When you plan activities you know will interest a child, you are saying to that child, "You are important to me, I heard your request, and I know you will like this."

The children in your program will change a lot during the year. In fact, they change each day as they develop physically, cognitively, and socially; learn new skills; and develop new interests. To promote children's sense of competence, you will need to observe frequently and change the environment, materials, and activities to reflect children's new abilities and interests.

Applying Your Knowledge

In this learning activity you will focus on one child and assess whether the four conditions that contribute to self-esteem are present in his or her life. Next, you will plan ways the school-age program can provide the conditions and thus help all children experience a sense of competence.

Encouraging Children's Competence

Child:_____   Age:_____   Date:_____

Describe how this child feels **connected** to his or her own body, family, friends, ethnic or cultural group, clubs, teams, and so on.

_____

_____

_____

_____

_____

Does this child have a sense of being **unique**? What are the personal qualities and attributes that make this child unique? Are they appreciated by others?

_____

_____

_____

_____

_____

Does this child feel **powerful**? What opportunities does the child have to use skills, make choices and decision, solve problems, be independent?

_____

_____

_____

_____

_____

Describe the **models** in this child's life. Does the child have clear values and personal standards for behavior?

_____

_____

_____

_____

_____

Review your responses and think about what the program can do to fulfill these conditions for all children in the program. Record your plans below.

We can help children feel *connected* by:

Supportive Interactions

_____

_____

_____

Activities and Experiences

_____

_____

_____

Program Schedule and Structure

_____

_____

_____

We can help children have a sense of being *unique* by:

Supportive Interactions

_____

_____

_____

Materials and Equipment

_____

_____

_____

Activities and Experiences

_____

_____

_____

Program Schedule and Structure

_____

_____

_____

We can help children feel *powerful* by:

Supportive Interactions

_____

_____

_____

Materials and Equipment

_____

_____

_____

Activities and Experiences

_____

_____

_____

Program Schedule and Structure

_____

_____

_____

We can provide children with *models* by:

Supportive Interactions

_____

_____

_____

Materials and Equipment

_____

_____

_____

Activities and Experiences

_____

_____

_____

Program Schedule and Structure

_____

_____

_____

Share your ideas with your colleagues and trainer.

SUMMARIZING YOUR PROGRESS

You have now completed all the learning activities for this module. Whether you are an experienced staff member or a new one, this module has probably helped you develop new skills for fostering children's self-esteem. Before you go on, take a few minutes to review your responses to the pre-training assessment for this module. Write a summary of what you learned and list the skills you developed or improved.

If there are topics you would like to know more about, you will find recommended readings listed in the Orientation in Volume I.

Your final step in this module is to complete the knowledge and competency assessments. Let your trainer know when you are ready to schedule the assessments. After you have successfully completed them, you will be ready to start a new module. Congratulations on your progress so far, and good luck with your next module.

ANSWER SHEETS

Fostering Children's Self-Esteem

1. **How did Mr. Denton build a positive and supportive relationship with each child?**

    a. He walked around the playground talking to individual children.

    b. He commented on what they were doing without making judgments.

    c. He offered assistance, then waited for the children's response.

2. **How did Mr. Denton's interactions with the children show respect and recognize real accomplishments?**

    a. He commented on Peter's climbing higher than ever before.

    b. He waited for Jaimie to finish her picture, then helped her hang it on the line.

    c. He talked to Bradley about his painting.

    d. He asked Diego if he wanted to talk about his book. When Diego looked up and nodded, he stayed to listen and discuss the book.

    e. He joined the volleyball game so the teams would be more evenly matched.

Developing a Positive and Supportive Relationship with Each Child

1. **How did this survey help children accept and appreciate themselves and others?**

    a. It gave children an opportunity to express their ideas and opinions.

    b. It showed the children different ideas and opinions present in the program.

    c. All the children's responses were accepted and included in the survey results.

Helping Children Accept and Appreciate Themselves and Others

2. **What did Ms. Kettler say and do to encourage children to accept and appreciate themselves and others?**

   a. She provided time in the schedule for the surveyors to report to interested children.

   b. She stepped in to end the presentation when the younger children lost interest.

   c. She suggested the surveyors hang up their charts and graphs where parents and other children could see them.

   d. She thanked the children for their hard work.

Providing Children with Opportunities to Feel Successful and Competent

1. **Why did Ms. Lamont ask if Ashleigh was planning to build the doll house at home or at the program?**

   a. She wanted to let Ashleigh know it would be okay to build the doll house at the program.

   b. She hoped Ashleigh would see the advantages of having more help for the project.

2. **How did Ms. Lamont help Ashleigh to feel competent?**

   a. She gave Ashleigh undivided attention.

   b. She listened to Ashleigh's long description of the doll house and what she planned to do.

   c. She told Ashleigh she had a good idea and involving other children would make it easier to carry out the project.

   d. She suggested Ashleigh discuss her idea with other children.

GLOSSARY

Autonomy	Independence; the stage when toddlers develop the ability to do things for themselves, make decisions, and explore the world.
Environment	The complete makeup of the indoor and outdoor areas used by school-age children. The environment includes the space and how it is arranged and furnished, routines, materials and equipment, planned and unplanned activities, and the people who are present.
Industry	Productivity; the stage when children develop and use their skills to accomplish tasks in school and in life.
Initiative	Self-motivation; the stage when preschool children come up with their own ideas and want to try them out.
Observation	The act of watching systematically and objectively what a child says and does to learn more about that child. The information gained from observation is used to plan activities and provide materials that address the child's temperament, needs, strengths, and interests.
Sense of self	Understanding who you are; how you identify yourself in terms of culture, environment, physical attributes, preferences, skills, experiences. A sense of self evolves throughout our lives as we continually revise our perceptions in response to our experiences and interactions with others.
Self-esteem	A sense of worth; a good feeling about oneself and one's abilities. Someone who feels connected to others, respected and valued, and able to do things successfully and independently is likely to have self-esteem.
Temperament	The nature or disposition of a child; the way a child responds to and interacts with people, materials, and situations in his or her world.
Trust	Security; the stage when infants develop deep feelings of comfort and confidence because their basic needs are met promptly, consistently, and lovingly.

Module 9:
SOCIAL

OVERVIEW

PROMOTING SCHOOL-AGE CHILDREN'S SOCIAL DEVELOPMENT INVOLVES:

- encouraging children to develop friendships and enjoy being with their peers;

- helping children understand and respect the feelings of others; and

- providing an environment and experiences that help children develop social skills.

Social development refers to the way children learn to get along with others and to enjoy the people in their lives. It begins when an infant responds to a familiar voice or the special touch of a parent or caregiver. It continues as toddlers first enjoy playing alongside each other and as preschool children learn to play in groups. By the time they become school-agers, children have developed a wide range of social skills that allow them to get along with their peers and to be successful members of groups—in school, on sports teams, and at the school-age program. While at times they may argue and fight, most school-age children really enjoy being with others. They are willing to make compromises so that their games and activities can continue.

Most school-age children have developed social skills.

Adults play an important role in promoting children's social development. School-age children enjoy spending time with their peers, so part of your job is ensuring there are plenty of opportunities for children to choose what they want to do—and who they want to do it with—during their time at the program.

Through their relationships with adults and involvement in program planning and operations, children can develop social skills. You also help children learn to respect the rights of others, so everyone can enjoy the benefits of being part of a community. You help them understand their feelings and you model accepted ways to express these feelings. As a school-age staff member, you can also provide opportunities for children to become meaningfully involved in their communities.

Children learn many skills through their participation in the school-age program.

Listed below are examples of how school-age staff demonstrate their competence in promoting children's social development.

123

Encouraging Children to Develop Friendships and Enjoy Being With Their Peers

Observe and listen to learn how individual children relate to others in the program. "Yesterday, I observed Inez teaching Frannie how to do a handstand. When Frannie fell, Inez told her, 'You almost had it that time. Try again.'"

Encourage children to help each other. "Peter, it looks like Todd could use some help carrying the street hockey equipment outside."

Include enough time for free play in the daily schedule so children can choose to play with friends during activities. "Jane, it looks like you and Torie are enjoying the new prop box."

Encourage children to solve their own conflicts. "You both want to use the computer. How can you share it or take turns using it?"

Accept children's need to establish their own identity as they create their own "culture" separate from adults. "Would you like to hear about the slang words that my friends and I used when I was your age? We used expressions such as out-of-sight, groovy, and dig it."

Observe and assist children who have difficulty being accepted by the group. "Jan, when you upset the Monopoly board on purpose, it scared the other children. Let's talk about some other ways to handle your anger when you lose a game."

Helping Children Understand and Respect the Feelings of Others

Identify your own feelings when appropriate. "Adults have disagreements with their friends, too. When I'm angry with one of my friends I try to discuss the situation to 'clear the air.'"

Accept children's feelings while helping them learn to control their actions. "It's okay to feel angry when John makes fun of you. You can tell him you're angry, but I can't let you hurt him."

Encourage children to value what makes each person a unique individual. "When Tenesha joined our group several children asked how they could learn sign language. Her mother suggested some videotapes she'd found helpful."

Use group meeting times to solve problems that involve all the children. "Several children have complained that things are missing from their cubbies. Does anyone have some ideas of what to do about the problem?"

Model positive ways to interact with others. "I have an extra pair of gloves you can wear when we go outside."

Involve children in establishing rules that encourage the use of social skills. "Before we see the play, let's talk about how to be a polite audience."

Provide books that help children deal with their feelings about friendship, conflicts, diversity, and similar topics. "Karen, I read this book when I was your age. What would you do if one of your friends lied to you?"

Plan multi-age activities that encourage cooperation and allow older children to play the role of leader and mentor. "Steven, would you show the younger children how to use the measuring cups and spoons?"

Provide a variety of objects and tools that encourage children to explore their world. "We have a microscope and magnifying glasses you can use to examine the sand dollars."

Provide opportunities for children to belong to groups. "Regan and Natalie want to learn more about the fish we saw at the aquarium, so they are starting an Oceanography Club. Let them know if you want to join."

Offer opportunities for children to participate in the community at large. "Homestead Farms has so many apples on their trees they want to donate some to the food bank. They would like some volunteers to help pick the apples."

Invite members of the community to the program to share their special knowledge and skills so children can feel connected to the world beyond the program. "Next week a bicycle repair person is coming to the program to talk about bike maintenance and safe riding tips."

Providing an Environment and Experiences That Help Children Develop Social Skills

Promoting Children's Social Development

In the following situations, school-age staff are promoting social development. As you read each one, think about what the staff are doing and why. Then answer the questions that follow.

Encouraging Children to Develop Friendships and Enjoy Being With Their Peers

Emilio and Charles, both in third grade, are sitting in a corner telling each other jokes. Mary approaches them and says, "The Dance Club reserved this area for our rehearsal today. Would you please move? We're going to need a lot of space and you might get stepped on where you are." Emilio and Charles get up and look around for another place to sit. Charles says, "How about the quiet area, Emilio?" The two boys proceed to the quiet area. After listening to a few minutes of joke-telling and raucous laughter, Paul looks up from his homework and says, "You guys are really noisy. Find somewhere else to hang out." "But we don't have anywhere else to go," replies Emilio. Ms. Stuart has been watching the boys look for a place to settle. She steps in to make a suggestion. "I appreciate the way you two are trying not to get in the way of other activities. Would you like to move the bean bag chairs to another part of the room." "Okay," says Charles, "but where can we put them?" "Look around to see where there's some empty space," says Ms. Stuart. "How about next to the science area? There's room next to the gerbils and fish." "Yeah," says Emilio. "We can tell jokes to the animals." Charles laughs at his friend's idea and each boy grabs a chair. Twenty minutes later Ms. Stuart sees them still nestled in their chairs laughing and enjoying each other's company. She says, "You two have been laughing at each other's jokes for a long time. You must be really good friends."

1. **Why did Ms. Stuart step in to help the boys find a place to be together?**

   _____

   _____

   _____

2. **How did Ms. Stuart support the boys' friendship?**

   _____

   _____

   _____

Ten-year-old Wendy is the leader for this week's group meeting. With Mr. Swensen's help she gathers the children in the large group area. Wendy follows the agenda used at every meeting. First, Mr. Swensen makes a few announcements about outdoor activities and some new board games. Then Wendy takes over. She asks if anyone wants to share something they did at the program this week that was really fun. Several children raise their hands. She calls on Shellie. "Ben and I played in the loft and pretended it was a fort." Zack interrupts, "You mean you hogged the loft all afternoon." Wendy calmly states the program's rule, "No interrupting when someone else is speaking." Zack responds, "I'm sorry. After sharing, can we talk about how long people can use the loft?" Wendy turns to Mr. Swensen. He nods his head and makes a note. Wendy continues with the sharing, "Does anyone else want to share?" After everyone who wants to has had a turn, Wendy announces, "Okay, now we can talk about problems and think of ways to solve them." Mr. Swensen steps in to help lead the discussion so Wendy can participate along with the other children. He says, "Zack, tell us about your concern and we'll try to think of some solutions. "Well," Zack begins, "I don't think it's fair for two kids to use the loft for the whole afternoon when other people want to use it, too. We need some rules."

Helping Children Understand and Respect the Feelings of Others

1. **What social skills did children use during the group meeting?**

_____

_____

_____

2. **How did the group meeting format help children express and understand their own feelings and those of others?**

_____

_____

_____

Providing an Environment and Experiences That Help Children Develop Social Skills

A small group of older children is making final plans for tomorrow afternoon's road cleanup. (As part of a community-wide program, the school-age program has adopted a stretch of road and promised to keep it free from litter. Children age 9 and over can participate.) Clay says, "This is my first time on the clean-up crew. What am I supposed to bring?" Janine responds, "Your signed permission slip, if you haven't brought it already. And, we each bring our own trash bag. The big green ones are the strongest ones. It's a good idea to wear gloves, like gardening or work gloves." Ms. Caruso joins the conversation, "Clay, we're really glad you are joining us. We have a lot of fun and we leave behind a clean road." "Yeah," says Rico. "We started a contest to see who finds the largest piece of trash. Last time I found a washing machine. It wouldn't fit in my bag, of course, so we had to call someone else to pick it up." Ms. Caruso goes over the rest of the plans, Janine explains that everyone will wear an orange safety vest, and the meeting is over.

At the end of the day Ms. Caruso hears Clay telling his mother, "Did you remember to sign the permission form for the road cleanup? Can we drive along Chatham Road to see how dirty it is today? Then tomorrow we can drive by and you can see how clean it is." Clay's mother smiles. She turns to Ms. Caruso and comments, "It's nice to see Clay excited about work. What's your secret?"

1. **How did the road cleanup help children become involved in their community?**

   _____

   _____

   _____

2. **How did Ms. Caruso make the clean-up task enjoyable for the children?**

   _____

   _____

   _____

Compare your answers with those on the answer sheet at the end of this module. If your answers are different, discuss them with your trainer. There can be more than one good answer.

Your Own Social Development

Adults use social skills every day. When you yield to another car in traffic, share your lunch with a colleague who forgot hers, or wait for your turn to speak at a staff meeting, you are using the social skills you learned as a child.

Sometimes you find yourself in situations where you need to adapt to a new group of people. Perhaps you just joined a choir or started a new exercise class. In both of these situations you use social skills to get to know the other group members and to adjust to the group's accepted ways of doing things. You may introduce yourself to individual members, ask for advice, and observe and follow what others do.

Some adults find it very difficult to adjust to new situations. Although this difficulty may stem from individual temperament or personality, perhaps these adults never really learned how to get to know new people when they were children.

One of the ways children learn about how society expects them to behave is by watching adults in a variety of interactions. When children see staff members working cooperatively, sharing feelings and ideas, having friendly conversations, and enjoying each other's company they are learning about social behaviors.

It is important that staff members find ways to interact—adult to adult—so children can observe them getting along with others. Sometimes staff members are so busy it's hard for them to find time to be "friends"—but when they model social behaviors for children, everyone benefits. The staff members can feel positive about their jobs and the people they work with, and the children can gain a more complete picture of adults. They see adults working out problems, sharing experiences, and cooperating with each other.

Adults use the social skills they learned in childhood.

Staff model positive social behaviors in their interactions with others.

129

Think about how you and your colleagues model social skills. Give some examples below.

Negotiating:

_____

_____

_____

_____

Cooperating:

_____

_____

_____

_____

Solving problems:

_____

_____

_____

_____

Sharing experiences:

_____

_____

_____

_____

Positive relationships at work make your job more enjoyable and rewarding. The social skills you use and model for children are as important for their learning as they are for your mental health.

When you have finished this overview section, you should complete the pre-training assessment. Refer to the glossary at the end of this module if you need definitions for the terms used.

PRE-TRAINING ASSESSMENT

Listed below are the skills school-age staff use to promote children's social development. Think about whether you do these things regularly, sometimes, or not enough. Place a check in one of the boxes on the right for each skill listed. Then discuss your answers with your trainer.

Encouraging Children to Develop Friendships and Enjoy Being With Their Peers

		I Do This		
		Regularly	Sometimes	Not Enough
1.	Observing and listening to learn how individual children relate to others in the program.	☐	☐	☐
2.	Encouraging children to help each other.	☐	☐	☐
3.	Encouraging children to solve their own conflicts.	☐	☐	☐
4.	Observing and assisting children who have difficulty being accepted by their peers.	☐	☐	☐
5.	Providing enough time in the daily schedule for self-selected activities so children can decide with whom they would like to be.	☐	☐	☐
6.	Accepting children's need to create their own identities as they use slang and create a "culture" separate from adults.	☐	☐	☐

Helping Children Understand and Respect the Feelings of Others

		Regularly	Sometimes	Not Enough
7.	Identifying your own feelings, when appropriate, to model acceptable ways to express feelings.	☐	☐	☐
8.	Accepting children's feelings while helping them learn to control their actions.	☐	☐	☐
9.	Encouraging children to value what makes each person a unique individual.	☐	☐	☐
10.	Using group meetings to solve problems that involve all the children.	☐	☐	☐
11.	Modeling positive ways to interact with people of all ages.	☐	☐	☐

Providing an Environment and Experiences That Help Children Develop Social Skills	I Do This		
	Regularly	Sometimes	Not Enough
12. Planning multi-age activities that encourage cooperation and allow older children to play the role of leader and mentor.	☐	☐	☐
13. Involving children in establishing rules that encourage use of social skills.	☐	☐	☐
14. Providing a variety of objects and tools that encourage children to explore their world.	☐	☐	☐
15. Providing books that help children deal with their feelings about friendship, conflicts, ethnic diversity, and similar topics.	☐	☐	☐
16. Providing opportunities for children to belong to groups.	☐	☐	☐
17. Offering opportunities for children to be involved in the community.	☐	☐	☐
18. Inviting community members to share their special knowledge and skills with the children.	☐	☐	☐

Review your responses, then list three to five skills you would like to improve or topics you would like to learn more about. When you finish this module you will list examples of your new or improved knowledge and skills.

_____

_____

_____

_____

_____

_____

_____

Begin the learning activities for Module 9, Social.

LEARNING ACTIVITIES

Learning Activity I.
Using Your Knowledge of Child Development to Promote Social Development[1]

IN THIS ACTIVITY YOU WILL LEARN TO:

- recognize some typical behaviors of school-age children; and
- use what you know about school-age children to promote their social development.

By the time they are school-age, children have already learned many social skills. Between the ages of 5 and 12, children become increasingly independent, yet are still emotionally dependent on adults. They need support and encouragement from the important adults in their lives—such as parents, teachers, and school-age staff—to help them develop and refine their social skills.

In his book *Playground Politics,* Dr. Stanley Greenspan describes three distinct phases children pass through during the school-age years. As they pass through these phases, children move from a preschool focus on fantasy and feeling to being more logical and able to reason, learn, and control their impulses. These important skills are used by children in their life at school, their relationships with parents and other family members, and in sports and other community activities. The three phases defined by Greenspan are described below.

"The World is My Oyster" (4½ to 7 years)

Greenspan describes the first stage (4½ to 7 years) as a time when children feel very important and powerful—the center of attention. They are fascinated by super heroes and heroines and imagine they too have special powers. Accept this type of play as normal for this stage of development and encourage children to put their "powers" to good use. Most of the time children at this stage know the difference between reality and fantasy; however, they may be afraid of scary figures such as witches, robbers, or monsters. Be available to listen to children who want to discuss

---

[1] Based with permission on Dr. Stanley Greenspan, *Playground Politics, Understanding the Emotional Life of Your School-Age Child* (Reading, MA: Addison-Wesley Publishing Co., 1993).

135

their fears. Ask follow-up questions to help them develop their own strategies for handling fears.

Children of this age still rely on their families as sources of security but they also work and play with other children. Through play they express feelings, use creativity, and make sense of the world. They are fascinated by rules and may make up their own games with very specific rules and routines. Friendships are important. Some children have a special friend who is the object of much attention and affection: "I want to get a sweatshirt like Taylor has." Other children may try to manipulate their friends, "You can't play with me now because Amy is my friend today." The school-age program can support friendships by providing many opportunities for children to choose who they want to be with. In addition, you can help children resolve their disagreements and discuss ways to "make up."

Children in this age group are likely to seek your attention and affection. They like to feel close to adults and enjoy your participation in their games and play. Respond warmly when children request your attention, even if you are busy: "Hi Sarah. I'm helping these children get started on their masks. I'll come look at your picture in a minute."

At this stage, many children are defining what it means to be a boy or girl. The program should have a wide variety of books that depict males and females in positive ways. You and your colleagues should avoid commenting on what girls and boys cannot do because of their gender and encourage children to try all the activities offered at the program. You can respond to comments such as "boys can't cook' or "girls can't climb up to the loft" by guiding children to broader views about what boys and girls can do. "Gee, I'm a man and I really like to cook." "Why do you think girls can't climb up to the loft?" Remember, you are a model for the children in the program. If they see you doing a variety of tasks—carrying heavy items, preparing snack, playing football—they will get the message that men and women are not limited by their gender.

Toward the end of this stage, children begin feeling and handling a variety of emotions: anger, jealousy, love, guilt, and competitiveness. They also experience empathy: feeling and acting concerned when another person is upset or hurt and sharing another person's happiness and excitement. Being able to experience and express emotions helps children move beyond their close ties to family and into a world where peer relationships are very important.

Some children hide their feelings from adults. On the surface they may seem calm and happy; however, they may actually be dealing with unexpressed fears and concerns. The school-age program can provide opportunities for children to express their feelings through writing, dramatic play, and art work. Books about feelings help children understand their own emotions and empathize with other people.

"The World is Other Kids" (7 to 9 years)

At this age (7 to 9 years), Greenspan observes, children still enjoy using their imaginations to try out different roles. However, they are more likely to pretend to be a real person—a teacher, an astronaut, a dancer—rather than an imaginary character such as Supergirl. They apply their growing knowledge and academic skills to their play. Children might create a puppet show based on *Charlotte's Web*, write a play about Thomas Jefferson, or paint a picture of an endangered species. They enjoy using prop boxes—a collection of materials focused on a theme—travel agent, television show, auto mechanic.

Children in this age group use their cognitive skills to analyze and negotiate their position within their peer group. Mindy might think, "Lara and Kia sat next to each other on the bus today and now they are playing together. Tomorrow I'll sit with Lara on the bus and then she'll play with me." Such a plan—designed to get Lara to like her—shows how Mindy applies high-level thinking skills to a social situation.

By the time they are eight, many children enjoy forming clubs based on shared interests. They want adults to be facilitators rather than leaders. You can provide suggestions, time, and materials, then step back to let children make and carry out their plans.

At this stage, children may include and exclude others, sometimes based on gender. "This club is for girls. No boys allowed." Some children who are excluded know what to do to make sure they are included. Although adults might cringe at their methods, children often use their negotiation and problem-solving skills to convince their peers to include them. "It's against program rules to keep me out of the Computer Club. Besides, I won't show you how to use the new drawing program if you don't let me join." Others may need some assistance from a sensitive adult, "Rita, I'd really like to learn to use the new drawing program. Will you join our club and show me how to use it?"

A typical characteristic of children this age is their difficulty accepting disappointments and losses. Some children feel a sense of personal loss when losing at Old Maid or checkers and take a long time to recover. This is a normal reaction at this age, not a sign a child is a "poor loser" or a "bad sport." As children's self-esteem grows they are less likely to tie their feelings of self-worth to performance in a game.

Children can be very competitive, accusing each other of cheating or upsetting a board game because the game wasn't going their way. Competition can also affect relationships; children may compete for the attention of a popular child or to spend time with a favorite staff member. When children find the competitive nature of school and sports activities overwhelming you may need to steer them to less-competitive activities. The program should encourage noncompetitive games without winners and losers. You can help children set and pursue individual goals so they can master skills and experience personal achievement.

Seven to nine year olds tend to define themselves in relation to others. They compare their appearance, school performance, physical abilities, and popularity in relation to that of other children. "Casey read a longer book than I did so he must be smarter." "I can't do a handstand, but Alicia can. I must be clumsy." Their self-esteem rises and falls based on the judgments of their friends. Sometimes they make cruel comments that are very painful. As children move into the next stage they continue to be aware of other people's judgments. However, they also base their sense of self on how they feel about themselves.

"The World Inside Me" (10 to 12 years)

Greenspan views children in the third stage (10 to 12 years) as learning to define themselves based on their own goals and values rather than how they are treated by their peers. They gain a sense of who they are that doesn't change with each new criticism or comment. Their interactions with family, friends, teachers, and others help them develop personal values. They begin to see who they are and how they fit in the world. Children in this age group are generally more secure in their feelings about themselves. They can show initiative, are usually cooperative, and appreciate others and their accomplishments.

Most children in this age group have entered or are on the edge of puberty. They are looking forward to growing up, but may also be uncomfortable with the physical changes their bodies are going through. If their bodies are changing at a rate much faster or slower than their peers they are likely to be self-conscious. The school-age program can encourage children to develop their talents and skills so their self-esteem is not tied to how slowly or quickly their bodies are changing.

This is an uneven time for the sexes. Girls may be up to two years ahead of boys in their progress towards physical and social maturity. As they become increasingly interested in the opposite sex they mimic teenage behaviors. Try to accept their harmless imitations and ignore those that can be annoying at times such as using slang or constantly talking about music, clothes, or celebrities.

At this age, children have a strong need to be accepted by their peer group. Even children with good judgment may be influenced by the group to do things they know are not appropriate. Negative peer pressure can lead to drug and alcohol use, early sexual activity, and gang membership. School-age staff are in an excellent position to help children define and stick to their own values even when their friends want them to do something else. You can help children practice how to respond when asked to do something they know is not right—for example, if asked to steal something to prove he or she isn't afraid a child could say, "But I am afraid. Afraid someone will think I'm so stupid I stole something." If you are aware of a child's anti-social behavior, discuss it with parents so children can get the help they need immediately.

This can be a frightening time for children as they become more independent and move into the world. Like toddlers, they may have two desires—to remain close to and dependent on their families as well as to grow up and do things on their own. In response to these confusing feelings, children may become more dependent or may rebel against rules and accepted ways of behaving. Involve them in planning the materials and activities offered by the program. Provide blank schedules so children can plan how to spend their time at the program. If possible, plan activities and set aside an area for this age group only. Try to keep your commands and instructions to a minimum. Instead, use indirect methods to give directions—a sign-up list for chores rather than assignments.

Ten to twelve year olds begin to experience feelings such as sadness and joy in a deeper way, much as adults do. They are aware of and interested in events outside their communities and are developing opinions. They can get fired up discussing topics such as saving the environment and helping the homeless. They can also experience empathy by imagining how they might feel if they lived through an earthquake or what they might do if they won the lottery. Children may talk to you about their feelings and may ask what you might do in similar situations. The program can also arrange for children to participate in community projects such as cleaning up a park or stream or making regular visits to a nursing home. Contact groups that might need volunteers and ask representatives to visit the program.

At this stage, children are beginning to be motivated by personal goals rather than out of desire for approval or fear of what will happen if they don't do what is "right." For example, a child may practice the piano because he or she wants to play well rather than to be praised by the teacher or to avoid being nagged by a parent. They also think about the future—What will the world be like? What will my life be like? Such thoughts can motivate their actions: I want to get a good job when I grow up, so I will do my homework today.

Children with good social skills are more likely to succeed in school and in life.

Success in school is closely related to a child's ability to cooperate, consider another person's perspective, and follow accepted rules and practices. Children are more likely to enjoy youth activities such as athletics and scouts if they are able to be a team member and contribute to group efforts. Their family life will be more rewarding if they can share and take turns with siblings and communicate their ideas and feelings to their parents.

Applying Your Knowledge

In this activity you record examples of the social development of children in your program. Three charts are provided; one for each of the three stages defined by Greenspan: $4^1/2$ to 7 years, 7 to 9 years, and 10 to 12 years. If you work with only one age group or do not have a full span of ages enrolled, provide examples that apply to your group.

> As you complete the charts that follow, keep in mind that many of the examples of children's behavior and staff responses apply to more than one age group. Developmentally appropriate programs are based on a knowledge of child development and are responsive to children's individual strengths, needs, and interests. Therefore, it is important to observe children regularly, and to use what you learn to individualize the program.

The World is My Oyster: 4½ to 7 Years

Typical Behavior	Example
Fascination with super heroes and heroines.	*Peter pretended to be a monster and chased Cindy and Pam.*
Work and play with other children; express feelings, use creativity and make sense of the world.	
Make up their own games with rules and routines.	
Have special friends.	
Enjoy being with adults.	
Are defining what it means to be a boy or girl.	
Feel and handle a variety of emotions; may hide feelings from adults.	

The World is Other Kids: 7 to 9 Years

Typical Behavior	Example
Pretend to be real people.	*Randi and Emma made up a play about being astronauts.*
Analyze and negotiate their positions within their peer group.	
Form clubs based on shared interests.	
Include and exclude others; may negotiate to be included.	
Have difficulty accepting disappointments and losses.	
Can be very competitive; may find competition overwhelming.	

The World Inside Me: 10 to 12 Years

Typical Behavior	Example
Gain a sense of who they are; develop personal values.	*Jamal told Bernard "I'm not the best guy on the team, but I really like to play."*
Have entered or are on the edge of puberty; may be uncomfortable or self-conscious.	
Mimic teenage behaviors.	
Want to be accepted by peers; can be negatively influenced by peer group.	
Want to be independent, but may sometimes be afraid of growing up.	
Are aware of and interested in community and current events.	
Motivated by personal goals.	

When you have completed as much as you can on these charts, share your answers with your trainer. Discuss what you and your colleagues can do to support children's social development.

Learning Activity II.
Promoting Children's Play

IN THIS ACTIVITY YOU WILL LEARN TO:

- observe how children learn and develop through play; and

- provide materials, time, space, and suggestions that allow children to make and carry out their own plans.

The Importance of Play

School-age children come to the program after a full day of "work" at school where most of their activities were planned and controlled by adults. Therefore, it is important for children to spend a good deal of their time at the school-age program engaged in unstructured play. Play is children's work—it helps them grow in all areas. Play gives children opportunities to develop physically, think and solve problems, learn to express themselves in acceptable ways, and build self-esteem. Play is also one of the most important ways in which children develop social skills. They learn to take turns, negotiate, share materials, understand how a friend feels, and express their emotions. In addition, play helps children try out grown-up roles and overcome their fears.

Children's play may include using their imaginations, organizing and leading others, researching special interests, making collections, playing board games, doing puzzles, working on crafts, using physical skills, or listening to music. The school-age program can offer children a change of pace—a place to relax, have fun, use their creativity, make their own decisions, practice and master skills, do things with other children, and do things by themselves.

Before continuing your reading spend a few minutes walking around to see what the children in your program are doing. Write down some examples of their play. An example is provided to get you started.

Example: *Jaron and Ian are feeding Scampy, the program's gerbil. Jaron holds Scampy while Ian offers her a piece of food. Jaron lets Scampy crawl up his arm and behind his ear. He laughs when she tickles his ear. Ian asks for a turn.*

_____

_____

_____

_____

_____

_____

Sara Smilansky identifies four kinds of play enjoyed by school-age children.[2] **Functional play** occurs when children explore and examine the properties of objects and materials and find out how things "work." By handling, experimenting, observing, listening, and smelling, children make discoveries. Doing science experiments, making designs with parquetry blocks, and baking bread are examples of functional play that might take place in your program.

Functional play allows children to make discoveries.

Through **constructive play**, children use materials—for example, blocks, modeling materials, recycled items, sand—to create a representation of something real or imagined. For example, children might create a farm with Legos, make a collage depicting life in space, or build roads in the sandbox.

Constructive play involves making representations of real or imagined things.

Games with rules include board games, many computer games, sports, or any type of play governed by a set of rules that everyone understands and follows. Depending on a child's temperament, he or she may enjoy playing board games with one or more peers. Some children just enjoy the game; others are driven to win. They may fight over the rules and they may have difficulty accepting when they lose. Playing games with rules provides opportunities for children to deal with competition and the strong feelings generated by winning or losing. You can help children work through their disagreements and handle feelings of anger and aggression. You can also introduce some games that do not result in winners or losers. Some children enjoy competing with themselves to better their previous scores or records. Interested children can make charts to keep track of their own progress.

[2]Based on Sara Smilansky and Leah Shefatya, *Facilitating Play: A Medium for Promoting Cognitive, Socio-Emotional, and Academic Development in Young Children* (Gaithersburg, MD: Psychosocial and Educational Publications, 1990).

School-age children enjoy socio-dramatic play focused on fantasy or the real world.

During the school-age years, children engage in socio-dramatic play at a level that is more complex than when they were younger. Their make-believe play may revolve around fantasy or focus on themes from the real world (past or present). Play episodes can extend over several days or weeks. This type of play is most closely related to social development. It is an important way for children to learn how to get along with their peers. When playing with each other, children share information, offer suggestions, and sometimes tell each other how to behave. Children who are naturally shy may find it is easier to be a part of a group when they can pretend to be someone else. The social skills developed through socio-dramatic play are used in almost all the other situations children encounter. For example, learning to follow the rules established by the group will help a child learn to play games and sports that involve rules.

Many school-age children enjoy planning and putting on their own plays and shows. You can provide writing materials for budding playwrights and books of creative drama activities and short plays. Children will make good use of props and dress-up clothes such as the following:

Shoes	Sunglasses	Boots
Handbags	Watches	Coats
Sweaters	Hats	Capes
Dresses	Shirts	Belts and suspenders
Skirts	Pants	Scarves
Aprons	Neckties	Fake fur pieces
Raincoats	Umbrellas	Eyeglass frames
Jewelry	Graduation Gowns	Brief cases

Older school-age children may involve younger ones in their productions, or they may put together a show, then perform it for the rest of the group. Writing a script, providing background music, and creating elaborate costumes can all be part of their play. Such projects may last from an afternoon to several weeks.

Create a variety of prop boxes to encourage children's socio-dramatic play.

One way to support children's socio-dramatic play is to create prop boxes—containers filled with materials related to a specific theme or type of play. Prop boxes can be used both indoors and outdoors. They are ideal for programs that operate in shared space because they are easy to set up and store. Young school-age children, who are still tied to home, enjoy prop boxes that allow them to explore family roles. Prop boxes for older children might be related to a shared experience, such as a behind-the-scenes tour of a supermarket. The box might include uniforms, empty food containers, a cash register, shopping baskets, and important that has happened in a child's life—dancing a role in *The Nutcracker Suite*.

Children will have ideas for prop box themes and can help collect the materials. Include related books (fiction and nonfiction) and pictures so children can fully explore their interests. Ask them to let you know when consumables such as pads of paper need to be replaced. Any sturdy container, perhaps decorated by the children, will do for storage of the props. Introduce new boxes to the group, then store them where children can have easy access.

Offer a variety of prop boxes so you can address a wide range of interests. Keep them out as long as children are interested. Some suggested themes and materials for prop boxes appear at the end of this activity.

School-age staff play an important role in supporting children's play by providing time, space, materials, and encouragement. The youngest children in the group may invite you to participate in their games and dramatic play. You can model how to be a graceful loser (or winner), review the rules at key moments in the game, introduce non-competitive versions of popular games, and ask open-ended questions to help children recreate experiences, "What are some of the things you usually do at the beach? What would you need to open an ice cream stand?"

Most older children prefer to make and carry out their own plans without a lot of adult involvement. Allowing children to be independent tells children that you feel confident they can do many things on their own. You don't have to completely ignore them. Instead, observe to see how things are going, encourage them to ask for what they need, and offer suggestions in a way that allows children to accept or reject them. "If you want to make curtains for your puppet theater, there's some fabric in the storage cabinet."

How school-age staff support play depends on what children ask for.

Applying Your Knowledge

In this learning activity you can use a checklist to assess how your program supports children's play. After completing the assessment, review the results and plan ways to improve the program environment and encourage children's play.

Supporting Children's Play: Checklist

Program Environment

1. The schedule includes long blocks of time when children can make and carry out their plans. ☐

2. Materials (e.g., radios to take apart, cooking ingredients and equipment, pegs and pegboards) are available for functional play. ☐

3. Materials (e.g., blocks, art and craft supplies, Legos, recycled items) are available for constructive play. ☐

4. Materials (e.g., board games, computer games, balls and sports equipment) are available to play games with rules. ☐

5. Materials (e.g., props, costumes, books of plays) are available for socio-dramatic play. ☐

6. There is space for children to store long term projects. ☐

7. The space can be arranged if necessary to make room for children's play. ☐

8. The program can provide additional materials in response to children's requests. ☐

Encouraging Children's Play

1. I join in younger children's games upon request. ☐

2. I help children learn the rules for games and sports. ☐

3. I help children handle feelings generated by wins and losses. ☐

4. I introduce non-competitive games. ☐

5. I give children the freedom to play on their own without adult involvement. ☐

6. I encourage children to ask for what they need to support their play: time, space, and materials. ☐

7. I offer suggestions in a way that allows children to choose whether to adopt them. ☐

8. I encourage children to carry out their own plans. ☐

9. I let children make their own mistakes and learn from them. ☐

10. I use information from observing children's play in planning. ☐

Review your responses to this checklist. List below any changes you'd like to make to improve the ways you and your program encourage play.

_____

_____

_____

_____

_____

_____

_____

_____

_____

_____

Discuss your ideas with your trainer and colleagues. Plan any changes you can make to more effectively encourage chidren's play.

Prop Boxes for School-Age Children[3]

Health Clinic

Gauze	Real stethoscope	Band-Aids	Beds
Cotton balls	Plastic eye droppers	Play thermometer	Stop watch
Height-weight chart	Dolls	Paper and pencils	Telephone
Prescription pads	Scale	Stretcher or cot	Hospital gown
Disposable tongue depressors	Red finger paint for blood	Cloth for making bandages	Health provider uniforms
Small suitcase or bag for medical supplies	Books on first aid and preventive health care		

Veterinarian

Stuffed animals	Pet carrying boxes	Collars and leashes	Food dishes
Items from health clinic list above	Books on pet care and animal behavior	Pet toys	

Unisex Hair Stylist

Large mirror	Hand mirrors	Hairpins	Towels
Rollers or curlers	Hair nets	Plastic basin	Scarves
Bobby pins	Hair clips	Barrettes and ribbons	Headbands
Manicure set	Emery boards	Magazines	Play money
Paper	Pencil	Shaving brushes	Shaving cream
Hair dryer and curling iron without cords	Hair care products (empty containers)	Hairbrushes and combs (wash after use)	Wigs mounted on wig stands
Aprons, large bibs, or smocks	Razors (toys or real ones without blades)		

School

Books	Chalk	Small blackboard	Pencils
Pencil sharpener	Paper pads	Rulers	Erasers
Attendance book	Red pencil	Stickers	Stamp and pad

---

[3] Adapted with permission from Cheryl Foster, "Dramatic Play Kits or Prop Boxes," in *Competency-Based Training Module No. 24: Dramatic Play* (Suppl. No. 5) (Coolidge, AZ: CDA Training Program, Institute of Human Development, Central Arizona College, 1982), pp. 41–46.

Office

Pencils	Pencil holder	Pencil sharpener	Waste basket
Paper and pads	Rubber stamps	Ink pads	Telephones
Phone books	Briefcases	Portfolios	Clip boards
Assorted junk mail	Adding machine	Files	Paper clips
Typewriter or keyboard (from recycling center)	Discarded business forms of many types	Portable file box to hold the props	Scissors
			Staples

Live Movies, TV, or Stage Production

Puppets	Paper money	Empty popcorn boxes	Paper pads and pencils
Supplies for making new puppets	Large carton with "window" and painted knobs	Colored paper for tickets or roll of expired movie tickets	Use with dress-up box to create costumes for dancers and actors

Beach

Sunglasses	Sun hats	Beach bags	Sea shells
Umbrellas	Picnic basket	Fishing poles	Portable radio
Playing cards	Swim goggles	Inflatable tubes	Flippers
Buckets and shovels	Sand molds	Frisbees	Plastic thongs
Blankets or beach towels	Empty suntan lotion bottles	Paper plates and cups and plastic utensils	Food (pictures or empty cans or boxes)
Books about beach plants and animals			

Gas Station and Automobile Repair

Work shirts	Caps	Tire pump	Hammers
Pliers	Screwdrivers	Oil funnel	Empty oil cans
Flashlights	Wiring	Air pump	Windshield wipers
Key ring and keys	Rags	Work gloves	Short lengths of hose
Motor parts (used and washed spark plugs, filters, cable sets, carburetors, gears)	Auto supply catalogs	Large and small boxes to make cars and/or miniature vehicles	Miniature tool set for use on miniature cars

Learning Activity III.
Promoting Children's Emotional Development[4]

IN THIS ACTIVITY YOU WILL LEARN TO:

- recognize the emotional milestones children need to master during the school-age years; and

- support children's emotional development.

The Foundations for Emotional Development

Dr. Stanley Greenspan has defined several early milestones that are the foundation for children's ongoing emotional development. Addressing these milestones begins in early childhood; however, they are more fully developed during the school-age years. Children who do not master these milestones may have problems—in school, at home, and in their relationships with peers. Greenspan's five milestones are described below.

"Security and the ability to look, listen, and be calm."

This milestone allows children to focus on work and activities. Most children begin learning this skill during the first few months of life. They enjoy being with their parents and caregivers; develop a regular schedule for sleeping; look and listen to their environment; and in general, feel comfortable with life. School-age children who have accomplished this milestone can sit and listen to instructions without looking around the room or thinking about something happening outside the window. Children who have not reached this milestone have difficulty focusing on their work or activities because they are distracted by what is going on around them. They may have difficulty selecting what they want to do—the numerous options may seem overwhelming.

"Relating: the ability to feel warm and close to others."

The second milestone allows children to enjoy being with others. It is based on the trust that normally develops during infancy as a child interacts with and depends on parents and other caregivers. In the early years most of children's learning comes from their relationships with others. Mastering the ability to relate to individuals as well as a group is important to learning. For example, infants begin to understand cause and effect when they learn crying will bring someone to their side or that smiling will

---

[4]Based with permission on Dr. Stanley Greenspan, *Playground Politics, Understanding the Emotional Life of Your School-Age Child* (Reading, MA: Addison-Wesley Publishing, 1993).

get a smile in return. The emotional experiences resulting from warm and close relationships help children understand more abstract concepts later in life.

A school-age child who feels warm and close to others can work independently and easily join a group at play. Children who aren't able to develop warm, trusting relationships are likely to have difficulty making friends and becoming part of the group. They may be wary of others, use aggression to get what they want, or play and work alone because they fear rejection.

The third milestone allows children to understand and respond appropriately to nonverbal cues. Children need to be able to pay attention and feel close to others before they can communicate with them. This milestone begins when infants learn that facial expressions and body language are signs of thoughts and feelings. Infants use this information to decide how they will respond. Thus, a child responds to a parent's frown by crying, or wiggles with delight in response to a parent's open arms. Children also use nonverbal communication to express what they want or need—for example, pointing at an object on the table so her older brother will get it for her.

"Intentional two-way communication without words."

School-age children who have mastered this milestone can observe nonverbal cues and accurately "read" the expectations, desires, and feelings of other people—for example, teachers, school-age staff, and peers. Children who have not mastered this milestone may misinterpret the actions of their peers and have trouble being accepted by the group. For example:

> Chaundra and Deanne are working on collages in the arts and crafts area. Deanne gets up to join a group of children making up a dance. Chaundra doesn't understand why Deanne left. She thinks Deanne doesn't like her. Actually, Deanne has been watching the other children for some time. She was waiting to see what kind of dancing they would be doing. Chaundra did not notice Deanne's quick glances at the dancers, sighs of boredom with her collage, and tapping the table in time to the music. Because Chaundra feels rejected, she calls after Deanne, "You can't leave. You didn't pick up your stuff." The other children turn to look at Chaundra. They want Deanne to join them so they take her side, "She already picked up." "That's your mess." Now Chaundra feels doubly rejected—by Deanne and by the dancers. She has no idea what went wrong.

"Emotional ideas."

This milestone allows children to use words to express their feelings. With this ability they can create mental pictures of what they want, need, or feel. When something happens that makes them feel angry they can give this feeling a name, rather than responding with tears, a tantrum, or pouting. The child who feels angry says to herself, "I am angry." Children who have mastered this skill can use it in dramatic play and in creative writing. They can imagine how a character might feel in a situation; then they assume that role or write about it.

Children who have not mastered emotional ideas may have trouble controlling their actions. They can't describe their feelings to themselves and don't know how to use words to express the ideas their feelings represent. They tend to act without thinking because they don't know they can have a feeling without an action. A person can feel sad without crying, angry without hitting, or frustrated without tearing up a picture. Instead of using words to express their feelings, they respond by hitting another child, throwing a bat, or crying. For example:

> Neil and Brianna are watering the garden with a hose. When Quentin walks by, Neil turns towards him, aims the hose, and says playfully, "Would you like us to water you, too?" Some water drips on Quentin's sneakers. Quentin grabs the hose from Neil and pushes him out of the way. Neil falls down in the garden as Quentin says, "You are so stupid." Quentin didn't notice the playful tone in Neil's voice. He didn't know how to express his feelings—anger at having water drip on his sneakers—so he pushed Neil and called him "stupid."

"Emotional thinking."

The fifth milestone enables children to understand the consequences of their actions. It involves the ability to link different kinds of ideas and feelings in order to understand how one relates to another. For example, a child might think, "I am angry because Terrence wouldn't play with me." This cause-and-effect thinking is also used in reading comprehension and understanding of arithmetic concepts.

An important part of emotional thinking is understanding that there are consequences to actions. Being able to consider consequences allows children to think about the future. They know what they do today will affect what happens tomorrow, and perhaps what happens into the future. This helps children learn to handle frustration, set aside immediate gratification for future rewards, and work hard at difficult tasks.

Children who can't use emotional thinking may have difficulty controlling their behavior or making future plans. They don't see how what they do today affects the future. For example:

> Francie spent the whole afternoon on the computer, even though Yancey repeatedly asked for a turn. The next day Yancey gets to the computer first. When Francie asks for a turn, he says, "No way. Yesterday you had enough turns for a week." Francie asks Ms. Dodd to intervene. "Yancey won't let me have a turn on the computer." Yancey tells his side to Ms. Dodd, who is sympathetic. She takes Francie aside and tries to explain why Yancey won't share the computer. Francie responds, "It's not fair. I want my turn."

How School-Age Staff Can Support Emotional Development

Although children develop in similar ways, each child is a unique individual. The child's physical characteristics, temperament, family, culture, sense of self, values, and experiences all play a part in learning to communicate, to get along with others, and become a productive member of society. To support emotional development, it's important to get to know each child in the group, spend one-on-one time, and participate in activities—rather than just planning and leading them. Greenspan recommends five techniques that help children master the emotional milestones described above. You probably already use many of them.

"Floor time" lets you and a child talk about whatever the child wants to discuss or do whatever the child wants to do. The child takes the lead, while you follow. Floor time allows a child to communicate, interact, and relate to another person. In a school-age program this might take place as you and a child do a puzzle together, play catch, or sit on the couch. Here is an example of floor time. Add an example from your own experiences in the blank space.

> As seven-year-old John throws the ball to Mr. Vigersky he says, "I messed up on my spelling test. I cried and some of my friends laughed at me. Do you ever cry?" Mr. Vigersky responds, "Yes. I cry sometimes if I'm sad or very disappointed. You must care a lot about your school work."

_____

_____

_____

_____

"Problem-solving time"* allows a child and staff member to work together to discuss and come up with possible solutions to specific difficulties. You might bring up an incident you observed, or raise a problem behavior that needs to be addressed. The goal is to help the child understand his or her behavior and interactions with others. This understanding helps the child anticipate and prevent problems in the future. Here is an example of problem-solving time. Add an example from your own experiences in the blank space.

> Ms. Jackson says to Amy, "Today I heard you swearing at me behind my back after I told you it was time to go in. Let's talk face to face about why you were angry and how you can express your feelings appropriately."

_____

_____

_____

_____

"Identifying and empathizing with a child's point of view" helps you understand the reasons for a child's behavior. You can then accept that the reasons make sense or help the child change his or her inappropriate behavior. Here is an example of identifying and empathizing with a child's point of view. Add an example from your own experiences in the blank space.

> Rashid explains to Ms. Barnes why he took the basketball away from another child. "Jordan doesn't need the ball because he's the best basketball player on our team. He doesn't need to practice any more. I do." Ms. Barnes says, "Rashid, I think you want to practice so you can score more baskets. You think Jordan is so good he doesn't need to practice. If the two of you play a game of one-on-one together, you can both practice."

_____

_____

_____

_____

*Helping children learn to solve problems is also covered in Module 10, Guidance.

"Breaking the challenge into small pieces" lets a child experience success. Completing one step successfully encourages the child to continue working on a difficult task. Being able to face a challenge one step at a time is a skill children can use in school, to write a research report; in a community activity, learning to skate; or at home, cleaning a messy room. Here is an example of a staff member helping a child break a challenge into small pieces. Add an example from your own experiences in the blank space.

> Ms. Hemming says to Catherine, "Learning to play tennis takes time. Perhaps you could begin by learning a basic skill—serving, forehand, or backhand. I can show you how to hold your racket and hit the ball. Then you can practice with me or a friend or hit the ball against the backboard."

_____

_____

_____

_____

"Setting limits" helps children feel safe. Limits tell children what behavior is acceptable and what the consequences are for unacceptable behavior. Limits must match the child's developmental stage. Here is an example of a staff member setting limits. Add an example from your own experiences in the blank space.

> Mr. Penn says to Yanni and Jessica, "I'm sorry to interrupt your drawing, but you left your board game out on the table. You need to put the pieces back in the box and return the game to the shelf. You can come back to your drawing after you put the game away."

_____

_____

_____

_____

The techniques just described are most helpful when used in your daily interactions with children, rather than at special times. They are part of the many appropriate practices you use in your work that help you get to know and understand what makes each child a unique individual. Knowing about each child helps you support his or her social and emotional growth.

Applying Your Knowledge

In this learning activity you keep a journal for five days, noting the times you use the techniques recommended by Greenspan for promoting children's emotional development. You record what happened and how the children responded. Include examples from each of the age groups defined by Greenspan (4½ to 7 years, 7 to 9 years, and 10 to 12 years). If you work with only one age group, try to include examples from as wide an age range as possible. Begin by reading the example that follows.

Promoting Emotional Development
(Example)

Dates: _December 4–8_

What Happened	How the Child Responded
I spent "floor time" with Seth (8 years). I listened to his story about a girl at school who keeps chasing him at recess. He wants her to stop, but he doesn't know how to tell her.	_Seth spent five minutes describing the girl who is chasing him. He was very concerned, but seemed relieved to be able to talk about the situation._
I observed Loren (10 years) watching Lisa (11 years) teach Rachel (12 years) a new dance. Lisa and Rachel were laughing and having a great time. Loren watched for a while then said, "You two look really stupid. You sure are uncoordinated." I tried to empathize with Loren's point of view to learn why she might have made her comment. I think she wanted to join Lisa and Rachel but didn't know how. I asked Lisa and Rachel if they would teach me the dance, then I asked Loren to join us.	_At first Loren said she didn't want to dance. After a few minutes I asked again. I said I needed lots of help to learn the steps. She shrugged her shoulders and joined us. I stayed for a while, then left the three girls dancing together._
Maria (6 years) seemed to be having a hard time finding something to do. We talked about her problem and the different things she might do. Some appealed to her and some didn't. I asked whether she wanted to be inside or outside.	_Maria decided to play in the sandbox outside because her friend Lisa (5 years) was already out there._

Promoting Emotional Development

Dates: _____

What You Did or Said	How the Child Responded

Discuss your journal entries with your trainer and your colleagues. Plan ways to continue encouraging children's emotional development.

Make additional copies of this form if you need them.

Learning Activity IV.
Helping Children
Relate Positively to Others

IN THIS ACTIVITY YOU WILL LEARN TO:

- tell when a child needs your help to make friends; and

- help individual children develop friendship-making skills.

Every child needs to have at least one friend to talk to; play, argue and make up with; and care for. Some children develop and use their social skills with ease. They are naturally outgoing and seem to know instinctively how to make friends and find a place in their peer group. They get a lot of pleasure from being with their friends. Other children may take longer to make friends, but once they feel comfortable, they join in activities and enjoy being with others.

Every child needs a friend.

There are children who find it very difficult to make friends. They frequently feel rejected. Such children often have low self-esteem and feel unloved. They may not have mastered Greenspan's emotional milestones as discussed in Learning Activity III. Because they aren't accepted by their peers, they have fewer chances to develop social skills. They cannot break the cycle of rejection. These children need adult assistance to learn how to make friends.

Most children who have trouble making friends fall into one of three categories. (These are very broad categories and should not be used to label children.) They are: shy or withdrawn, overly aggressive, or rejected by their peers. If you have a child in your program who has difficulty making friends, you can make a big difference in that child's life by helping him or her to break the cycle of rejection. Being able to make and keep friends is a skill children will use throughout their lives.

You are likely to have one or two children in your program who appear to be very shy or withdrawn. Before offering assistance, it is important to observe to see if the child is simply moving at a slower pace than others in the group. Some children prefer doing a solitary activity—for example, painting at the easel—before they

Helping Shy or Withdrawn Children Make Friends

are ready to join a group activity—for example, making a mural. Some need to sit back and observe other children to learn how to become part of the group. They may begin by joining in an activity with one or two children. Then, after becoming more at ease, they can participate in a large group activity.

There are some children, however, who are so shy or withdrawn they need you to step in. Your assistance will be most helpful if it is offered indirectly, without making it obvious to anyone else that assistance is being offered. If Mary and Billy are very shy, then saying things to the other children such as "be nice to Billy" or "can you let Mary play too?" are not helpful. These tend to make the two shy children feel self-conscious or embarrassed. The other children may go along with the suggestions for a time, but Billy and Mary will not develop the social skills they need to cope by themselves.

Try these suggestions.

The following are some suggestions for helping shy or withdrawn children make friends.[5]

Observe, observe, observe. Watch what the child does and says, who the child talks to, and who the child watches. When playing a game of solitaire, is the child fully engaged or also watching a group of children playing Sorry? Observe to find out what the child likes to do, where his or her favorite places are, whether the child behaves differently outside, and what skills and interests the child has.

Establish a connection with the child. Talk about what the child is observing. "It looks like they're having fun with the hula hoops." If the child responds, you can continue the conversation. "Do you think you could keep one twirling that long? There are some more hoops in the storage shed. Would you like to get one for yourself?" You might also comment on what the child is doing. "I've noticed how much you enjoy using the Legos." Such comments convey that you are paying attention to the child.

Encourage the child to express his or her ideas and feelings. Notice when a child is particularly engaged in an activity and try to build on this interest. "Leila, you know just how to handle our guinea pigs. How do you know so much about them?"

Use what you know about the child's interests to create special situations. For example, if you know Jeff really likes to cook, suggest he help you organize a Cooking Club that will involve several children working together. Ask Jeff to

---

[5]Adapted with permission from Dennie Palmer Wolf, ed., *Connecting: Friendship in the Lives of Young Children and Their Teachers* (Redmond, WA: Exchange Press, Inc., 1986), pp. 58-62.

help you plan the club and suggest specific assignments for him to carry out to keep him involved.

Help children find good friends. Just as there may be several shy or withdrawn children in your program, there also may be several who are socially competent and sensitive. Try asking one of these children and a "shy" child to help you do a task. "Dean, could you please help Tommy and me carry the equipment outside?" Or let both children know about an activity you know both would enjoy. "Dean and Tommy, I know you both like woodworking. We have a new supply of wood and some new hand drills."

Help the child understand his or her feelings. "It's perfectly normal to want to spend time alone when you don't know the other children too well. After a while you'll feel more comfortable and be ready to join in the group activities."

Helping Overly Aggressive Children Make Friends

In any group of children there may be a few who are not able to control their behaviors. One reason may be that they are not able to give words to their feelings. (Greenspan's "emotional ideas" milestone). These children might use aggression as a means to express their unhappiness or to get their own way. They may not know how to take turns, negotiate, or cooperate with others. They don't understand how to meet their own needs within the context of the group. Other children may not include them in their activities because they are afraid of their aggressive outbursts.

Staff also may have trouble relating to children whose behavior is overly aggressive. It's natural to want to avoid a child who frequently hurts others or uses force. But because school-age staff are professionals, they must learn to overcome their negative feelings about an aggressive child. It may help to remember that the children who hit or bully other children may be troubled or in pain, emotionally. They may feel unhappy or insecure, and they need help to learn positive ways of relating to other children. These children must feel safe and cared for before they can develop self-esteem and the social skills to make friends and play with other children.

The following are some techniques for helping children who behave aggressively to find new ways of relating to others.

Try these suggestions.

Help the child understand the consequences of his or her actions. "I think you want to play Uno with Crystal and Susan. But when you refuse to follow the rules it makes them angry. Then they don't want to play with you."

163

Help a child gain control over his or her negative feelings. "Shawn, I know you are frustrated because you didn't get a hit, but you may not throw the bat. Try taking several deep breaths. That will help you to calm down before it's your turn at bat again."

Spend five or ten minutes alone with the child ("floor time"). Wait until the child is no longer exhibiting aggressive behavior. "David, let's play cards. Will you teach me how to play the new game the other kids are playing?"

Use the child's positive characteristics and interests to help him or her be accepted by the group. "Blake, you collected some beautiful leaves. Can we put them on the table in the science area where everyone can see them?"

Set limits. At times, overly aggressive children are frightened by their own inability to control their behavior. Setting and adhering to clear limits helps them feel secure at the program, and feeling secure helps them be ready to learn more appropriate behaviors.

Helping Rejected Children Make Friends

Some children are regularly rejected by their peers. These children, who may be loud, clumsy, or bossy, do not know how to get involved with other children. For example, while working on a puzzle, Mark tells the other children, "I'll do the edges. Barbara you do the sky and Brett will do the trees." The other children resent being told what to do and drift to other activities, leaving Mark to do the puzzle by himself. Children who are frequently rejected are often unaware of the effects of their behavior on others. They seem to want to play with others, but don't know how to get involved. You may hear a lot of complaints about these children. "She's always butting in." "He talks too loud." "She thinks she's in charge of us."

Many of the techniques for helping shy or aggressive children are also effective for helping a child who is rejected. Often these children are highly intelligent and have some social skills but may not know how to use them. Some find it easier to interact with adults than their peers and tend to spend more time with the staff than with other children. Even if the staff find such children engaging, it is crucial for them to develop the ability to be a part of their own peer group. Observe these children to find out who in the group does accept them. Then find ways to include them in group projects.

The following are some suggestions for helping children who are often rejected to make friends.[6]

Teach the child how to ask questions to find out what a group of children are doing before joining in. "What are you playing?" "Who are you pretending to be?" "What are you making?"

Encourage the child to discuss his or her feelings about being rejected. "You look sad, Cynthia. Can you tell me what happened?" Telling what happened may help the child understand why she was rejected by the others.

Coach the child on how to follow accepted social practices. For example, if Felipe takes too long deciding what he wants for snack (which annoys the other children), Ms. Jenssen could say, "Felipe, step out of line while you are deciding what you want to eat. The children will let you back in line once you have decided. That way the others can get their snack."

Help the child figure out a way to be included in activities. For example, Mr. Donovan notices Cassie trying to join the soccer game. The other children say, "We've already started. It's too late." As a disappointed Cassie walks away, Mr. Donovan suggests, "The blue team has fewer people than the red one. You could offer to join the blue team." Cassie returns to the field and says, "I can play on the blue team to make the teams more even. Okay?"

Applying Your Knowledge

In this learning activity you will think of a child in your program who needs help learning to make friends. Observe this child for five minutes at several different times of the day. Review your notes and summarize your thoughts about the child. Use this new information and the suggestions in this learning activity to plan ways to help the child develop friendships. Implement your plan over the next week and record what happens. Begin by reading the example that follows.

---

[6] Adapted with permission from Dwight L. Rogers and Dorene Doerre Ross, "Encouraging Positive Social Interaction Among Young Children," *Young Children* (Washington, DC: National Association for the Education of Young Children, March 1986), pp. 15-16.

Helping Individual Children Develop Friendships
(Example)

Child: _Alexa_   **Age:** _9 years_   **Dates:** _April 15-17_

Observation Notes	Summary
Time: _3:20 p.m._ Alexa gets snack. Looks around room. Sits at end of table. Charmaine and Donna at other end, talking, laughing. Alexa looks up, watches for few minutes. Charmaine looks up, smiles at Alexa. Alexa finishes snack, cleans up, goes to reading area.	Alexa seems to be interested in Charmaine and Donna, but she didn't smile back. Perhaps she didn't notice.
Time: _7:20 a.m._ Alexa walks through door. Hangs up coat, puts bag in cubby. Looks around room. Walks to bean bag chair. Sits down. Watches Donna and Trent playing checkers. Says, "Can I play the winner?" Donna laughs, "That will be me!"	Alexa seems to be reaching out. She took a chance by asking to play the winner of the checkers game.
Time: _3:40 p.m._ Alexa and others in group meeting. Mr. Lawrence describes afternoon activities. Says there will be a softball game. Alexa smiles. Donna stands up, pretends to throw the ball. Alexa laughs.	Alexa seems to want to play softball. She also seems to enjoy Donna's playfulness.

Plan:

I will continue observing Alexa to find out what she likes to do and talk to her about her special interests. I will also talk with other staff members to learn more about Alexa.

I will plan an activity of interest to both Alexa and Donna and try to get both girls involved.

I will try to involve both Alexa and Donna in completing a task.

Results (after one week):

I learned a lot about Alexa. Although she is a quiet child she enjoys sports and has strong physical skills. She also enjoys creative activities—she spends a lot of time in the arts and crafts area.

I planned a softball clinic and both Alexa and Donna volunteered to help teach the younger children some basic skills. They seemed to enjoy each other.

I asked Alexa and Donna to take inventory in the arts and crafts area and list the supplies we need. They spent most of the afternoon doing their job and getting to know each other.

Helping Individual Children Develop Friendships

Child: _____   **Age:** _____   **Dates:** _____

Observation Notes	Summary
Time: _____	
Time: _____	

Make additional copies of this form if you need them.

Review your observation notes and summaries as well as the suggestions you have read. Develop a plan for helping this child. Implement your plan over the next week and then record the results.

Plan:

_____
_____
_____
_____
_____
_____
_____
_____

Results (after one week):

_____
_____
_____
_____
_____
_____
_____
_____

Talk to your trainer about how you helped this child develop friendships.

Learning Activity V.
Building a Sense of Community

IN THIS ACTIVITY YOU WILL LEARN TO:

- create a sense of community in the school-age program;

- hold group meetings that allow children to use their social skills; and

- provide opportunities for children to be involved in the community at large.

The school-age program is a community unto itself, with children and staff as its members. Ideally it is a positive social environment in which all children feel they belong and know that their contributions are valued and respected. Such a community allows children to develop the social skills they will need to succeed in life.

The school-age program is a community.

By the time they reach the school-age years, most children have a wide range of social skills. They know how to share, take turns, empathize, compromise, cooperate, and express feelings using words. These skills are further developed during the school-age years. In addition, children are ready to learn more sophisticated social skills such as accepting different points of view, listening when others are speaking, respecting another person's personal space and belongings, working as a member of a team, and using conflict resolution techniques to solve problems and resolve disagreements. Children will use these and other social skills throughout their lives—in school, on the job, in their communities, and as they create families of their own. As they participate in the program each day, staff can provide many opportunities for children to develop and use social skills as members of a community.

Here are some ways you can build a sense of community in your program.

Try these suggestions.

Invite children to participate in program planning. They can help form new clubs, select new materials and games, suggest places to go for field trips, and assess which activities and interest areas are working and which ones need to be changed. (See Module 11, Program Management for more information on involving children in planning.)

Include some materials and activities that are enjoyed by children of different ages. Multi-age activities encourage older and younger children to get to know and appreciate each other. Older children can practice leadership skills and feel good about being able to pass on their skills and knowledge. Younger children can get new ideas from the older ones and just enjoy receiving attention from someone older.

Offer some materials and activities that require specific skills and abilities. This practice demonstrates respect for children's individual interests and abilities. For example, a high level of skills are needed for some team sports, crafts, or science experiments. Conversely, offer some materials and activities that address the needs of children with skills that are less developed.

Encourage children to form clubs to explore their special interests. Clubs are an excellent way for children to use leadership and other social skills. After helping the club get off the ground, step back and encourage the children to take over the club's activities. Let the children know you are available to offer materials and other assistance, if needed. Respect their ability to do things for themselves.

Include children in discussing and developing program rules and consequences. Children are more likely to follow rules when they are involved in creating them and understand why the rules are needed. It's also important to respond when children complain that rules are too restrictive. Children gain new skills and abilities over time, and rules that once were important may no longer be needed. (See Module 10, Guidance, for more information on how to involve children in setting rules and limits.)

Identify real jobs children can do to help the program run smoothly. Involve children in identifying what jobs are needed. You can suggest some of your own such as cleaning the rabbit's cage or surveying children to find out what books they would like to have on hand.

Establish a buddy system to help new children adjust to the program. "Buddies" can give a tour of the program, explain the schedule and routines, and participate in activities with the newcomer for a few days.

Model social skills as you interact with colleagues and children. Use the language and actions you would like children to use. For example:

- use polite words such as please, thank you, and excuse me;

- ask for permission before interrupting a child;

- step in when a colleague needs assistance—"I'll wipe up the spilled juice while you get some more from the refrigerator."

Group Meetings

Group meetings are times to share, provide information everyone needs to hear, sing songs, review the schedule, discuss and solve problems, and plan activities. One great advantage of holding meetings is that they build a sense of community. How often you hold them depends on group size, program format, and whether children enjoy participating. In smaller programs, all children and staff meet together; in larger programs, different age groups (or multi-age groups) may meet separately so all children can have a chance to express their ideas. It's probably best not to hold meetings as soon as children arrive at the program. Most children need some time to talk with their friends, burn off energy, and have a snack. If holding meetings every day becomes chaotic, plan them biweekly or weekly and try shortening the time.

Many children enjoy and gain security from predictable events so it is a good idea to follow the same routine for each meeting. Rituals such as singing the same song at every meeting give children a sense of belonging. The school-age program feels like a familiar place. Some older children may balk and find the rituals "stupid." Others will be upset if the routine is changed because it is a source of comfort, even if it is "stupid."

Group meetings are excellent opportunities for staff and children to use their social skills. Remaining quiet while someone else is speaking, taking turns expressing an opinion, listening without interrupting, and compromising so the group can reach consensus are all skills used during group meetings.

At the beginning of the program year and periodically as needed, it is critical to set and review the ground rules for group participation. These guidelines, developed with the children, might include items such as the following:

It is important to establish and review the ground rules for group meetings.

- Try to meet at the same time and make sure meetings are short—for example, the first and third Mondays of the month from 3:30-4:00 p.m. Keep to this schedule unless the group wants to continue a discussion past the usual ending time.

- Sit in a circle so everyone can see one another. (This encourages children to speak to each other, not just to the leader.)

- Raise your hand if you want to speak. The group leader—either a child or a staff member—will recognize you.

- Remain quiet when someone is speaking. Pay attention and listen closely to what they have to say.

- Accept all ideas and suggestions. There are no right or wrong ideas or suggestions.

- Allow people to pass if they don't want to speak.

- If someone needs to leave the meeting, they should do so without disrupting the others.

Children can practice leadership skills in group meetings.

You can encourage children to lead and be actively involved in group meetings. For example, when a child has a specific concern he or she can raise it with the group and ask for their suggestions for solving it. Some children find it very easy to speak to the group and may tend to dominate the discussions. Others find it uncomfortable to share their ideas in a large-group setting. Such children may find it easier to write down their ideas, which you can then read aloud, or they may be willing to speak up in a smaller group. With practice and continued participation, children's reluctance to speak up may decrease over time.

Encouraging Involvement in the Larger Community

An important accomplishment for school-age children is learning that they belong to many different communities. Younger school-age children begin to see themselves as members of their local community. As they get older, children use community resources, take part in activities such as scouts and athletics, and contribute to projects such as neighborhood clean-ups or food drives. The oldest children in your program, 11- and 12-year-olds, are likely to be aware of national and world affairs. Some older children read newspapers and magazines and watch the news. They are becoming increasingly aware of current events and want to be involved in their world.

The school-age program can encourage children's involvement in the larger community in a number of ways. Field trips to museums, parks, and libraries help them get to know their community. Many businesses and government agencies offer behind-the-scenes tours of their facilities. Children can see first-hand the steps involved in bottling soda, writing and publishing a daily newspaper, or disposing of garbage. Such trips help children understand "how things work" and introduce them to potential future careers.

Inviting community members to visit the program is another way to expose children to careers and spark their interests in the larger community. Guest presenters might include a health professional, an aerobics instructor, a firefighter, and a veterinarian. Apprenticeships where children spend time with a mentor who introduces them to a profession can greatly expand children's knowledge of the world and inspire them to think about a career.

Some school-age programs are able to coordinate with other groups offering activities such as scouts, team sports, gymnastics, dance, or art classes. These might be held in the same building as your program, or at a nearby location. Interested children can attend, with their parents' written permission. Special interest clubs offered by the school-age program also offer opportunities for children to expand their understanding of the world at large.

Coordinate with community programs for school-age children as often as possible.

The school-age program can offer children opportunities to contribute to the larger community. Some examples follow:

Try these suggestions.

- Knitting hats and mittens to donate to a homeless shelter.

- Making regular visits to a nursing home or hospital to assist residents or patients by writing letters, telling jokes, reading, or just talking to them.

- Making audiotapes of favorite books for community groups such as child care or Head Start programs, the local library, or the children's ward at a hospital.

- Spending an hour a month, supervised by staff or parent volunteers, picking up litter on a stretch of road.

- Helping address and stuff envelopes for a community fundraiser.

- Putting on a talent show and donating the money raised to an organization that helps victims of natural disasters.

- Writing to national and international environmental groups to learn about ways to preserve natural resources and prevent pollution.

Projects such as these might involve some or all of the children. Finding ways to involve all children, at whatever level is appropriate for them, helps make the school-age program feel like a community. For example, once a month children might make sandwiches for a homeless shelter. Each age group could have a different role: the youngest age group bags the sandwiches after the middle age group makes them, and the oldest age group shops for the ingredients and delivers the finished sandwiches.

Applying Your Knowledge

In this learning activity you plan and implement a strategy for involving children in the community at large. Your strategy can involve the full group, target a specific age group, or respond to children's interests. Invite children to help you plan and carry out your strategy, then answer the questions that follow. Begin by reviewing the example.

Involving Children in the Community at Large
(Example)

Planners: _Members of the Puppet Club_

Date: _February 6-17_

Describe your strategy:

Putting on a puppet show for the Head Start children.

Why did you select this strategy?

The Puppet Club has made some interesting puppets and produced some funny plays.

Several children in the school-age program have siblings in Head Start.

This strategy can involve children of different ages.

How will this strategy involve children in the community at large?

It will allow children from the school-age program to contribute to Head Start. Many of the school-age children are Head Start graduates and feel strong ties to the program.

Which children do you anticipate being involved?

Members of the Puppet Club and anyone else who is interested.

What will you and the children do?

Contact the Head Start director to find out if she is interested in having a puppet show. Ask which puppets and plays the children would like. Set a time for the show.

Practice until "perfect," then take our show "on the road."

Carry out your plan, then answer the questions below.

What happened?

The Head Start director and teachers were pleased the school-age children wanted to put on a puppet show. They asked us to come in about ten days.

The Puppet Club selected a play they had adapted from a favorite book. They added a few new characters.

The club practiced every afternoon. Several children worked on the new puppets.

The club performed their play. The children and teachers were very pleased. They asked if the children could come back to do another play.

The Puppet Club members told everyone about their experience at the next group meeting. The other children seemed very interested in working with Head Start and other programs such as Daisy and Cub Scout troops.

What would you change, if anything, about this strategy?

There are lots of ways the school-age children could contribute to the community. We could expand this strategy to involve more children and different kinds of contributions.

Involving Children in the Community at Large

Planners: _____

Date: _____

Describe your strategy:

_____

_____

_____

Why did you select this strategy?

_____

_____

_____

How will this strategy involve children in the community at large?

_____

_____

_____

Which children do you anticipate being involved?

_____

_____

What will you and the children do?

_____

_____

_____

Carry out your plan, then answer the questions below.

What happened?

_____

_____

_____

What would you change, if anything, about this strategy?

_____

_____

_____

Discuss this activity with your trainer and your colleagues.

SUMMARIZING YOUR PROGRESS

You have now completed all the learning activities for this module. Whether you are an experienced school-age staff member or a new one, this module probably has helped you develop new skills for promoting social development. Before you go on, take a few minutes to summarize what you've learned.

- Turn back to Learning Activity I, Using Your Knowledge of Child Development to Promote Social Development, and add specific examples to the charts of what you learned about helping children gain social skills while you were working on this module. Compare your ideas to those in the completed charts at the end of the module.

- Next, review your responses to the pre-training assessment for this module. Write a summary of what you learned, and list the skills you developed or improved.

Next, review your responses to the pre-training assessment for this module. Write a summary of what you learned, and list the skills you developed or improved.

_____
_____
_____
_____
_____
_____
_____
_____
_____
_____
_____
_____
_____

If there are topics you would like to know more about, you will find recommended readings listed in the Orientation in Volume I.

Your final step in this module is to complete the knowledge and competency assessments. Let your trainer know when you are ready to schedule the assessments. After you have successfully completed them, you will be ready to start a new module. Congratulations on your progress so far, and good luck with your next module.

ANSWER SHEETS

Promoting Children's Social Development

1 . **Why did Ms. Stuart step in to help the boys find a place to be together?**

   a. She recognized it was important for Emilio and Charles to have an opportunity to be with each other, just enjoying each other's company.

   b. She could see they were feeling frustrated because they had already moved twice.

2 . **How did Ms. Stuart support the boys' friendship?**

   a. She helped Emilio and Charles find a place where they wouldn't be in anyone's way.

   b. She commented on their supply of funny jokes.

Encouraging Children to Develop Friendships and Enjoy Being With Their Peers

1 . **What social skills did children use during the group meeting?**

   a. They took turns speaking.

   b. They listened while others were speaking (except Zack).

   c. Wendy used leadership skills.

2 . **How did the group meeting format help children express and understand their own feelings and those of others?**

   a. They followed the same agenda and rules they use every day so they knew they would have a turn to express their feelings.

   b. Wendy reminded Zack of the rule about not interrupting others.

   c. They had a specific time to raise problems and talk about solutions.

Helping Children Understand and Respect the Feelings of Others

Providing an Environment and Experiences That Help Children Develop Social Skills

1. How did the road cleanup help children be involved in their community?

   a. The program has joined a community-wide effort to help keep the roads clean.

   b. The cleanup takes place away from the program.

   c. When they drive on this road, children can feel proud they have helped keep it clean.

2. How did Ms. Caruso make the clean-up activity enjoyable for the children?

   a. She started a contest to find the largest piece of trash.

   b. She let Clay know the children's work was appreciated.

GLOSSARY

Peer

A friend or companion who is the same age, at the same developmental level, or otherwise linked by similar characteristics.

Social development

The gradual process through which children gain the ability to use social skills such as—sharing, cooperating, experiencing empathy, and reaching consensus—needed to interact positively with others and to contribute to society.

Module 10:

GUIDANCE

OVERVIEW

GUIDING SCHOOL-AGE CHILDREN'S BEHAVIOR INVOLVES:

- providing an environment that encourages children's self-discipline;

- using positive methods to guide individual children; and

- helping children understand and express their feelings in acceptable ways.

Children need adults to guide them—to help them learn what behaviors are acceptable and what are not, and to help them learn to live cooperatively with others. How you as an adult offer this guidance depends on your goals. What kind of adults do you want children to become? Do you want them to behave a certain way out of fear, or because they have learned what is acceptable and what is not?

Children need adult guidance.

Self-discipline is the ability to control one's own behavior. People who are self-disciplined make independent choices based on what they believe is right. They are able to balance their own needs with those of others. They can accept the results of their actions.

Children are not born with self-discipline. Adults need to provide positive guidance that teaches children to make their own decisions, tell the difference between right and wrong, solve problems, and correct their own mistakes. This module is about guiding children's behavior in ways that help them develop self-discipline.

There is a reason for all behavior—and children misbehave for many different reasons. Gina may be at a developmental stage where she needs to test the limits of her own control. Carson may be forced into a schedule that conflicts with his natural rhythm. Haki may be confused because his parents have different rules and expectations than those at the program. Nancy may be having difficulty coping with her father's illness. Sometimes children behave inappropriately simply because they are bored, tired, curious, or frustrated.

There are reasons for children's behavior.

To help children learn self-discipline, it is important to think about the reasons for their behavior. For example, you may ask a child to stop playing a board game because he or she keeps throwing the pieces on the floor. Later, you also need to think about why the child was throwing the pieces. When you identify the need the child is expressing (for example, "I want to play with my friend, but I don't understand the rules") you can then try to meet that need. When you do have to take something away (the opportunity to play the game), you must later replace it with what the child needs (the opportunity to have an adult explain the rules).

Because adults are powerful, they can make children behave in certain ways. But children who are punished or forced to behave in certain ways, and punished when they don't, learn the following lessons:

- I am a bad person.

- I need to watch out for adults.

- I had better not get caught.

These children are likely to behave only when someone is watching. Their goal is to avoid being punished. They do not learn to value acceptable behavior for itself, and they do not learn self-discipline.

Positive guidance encourages self-discipline.

If you have developed a supportive relationship with the children in the program, you are already doing a lot to promote self-discipline. Children depend on you and want your approval. They look to you to help them learn what is acceptable and what is not. If you involve children in setting program rules that fit their developmental and individual needs, they are likely to learn and follow the rules easily. If you are consistent in applying rules, children will try to follow them. If you set up an environment that supports self-control, children will find it easier to achieve. If you look for the reasons behind their behavior, you may be able to help children learn acceptable ways to express their feelings. And if you learn some positive techniques for guiding children, you will help them develop self-discipline.

Listed on the next page are examples of how school-age staff demonstrate their competence in guiding children's behavior.

Make sure there are no safety hazards in the environment. "Thank you for pointing out that the aquarium table is wobbling. Someone could have bumped into it and tipped it over. We can move the aquarium to a safer location until the table is fixed."

Store materials and equipment within children's reach. "It's time to clean up. Please put the blocks back on the shelf now. You can build with them again tomorrow."

Speak to children with the same tone and respect they use with adults. "Please write down your ideas for our next field trip and put them in the suggestion box. Carrie and Peter will tally the results so we can discuss the top three choices at our next group meeting."

Arrange the materials and furniture to encourage appropriate behavior. "When Sandy wants to be alone, she likes to sit in the reading nook."

Involve children in making the program's rules. "The school year is ending, so the program will be open full time for the summer. Could you please help me get everyone together so we can talk about the rules we will need for summer activities."

Plan a schedule that includes many opportunities for children to choose what they want to do. "Good morning, Derek . Breakfast will be ready in 20 minutes. What would you like to do until the food is ready?"

Involve children in planning activities and selecting materials and equipment that match their skills and interests. "Tell me about some of the things you like to do. You might be able to do some of them at the program."

Plan some games and activities that encourage cooperation rather than competition. "In today's Cooking Club we'll be making two big pots of vegetable soup. One is for us and one is to share with the senior citizen's center."

Hold conversations in private when you need to discuss a child's misbehavior. "Drew, I need to talk with you privately for a minute."

Allow children to experience the natural and logical consequences of their actions. "Marisa, your sculpture was damaged when it got knocked off the table. Next time let's try to remember to store fragile projects on the top shelf."

Providing an Environment That Encourages Children's Self-Discipline

Using Positive Methods to Guide Individual Children

Consider the reasons for a child's behavior. "Renée (11 years) seems to be getting into a lot of fights with other children. Maybe she needs more one-on-one attention from a staff member."

Give genuine, positive praise for appropriate behavior. "Yancey, I've noticed Marvin wants to do everything you do. You were really patient with him when you showed him to how draw Donald Duck."

Redirect children to acceptable activities. "Susan and Nina, your singing is disturbing the children who are reading. Could you please use softer voices or move your practice session to the other side of the room?"

Offer assistance to children who are screaming or thrashing because they are out of control. Help them to calm down so they won't hurt themselves or others. "I can see you are feeling very upset. Take my hand. We'll sit on the couch for a few minutes until you feel ready to talk about what happened."

Use simple, positive reminders to state and restate rules. "Use the safety equipment when you're playing street hockey."

Give children time to handle disagreements on their own. "Patrick and Brandon sometimes bicker with each other when they play chess. They tend to work out their disagreements without adult assistance."

Helping Children Understand and Express Their Feelings in Acceptable Ways

Listen when an angry child needs to talk about his or her feelings. "Jane, can you tell me about what made you feel angry? I will listen very carefully."

Tell children you accept their feelings, even when their actions are not acceptable. "Tad, I think you felt embarrassed when you struck out, but it's not okay to throw the bat. You'll have to miss your next turn up to bat."

Model acceptable ways to express negative feelings. "I've asked you twice to please lower your voices. Your loud voices are making my headache worse."

Teach children how to use conflict resolution techniques to settle their differences. "Aaron and Wesley, I can see that you both think you are 'right.' Cool off for a few minutes, then you can discuss what happened and what you need to do to solve your problem."

Provide creative outlets for expressing feelings. "Sometimes it helps to write a letter to the editor explaining how you feel. The address for the newspaper is on the bulletin board."

Talk to children about their concerns, feelings, interests, and activities at home and school. "Janet, how was your weekend? Did you have fun at your ice-skating party?"

Use group meetings at times when children can raise concerns and develop solutions. "You can bring up your concern about the trash on the playground at our meeting. We'll work together to come up with a solution."

Work with parents to help a child with a challenging behavior learn acceptable ways to express feelings. "Mr. Harper, Shellie had a great day today. I think our strategies for helping her use words to express her feelings are really working."

Guiding Children's Behavior

In the following situations, school-age staff are guiding children's behavior. As you read them, think about what the staff are doing and why. Then answer the questions that follow.

Providing an Environment That Encourages Children's Self-Discipline

Katy asks Ms. Mingus if the program can get some new board games. Ms. Mingus looks puzzled. "I thought we had a pretty good selection of games, Katy. Which new ones do you think we need?" Katy responds, "Well, we don't need new games. Just new copies of the ones we already have. Lots of times when we try to play a game some pieces are missing. Like when Jessica and I wanted to play Connect Four we couldn't, because someone took the checkers." Ms. Mingus says, "This sounds like a problem with the way we are storing and taking care of the games. Before we buy new ones, we need to think of a better way to take care of the games we have. Would you like to help organize the games?" Katy agrees and asks Mike and Terrence to help her

By the time Ms. Mingus joins the children they have placed all the games on a table with the lids off. Most of the boxes are ripped and pieces from some games have made their way into the boxes of others. It looks like a big job. She asks the children if they need anything. Katy asks for some strong tape to repair the boxes. Terrence asks for some small plastic bags. "You know," he says, "the kind with zippers on the top." Ms. Mingus tells the children where they can find both tape and plastic bags. She asks if they need any more help. "No thanks, " says Mike. "I'm good at getting organized." Ms. Mingus says, "While you're sorting and repairing, you can also think about how to store these games from now on. Our old system didn't work very well."

1. **How did Ms. Mingus demonstrate respect for the children?**

_____

_____

_____

2. **How did Ms. Mingus encourage children's self-discipline?**

_____

_____

_____

Using Positive Methods to Guide Individual Children

Kendall is the last child off the bus today. She walks slowly to the door. Ms. Anton greets her, "Hi, Kendall. You're our last customer today!" "So what," replies Kendall, dragging her backpack along the floor. Ms. Anton thinks to herself, "That's not like Kendall. Perhaps something is bothering her." She follows Kendall inside. Kendall is stuffing her belongings into her cubby. "These cubbies are too small," she says to nobody in particular, but within Ms. Anton's hearing. Later, at the Newspaper Club's meeting, Kendall sits by herself on the edge of the group. Ms. Anton watches her out of the corner of one eye. Throughout the meeting Kendall fidgets, looks at the clock, stares at the floor, and avoids participating. Again Ms. Anton wonders what's going on, "Kendall is usually very outspoken. I'd better see if she wants to talk." After the meeting Kendall returns to her cubby, takes out her backpack, and drags it to the quiet area. Ms. Anton catches up with her there. "Kendall," she says, "if you're not too busy, can we talk for a minute? I'd like to hear more about the social studies project you described last week." Kendall responds, "Of course I'm busy. All the sixth grade teachers think we have nothing else to do but their stupid homework. I'm never going to get it all done." Ms. Anton puts her hand on Kendall's shoulder, "I can hear that you feel overwhelmed. Can I join you at the homework table? We can work together to make a plan for getting the work done." "Okay," says Kendall, almost in tears, "That sounds like a good idea." Ms. Anton sits with Kendall and helps her make a schedule. Once Kendall sees the workload is manageable, she relaxes and tells Ms. Anton how her social studies project is going. "Yesterday we wrote a list of all the things we're going to take on our journey down the Nile. . . "

1. How did Ms. Anton know Kendall was upset?

_____

_____

_____

2. How did Ms. Anton's guidance help Kendall learn self-discipline?

_____

_____

_____

Helping Children Understand and Express Their Feelings in Acceptable Ways

Nicky and Brad are working together on a mural. "Nicky," says Brad in an angry voice, "I'm doing the fish underneath the ocean. You're supposed to be doing the boats on top." "I want to do the fish, too," says Nicky. "Why can't I do some fish and some boats?" "Cause your fish don't look like mine and you're wrecking the mural," replies Brad, his voice getting louder. "I'm going to get Mr. Franklin." Mr. Franklin hears his name and walks over to the boys. "Did I hear my name?" he asks. Brad and Nicky both talk at once trying to tell their side of the argument. Mr. Franklin asks the boys to be quiet so he can make a suggestion. "How about if you go sit on the couch and discuss your problem? If you haven't solved it in three minutes, you can set the timer again, or ask for my help." The boys agree to try to solve their problem without his help. They get the timer off the shelf and head for the couch. Three minutes pass very quickly. Mr. Franklin looks up from a game of chess with another child and sees Nicky and Brad back at work on the mural. When the game is over he asks the boys, "How did you solve your problem?" he asks. "It was easy," says Brad. "I'm going to draw fish and Nicky is going to draw sea creatures, like eels and octopus. Tomorrow we'll both do boats." Mr. Franklin complimented the boys, "You did a great job solving your problem. You worked it out quickly so now you can have fun doing your mural."

1. **Why did Mr. Franklin suggest the boys sit down on the couch to discuss their problem?**

   _____

   _____

   _____

2. **How did Mr. Franklin help the boys express their feelings in acceptable ways?**

   _____

   _____

   _____

Compare your answers with those on the answer sheet at the end of this module. If your answers are different, discuss them with your trainer. There can be more than one good answer.

Your Own Self-Discipline

Often behavior is automatic. You don't stop to think about what you should do; you just do it. When you put money in a parking meter, come to work on time, or thank a store clerk, you are probably acting without thinking about what you are doing. You have learned and accepted certain rules of behavior and, because you have self-discipline, don't need to be reminded of them.

Some behavior is automatic.

Self-discipline guides your behavior at work in many ways.

- You let your supervisor know when you're sick so a substitute can be called.

- You let a colleague know you are angry with her by telling her what you feel.

- You volunteer to help a colleague who's having difficulty understanding a child's behavior.

- You don't make long-distance calls on the program's phone.

List below a few examples of how self-discipline guides your behavior at work:

_____

_____

_____

_____

_____

Self-discipline also guides your behavior at home.

- You remember to water the plants because you know they'll die if you don't.

- You clean the frying pan so it will be ready to use in the morning.

- You say no to a second piece of cake because you shouldn't have so much sugar.

List some examples of how self-discipline guides your behavior at home:

_____

_____

_____

_____

_____

Think of a time when you did not show self-discipline. What affected your loss of control?

_____

_____

_____

_____

_____

What does this tell you about what children need to gain self-discipline?

_____

_____

_____

_____

_____

Some adults have problems making their own decisions about how to behave. They are most comfortable when they have rules and guidelines to follow. They may respond only to promises of rewards or threats of punishment. Perhaps they come to work on time only because they're afraid of being fired or having their pay docked. When these adults were children, they probably didn't have many opportunities to make their own decisions. They weren't able to develop inner controls.

Staff can model self-discipline.

Being in control of your behavior usually leads to higher self-esteem. Having good feelings about yourself will make you a more effective and skilled school-age staff member. Your self-discipline is a good model for the children. They will learn a lot from being in the company of a responsible, competent person.

When you have finished this overview section, you should complete the pre-training assessment. Refer to the glossary at the end of this module if you need definitions for the terms used.

PRE-TRAINING ASSESSMENT

Listed below are the skills school-age staff use to guide children's behavior. Think about whether you do these things regularly, sometimes, or not enough. Place a check in one of the boxes on the right for each skill listed. Then discuss your answers with your trainer.

Providing an Environment That Encourages Children's Self-Discipline

	I Do This		
	Regularly	Sometimes	Not Enough
1. Following a daily schedule that allows children to choose their own activities.	☐	☐	☐
2. Making sure there are no safety hazards in the environment.	☐	☐	☐
3. Storing materials and equipment within children's reach.	☐	☐	☐
4. Involving children in setting limits and making rules.	☐	☐	☐
5. Involving children in planning activities and selecting materials and equipment that match their skills and interests.	☐	☐	☐
6. Planning some games and activities that encourage cooperation rather than competition.	☐	☐	☐
7. Arranging the environment to encourage appropriate behavior (for example, creating clear traffic patterns so children don't get in each other's way).	☐	☐	☐
8. Speaking to children with the same tone and respect you use with adults.	☐	☐	☐

Using Positive Methods to Guide Individual Children

I Do This

	Regularly	Sometimes	Not Enough
9. Considering the possible reasons for a child's behavior.	☐	☐	☐
10. Redirecting children from inappropriate to appropriate activities (for example, suggesting to children who are "horsing around" they go outdoors or to the gym to use some energy).	☐	☐	☐
11. Giving children opportunities to handle their disagreements without adult assistance.	☐	☐	☐
12. Stating directions and reminding children of rules in positive terms (for example, "walk to the gym").	☐	☐	☐
13. Giving genuine, positive praise for appropriate behavior.	☐	☐	☐
14. Discussing children's misbehavior in private conversations.	☐	☐	☐
15. Allowing children to experience the natural and logical consequences of their actions.	☐	☐	☐
16. Offering assistance to children who are out of control.	☐	☐	☐

Helping Children Understand and Express Their Feelings in Acceptable Ways

	Regularly	Sometimes	Not Enough
17. Listening to and accepting children's angry feelings while helping them understand the consequences of expressing those feelings inappropriately.	☐	☐	☐
18. Talking to children about their day at school, their friends, their concerns, and their feelings.	☐	☐	☐
19. Holding group meetings during which children can raise concerns and grievances and work together to develop solutions.	☐	☐	☐

**Helping Children Understand and Express
Their Feelings in Acceptable Ways** (continued)

	I Do This		
	Regularly	Sometimes	Not Enough
20. Modeling appropriate ways to express negative feelings.	☐	☐	☐
21. Providing creative outlets such as writing, painting, and staging puppet shows for expressing strong feelings.	☐	☐	☐
22. Working with parents to help a child with a problem (such as getting into physical or verbal fights) express his or her feelings in acceptable ways.	☐	☐	☐
23. Teaching children how to use conflict resolution techniques to resolve their differences.	☐	☐	☐

Review your responses, then list three to five skills you would like to improve or topics you would like to learn more about. When you finish this module, you can list examples of your new or improved knowledge and skills.

_____

_____

_____

_____

_____

Begin the learning activities for Module 10, Guidance.

LEARNING ACTIVITIES

Learning Activity I.
Using Your Knowledge of Child Development to Guide Behavior

IN THIS ACTIVITY YOU WILL LEARN TO:

- recognize some typical behaviors of school-age children; and

- use what you know about children to help them learn self-discipline.

Understanding children's behavior is the first step in helping them learn self-discipline. By learning what children can and can't do at each stage of their development, you are more likely to have appropriate expectations for their behavior. Knowing what behavior is typical at different ages allows you to provide guidance that reflects developmental characteristics. For example, if you know it is typical for 5- to 7-year-olds to have difficulty sharing, then you can provide duplicates of their favorite play materials. If you know it is typical for 11- to 12-year-olds to test the limits, you will not take it personally if they talk back to you.

It is important to have age-appropriate expectations for behavior.

Most school-age children understand the difference between right and wrong. The reasons they give for doing what is "right" may differ depending on their stage of development. Lawrence Kohlberg and other researchers have studied how children in the United States and other countries make moral decisions. His theories state that moral development occurs at the same time as cognitive development. As children gain cognitive skills, they use these skills to make more advanced moral decisions. The levels and stages of moral development defined by Kohlberg include the following:[1]

Moral development occurs at the same time as cognitive development.

Level 1: Preconventional Moral Reasoning

Stage 1: Children behave because they want to avoid punishment.

Stage 2: Children's behavior is related to rewards and self-interest. Something is the "right" thing to do if it makes the child feel good or if it results in a reward.

Many of the younger children in your program are likely to be at this stage.

---

[1] Lawrence Kohlberg, *The Philosophy of Moral Development* (New York: Harper & Row, 1987).

Level 2: Conventional Moral Reasoning

Stage 3: Children follow certain rules and limits as set by others—usually adults such as parents and teachers. They follow the rules in order to receive praise for being "good" or to maintain order.

Stage 4: Children have developed an understanding of concepts such as obeying the law, applying justice consistently, doing something because it is your duty, and maintaining the social order.

The older children in your program are likely to use Level 2 moral reasoning.

Level 3: Postconventional Moral Reasoning

Stage 5: Individuals understand the relative nature of personal values and society's laws. They understand the importance of laws to society, but also recognize there are times when laws must be changed.

Stage 6: Individuals make moral decisions based on a belief in human rights. The individual might imagine him or herself in a similar situation and make the decision accordingly.

Level 3 moral reasoning is used by a small percentage of adults and almost never by children.

Think of Kohlberg's theories when guiding children's behavior.

Kohlberg's theories do not explain all of the reasons for children's behavior. However, it is helpful to keep them in mind when explaining the reasons for certain rules or limits or when considering how to respond to children's misbehavior. An example follows.

In preparation for a field trip to a large museum, the staff meet with the children to discuss the rules for the trip. One rule is children will pick a partner and stay with that person during the trip. Mr. Granger explains, "This rule is needed so we can keep track of the children. Children who do not stay with their partners will miss the next field trip." On the trip, most of the children follow this rule, however they have different reasons for doing so.

A child at Stage 1 stays with his partner because he is afraid he will not get to go on the next trip if he doesn't.

A child at Stage 2 stays with her partner, a good friend, because she wants to have a good time on the trip.

A child at Stage 3 stays with his partner because he wants to please the staff.

A child at Stage 4 stays with her partner because she knows obeying the rule makes it easier for the staff to keep track of the group.

To learn more about how children develop moral reasoning skills, consult the resources listed in the Orientation.

Applying Your Knowledge

The charts that follow list some typical behaviors of children at ages 5 to 7, 8 to 10, and 11 to 12. Included are behaviors relevant to helping children develop self-discipline The right column asks you to identify ways staff can use this information to promote self-discipline. Try to think of as many examples as you can. As you work through the module, you will learn new strategies and you can add them to the charts. You are not expected to think of all the examples at once. If you need help getting started, turn to the completed charts at the end of the module. By the time you complete this module, you will find you have learned many ways to guide children's behavior.

> As you complete the charts that follow, keep in mind that many of the examples of children's behavior and staff responses apply to more than one age group. Developmentally appropriate programs are based on child development and are responsive to children's individual strengths, needs, and interests. Therefore, it is important to observe children regularly, and to use what you learn to individualize the program.

Understanding and Responding to 5- to 7-Year-Old Children

What 5- to 7-Year-Old Children are Like	How Staff Can Use This Information to Promote Self-Discipline
They can think through problems in their minds.	*When children disagree, encourage them to use their thinking skills to resolve their differences. Ask open-ended questions to extend their thinking—"What might happen if . . .?" "What other ways could you do that . . .?" Give children plenty of time to think through problems on their own. For example, when two children decide to play a board game, watch as they discuss the rules rather than stepping in to explain them.*
Their attention span increases.	
They may still have difficulty sharing and taking turns.	
They may have difficulty controlling their behavior in group situations.	
They like teamwork and following rules. They may disagree about what rules say and what is "fair."	
They become more and more independent.	
They may hide their feelings, fears, and worries from adults.	

Understanding and Responding to 8- to 10-Year-Old Children

What 8- to 10-Year-Old Children are Like	How Staff Can Use This Information to Promote Self-Discipline
They expand and use their reasoning skills to solve problems, negotiate, and compromise with peers.	*Teach children to use conflict resolution as a way to work through problems. When children try to get you to solve their differences, encourage them to assume responsibility for resolving their differences. Model techniques such as negotiation and compromise as you work with children.*
They develop their own games with complicated rules and may fight when they think someone has broken the rules.	
They learn to express their anger and frustration in acceptable ways.	
They learn to use good judgment.	
They learn to accept responsibility for their actions.	
They do more and more on their own, without adult supervision or direction.	

Understanding and Responding to 11- to 12-Year-Old Children

What 11- to 12-Year-Old Children are Like	How Staff Can Use This Information to Promote Self-Discipline
They are able to negotiate, compromise, and solve problems.	*Teach children how to present and support their opinions when they differ with those of a friend. Help them learn to listen to another person's point of view.*
They may test program rules and adult authority and talk back to staff members.	
They may be in a hurry to grow up and may mimic teenage behaviors.	
They may have their judgment tested by strong peer group influences.	
They may "swear" because they think it is "cool." These words are generally used in daily conversations with their peers rather than in anger.	
They may test the limits of their physical skills.	
They begin to think in abstract terms; they can think about the consequences of their actions.	

When you have completed as much as you can of these charts, discuss your answers with your trainer. As you do the rest of the learning activities, you can refer back to the charts and add more examples of how school-age staff promote children's self-discipline.

Learning Activity II.
Creating an Environment That Supports Self-Discipline

IN THIS ACTIVITY YOU WILL LEARN TO:

- arrange the environment in ways that support positive behaviors; and

- encourage children to be involved in planning and making decisions about program operations.

A supportive environment for school-age children includes both physical and social elements that are responsive to children's needs, skills, and interests. Physical elements include well-stocked interest areas, materials stored where children can reach them, and displays of children's work. Social elements include practices such as including children in planning sessions, allowing children to choose the activities they want to do, and talking politely to children—even when reminding them of a program rule. When the physical and social environments are well-planned and demonstrate respect for children's abilities, many potential behavior problems can be prevented.

Well-planned environments can prevent behavior problems.

As discussed in Module 3, Program Environment, it is important to arrange the indoor and outdoor areas used by the program so children can choose their own activities. They can play alone or with friends and can use the interest areas with little or no adult assistance. This structure gives you and other staff members time to observe children, talk with them, and provide assistance to those who ask for help.

The physical environment should allow children to make choices.

Examples of how the physical environment can prevent behavior problems follow.

Try these suggestions.

Individual cubbies are available so children can store personal belongings. Children know items in the cubbies are "off limits," so disagreements about using other's belongings without permission are avoided. Also, children learn to take care of their own things and those of the program.

The daily schedule is posted at children's eye level. Children can see, for example, that permission slips need to be in by tomorrow for next week's field trip. Staff also remind children verbally, as some children remember better from listening rather than reading. Children tend to feel more secure when they know what's going on at the program.

Supplies for cleaning up spills and messes are stored where children can reach them. Children know it is their responsibility to use brooms, mops, paper towels, and sponges to clean up their spills. Staff help children learn the consequences of their actions, "You filled the pitcher too close to the top and the water left a trail from the sink to the aquarium. Please get the mop and wipe up the water."

Materials that are used together are stored together. Children are able to find what they need to carry out their plans. Clean-up time goes more smoothly because the materials are stored near where they are used.

Materials are stored where children can reach them. Children feel independent because they do not have to wait for adults to get out the materials and supplies.

There are comfortable places to sit and read or talk with a friend. A pile of pillows, an old stuffed chair, or a couch is available so children can relax, relieve stress, or spend some time alone when they need to take a break from the group or regain their composure.

There are clearly defined spaces for different activities and clear traffic patterns. This prevents children from getting in the way of each other's play and projects. Children can play or work without being interrupted. Conflicts that result from a child accidentally getting in the way of another are avoided.

The environment can be rearranged to accommodate changing needs and interests. Interest areas that children no longer use are replaced with new ones that children have asked for. Children don't get bored because the environment provides opportunities to learn new skills.

The outdoor play area is used for a variety of activities. Club meetings, talking to friends, cooperative games, sports, gardening, and reading take place outdoors. Many children benefit from spending part of the day outdoors. The fresh air and open spaces are energizing after spending most of the school day indoors. Being outdoors helps children expend energy that might otherwise be used in less positive ways.

A positive, cooperative social atmosphere can also help prevent problem behaviors. Involving children in program operations recognizes their important contributions and gives them a sense of responsibility. Talking with individual children; holding group meetings; listening to children's complaints, concerns, and suggestions; and responding to children's requests all let them know their participation is valued.

Some examples of ways the social environment can prevent behavior problems follow.

Children are involved in making decisions that affect the program. "Someone has offered to give us a guinea pig as a pet for our program. Do you think we should accept him?"

Staff notice children's interests and try to reflect them in the program's activities. "I heard some of you talking about the kite festival that's coming up. Would you be interested in starting a Kite Club?"

Staff use a normal tone and volume when speaking with children; they stand close by so they don't have to yell to be heard. "Ask Hannah to let go of the hula hoop and tell her you aren't through using it."

Cooperation is valued and praised. "That was quite a mess when Larry dropped the box of toothpicks. Thank you for helping him pick them up."

Children participate in the daily routines that keep the program running smoothly. "In addition to clean-up and snack, the jobs you can volunteer to do are mixing paint, changing the bulletin board, cleaning the rabbit's cage, and setting up a woodworking area."

Children are involved in setting the program's rules and limits. "Before the Cooking Club begins 'cooking' we need to make some safety rules. Cherie has offered to write down your suggestions."

Children are encouraged to help each other. "Sharon, can you show Justin how you made your basket? He's having a hard time getting started."

Staff teach children cooperative games and minimize competition in other activities. "Those of you who drew safety posters worked very hard. If we post some of them now, then rotate them throughout the year, we'll be able to display everyone's work."

A positive social atmosphere can also prevent behavior problems.

Try these suggestions.

When problem behaviors occur again and again in your program it is important to look for patterns. When do problems occur? In what areas of the environment—indoors and outdoors—do problems surface? Which children are involved? What are the children usually doing? Take turns observing, then discuss your observations with your colleagues. Look for the cause of the problem behavior. For example:

> The arts and crafts area has been the site of several arguments this week. The staff take turns observing children in the area to see what might be causing the problems. At the end of the week they meet to discuss their notes. They conclude that problems occur when: there are more children than chairs; children get in each other's way; children have to wait to use scissors, glue, and some of the other materials and equipment. They also conclude that children painting at easels are not involved in the disagreements; and children sitting at tables making collages, using clay, painting with water colors, and working on quilting squares are frequently involved in disagreements. They decide to provide more scissors and glue immediately. In addition, they post a notice of a meeting to involve children who use the area frequently in solving the other problems. Children attending the meeting agree on the following strategies: expand the area to include part of the space now set aside for hobby displays—this area is not being used; designate each of the three tables for different activities so children can share tools and materials; meet again in one week to discuss how things are going.

Observe the program to identify possible causes of problem behavior.

When the physical and social environments are "working," children are busy and happily engaged in play and activities. Fights are few and the school-age program is a pleasant place to be. In contrast, when the environment is not well-planned, children may be frustrated and unable to enjoy their out-of-school time. Of course, there are many possible causes for children's misbehavior; however, it's a good idea to consider how the environment might be contributing to the problems.

Applying Your Knowledge

In this learning activity you consider how aspects of the physical and social environment can affect children's behavior. You look at some typical behavior problems and how the environment can be the cause or the solution. Read the examples below, then use the chart that follows to plan ways to change the environment to address common behavior problems.

Creating an Environment That Promotes Self-Discipline
(Example)

Children's Behavior	Possible Problems in the Environment	How You Might Change the Environment
Some children form cliques and exclude others from their group.	*There is too much emphasis on competition. Staff members may be reluctant to get involved when children pick on someone because they think it will make it worse for the child who is excluded.*	*Encourage a more cooperative atmosphere. Have children do chores together, teach them cooperative games, eliminate contests, and meet with the cliques to help them understand their behavior is hurtful to others.*
The younger children in particular wander around with nothing to do.	*Materials may be stored out of the reach of the younger children. Activities may be geared towards older children. Older children may be excluding the younger ones.*	*Make sure materials are stored on open shelves where all children can reach them. Review the daily schedule to make sure there are age-appropriate activities for all children. Plan activities such as blowing giant bubbles that encourage children of different ages to get to know one another.*
Group meetings often become shouting matches between children with opposing points of view.	*Staff members may raise their voices when trying to get children's attention. There may be no guidelines for speaking out during a group meeting. Children may need the staff to impose some structure so they can learn to share their opinions calmly.*	*Work with children to develop some guidelines for speaking out in group meetings. Agree on consequences (losing your turn to speak for a day) for children who don't follow these rules. Make a pact with other staff to use a normal voice level at all times.*

Creating an Environment That Promotes Self-Discipline

Children's Behavior	Possible Problems in the Environment	How You Might Change the Environment
Children accuse each other of cheating when playing board games.		
Children get into fights when they can't use a material or piece of equipment.		
Children begin projects but do not finish them.		
Children make fun of others because something about them is different.		
Children can't find their belongings when it's time to go home.		

Check your answers with the answer sheet at the end of this module and discuss them with your trainer. There can be more than one answer.

Learning Activity III.
Guiding Children's Behavior

IN THIS ACTIVITY YOU WILL LEARN TO:

- use positive approaches to guide children's behavior; and
- use strategies tailored to an individual child's needs.

Often the words punishment and discipline are used to mean the same thing, but they are actually very different. Punishment means controlling children's behavior through fear. It makes children behave because they are afraid of what might happen to them if they don't. Children who are punished may stop their negative behavior temporarily, but they are not learning to use self-discipline. Instead, punishment may lead to or reinforce their bad feelings about themselves.

Discipline and punishment are very different.

Discipline means guiding and directing children toward acceptable behavior. The most important goal of discipline is to help children learn how to control their own behavior. Self-control is not a skill children are born with. It is learned through daily interactions with other children and adults. Learning self-discipline takes a lot of time, but it is time well spent. Children who are self-disciplined tend to be more successful in school and in life. They can set goals and take the steps needed to accomplish them. They find it easier to get along with their peers and with adults.

Often, children do not understand their feelings or how to express them. Even children with highly developed verbal skills may not understand feelings and may find it hard to express them with words. When children break the program's rules, talk back to adults, refuse to participate, destroy materials, or bicker with their friends, it is important to think about what their behavior means. What is the child trying to express? You can then respond in ways that help children control their behavior. Children's behaviors may be "telling" you many different things:

Children express feelings through behavior.

- "I feel lonely because my friend is playing with someone else. That's why I can't find anything to do."
- "I am angry because today at school my teacher yelled at me for no reason. That's why I lost my temper and hit Shawn."

- "I am afraid the other children will laugh at me when it's my turn at bat. That's why I went back inside without telling anyone."

- "I want my story to be perfect. That's why I keep ripping up my papers."

- "I need some limits because I'm not sure what it means to be an "almost teenager." That's why I'm using swear words."

- "I can't do what you asked me to do. That's why I said you are mean and none of the kids like you."

Accept children's negative feelings.

It's also important for adults to recognize and accept children's negative feelings. We all have days when we feel bad or don't want to do certain tasks. You can help children learn to recognize when they aren't feeling good. You can also provide ways for children to express their feelings without hurting themselves, other people, or the program's materials. When you see children are feeling frustrated, you can redirect them to listen to a soothing tape, run around the playground a few times, or read in the quiet area. These are soothing activities that help many children feel better.

Some inappropriate behaviors are accidental or careless more than deliberate. For example, a child may accidentally spill paint and then laugh when asked to clean up. Respond to such behaviors firmly but quietly; you don't need to dwell on them if they aren't part of a pattern of limit-testing behaviors.

Learning Activities I and II discussed how some problem behaviors can be avoided by having appropriate expectations for children's behaviors and by creating a supportive environment. Anticipating and planning for possible problems is another prevention technique. For example, if children are going to the bowling alley, staff can prevent potential problems by reviewing the procedures for walking there and the expectations for children's behavior at the alley. If a child has difficulty handling change, staff can explain that this week's trip to the swimming pool will take place on Thursday, not Wednesday.

Try these suggestions.

There are times when staff need to directly guide children's behavior. No single approach works for every child or every situation. The approach used should relate to the child and to the problem. The following positive guidance approaches are suggested:

Help children use problem-solving skills to develop solutions. "Gene, I can see you and Carlos are having a hard time agreeing on how to build the space station. How can you both have a chance to use your ideas?"

Talk with children privately away from the rest of the group. "I'd like to discuss your behavior during the gymnastics show. Let's talk privately for a few minutes."

Use a pre-arranged individual signal to remind a child to use self-control. "If I see you need some help controlling your temper I'll pull on my ear lobe. Then you can take a couple of deep breaths or close your eyes for a minute until you relax."

Focus on the child's behavior, not on the child. "Thank you for helping us carry the bag of balls in from the field," rather than "you're a good girl for being so helpful."

Help children understand the consequences of their actions and help them make amends. "Tim, I know you were fooling around and didn't mean to do harm, but Lisa is angry with you because you wrote on her picture. What can you do to make it up to her."

Assume the role of the authority only when necessary—but do so firmly. Your firm voice will help children learn to obey automatically in certain situations. "Don't move, Chaundra! A car is coming."

Gain control of your own angry feelings before disciplining a child. Ask for help from a colleague when needed. "Ms. Reynolds, Jennifer has talked back to me one too many times. I need to calm down for a few minutes. Could you please cover for me?"

Intervene in children's conflicts when necessary to prevent injuries. "Trinh and Kyle, I can't let you hurt each other. You need to leave the game so you can resolve your disagreement. Use your words to communicate with each other, not your fists. Kyle, you can go first. Trinh will listen to you without interrupting. Then it will be Trinh's turn to talk while you listen."

Applying Your Knowledge

In this learning activity you keep track of how you guide the behavior of an individual child over a five-day period. Take notes on what you see the child doing and how you respond. After reviewing your notes, plan ways to use the information to help the child develop self-discipline. Begin by reviewing the example on the next page.

Guiding Children's Behavior
(Example)

Child: _Martha_   **Age:** _8 years_   **Dates:** _January 19-23_

Day One

Martha was playing hopscotch with Leah. Stacy tried to join them. Martha told Stacy she couldn't play because she didn't know how. Stacy and Martha got into a pushing match. Stacy fell down. I walked over and asked Stacy if she was okay. She was so I asked the girls to talk about what happened. The three girls all talked at once. I asked Martha to come with me for a few minutes. We sat under the oak tree and talked about what happened. Martha said she was angry because Stacy always "hogs" Leah and she never gets to play with Leah alone. We talked some more about feelings—hers, Leah's, and Stacy's. Martha asked if I would help her talk to Stacy about what happened. I agreed to help.

Day Two

Martha bumped into Aaron and his juice spilled on his shirt. She immediately apologized and helped him clean off the shirt. Later, I praised her for the way she handled herself.

How can you use what you learned about this child to promote self-discipline?

Martha has strong verbal skills. She is able to talk about her feelings and knows how they are connected to her behavior. It seems like talking about a problem behavior is an appropriate way to guide Martha's behavior.

Martha can consider other children's feelings and make amends for her actions, even if they were unintentional. This skill can be reinforced through genuine praise for her actions.

Guiding Children's Behavior

Child: _____   Age: _____   Dates: _____

Day One

_____

_____

_____

Day Two

_____

_____

_____

Day Three

_____

_____

_____

Day Four

_____

_____

_____

Day Five

_____

_____

_____

How can you use what you learned about this child to promote self-discipline?

_____

_____

_____

_____

_____

Discuss this activity with your trainer.

Learning Activity IV.
Teaching Children to Use Conflict Resolution Techniques[2]

IN THIS ACTIVITY YOU WILL LEARN TO:

- teach children how to use conflict resolution techniques; and

- encourage children to resolve conflicts with minimum adult assistance.

Conflicts arise in any group situation.

Conflicts are part of life in a school-age program. They arise between children or between children and staff. When handled effectively, they can be productive and lead to better communication and program improvement. Most conflicts are disagreements about one of the following:

Resources—two or more people want something in short supply. The resource might be materials or equipment, the friendship of a popular child, or your attention. Generally, these conflicts are easy to resolve. Two children fighting over who can sit next to you during a group meeting, might be arguing over a scarce resource—closeness to you.

Needs—for power, friendship, self-esteem, achievement, or a sense of belonging. These can be difficult to resolve because it may be hard to identify the reasons for the conflict. Two children arguing over whose kite flies the highest might be expressing a need for achievement—to have made the "best" kite.

Value clashes—include disagreements over personal beliefs, the right way to do something, or the relative importance of a task. These are the hardest to resolve because individuals feel their sense of self is threatened. Children fighting about which basketball team will win a game may be expressing conflicting values—each child believes a different team to be "best."

When resolving conflicts, begin by determining what type of disagreement is taking place. When a conflict falls into more than one category, respond first to the one that is easiest to resolve. For example, the two children fighting over who gets to sit next to you appear to be fighting over a "resource"—your time and attention. After dealing with this conflict, others may arise that

[2] Parts of this learning activity are based with permission on William J. Kreidler, *Creative Conflict Resolution* (W. Glenview, IL: Scott, Foresman and Company, 1984).

indicate the conflict is also about needs—the children need more individual attention from staff.

Conflicts may be reduced when the school-age program fits the following description:

School-age programs can reduce conflicts.

The program has a cooperative atmosphere. Many activities encourage children to work with each other. There are some competitive games and contests, but these are balanced with opportunities for children to explore materials and try out new activities. Children learn to work cooperatively. Cooperative behavior is encouraged and rewarded. They focus their energies on enjoying games and sports and are not overly concerned with winning and losing.

Staff and children demonstrate tolerance. Children know how to be nice to each other and to the staff. Prosocial behaviors such as empathy and taking turns are encouraged and rewarded. When cliques form that exclude children from play, adults step in to try to encourage different ways to have fun. Individuals value and respect other children's talents and accomplishments. Diversity is valued.

Children and staff have good communication skills. They know how to express their needs and feelings effectively. There are many opportunities for children to be meaningfully involved in program planning and operations. Children know how to listen to each other, and they understand each other.

Feelings and emotions are expressed appropriately. Staff and children express their anger and frustration by using words to tell others how they feel. Self-discipline is encouraged and rewarded.

Staff have appropriate expectations for children's behavior. They use their authority sparingly. There are a few simple rules, the program is loosely structured and flexible, and there is an atmosphere of trust and respect. Children behave because they helped make the rules and they understand the reasons for the rules.

Children and staff use conflict resolution to discuss and develop solutions to conflicts. Conflicts are resolved quickly and fairly, with the full participation of the children and staff involved.

The most common form of conflict resolution is mediation. Staff help children work out their problems in the presence of a calm, objective observer who will ensure fairness. Fairness is very important to school-age children. To be effective, mediation can take a long time. It is productive time, however, for it helps children develop skills they can use to solve future problems by themselves. Mediation includes the following steps:

Many conflicts can be solved through mediation.

- Each child tells his or her side of the story without interruption.

- Each child describes the problem, then what happened in the conflict.

- If the problem still exists, children develop possible solutions.

- If the problem no longer exists, children are asked if there were other ways to solve the problem than the one they chose.

You can use reflective listening to help children resolve their disagreements.

Another technique used to clearly define or end a conflict is reflective listening. Staff members listen to children as they describe the conflict and what happened, then reflect the statements back to the children using statements such as, "Sounds like. . .," "In other words. . .," "I hear you saying that. . ." It is important to reflect the child's feelings as well as the facts of the situation. Children then agree or disagree with the staff member's statement. Often, the use of reflective listening is sufficient to resolve the conflict.

An example follows.

> Raeshawn and Theresa have been rehearsing the dance they plan to perform at next week's talent show. Raeshawn says, "We've practiced enough. I want to go outside to play volleyball." Theresa disagrees, "We need lots more practice. I don't want to make a fool of myself. You can play later." Raeshawn responds, "That's what you think. I'm going outside." Theresa faces Raeshawn and yells, "No." Raeshawn steps back and says, "You're not my boss." Mr. Suarez steps in, "Can someone tell me what's happening? Theresa, you can go first."

> Theresa: "She promised to dance in the talent show with me, but now she won't practice and I don't want to look stupid in the show."

> Mr. Suarez: "I hear you saying that Raeshawn agreed to dance with you, but she doesn't want to practice and you're worried about looking stupid. Is that right?"

> Theresa: "That's right. I don't want to look stupid."

> Mr. Suarez: "Theresa, describe what happened."

> Raeshawn: "I said I would dance in the talent show with her, and we practiced for half an hour. Now I want to go outside and she won't let me."

> Mr. Suarez: "You agreed to be in the talent show, you practiced for half an hour, and you think you know the dance well enough. You want to go outside, but Theresa won't let you. Is that right?"

Raeshawn: "That's partly right. I think we practiced enough for today. I want to go outside and she won't let me."

Mr. Suarez: "It seems like you both want to be in the talent show together but you disagree about how much you need to practice. Maybe you could agree on a practice schedule that both of you could live with."

Raeshawn: "Okay. As long as it doesn't mean more today. I want to do something different."

Theresa: "Okay. Can we practice every day for half an hour?"

There are a number of conflict resolution techniques you can teach children. After practicing the techniques children will be able to use them on their own.

Storytelling—This technique can help children step back from the conflict so they can discuss the problem without feeling threatened. It is most effective with younger children. Retell what happened in the form of a story, "Sherrie and Wanda both wanted to try out the new computer program." Stop frequently to ask for input from the group. Encourage them to be very specific, "How could they both get what they wanted?" Include their suggestions in the story. If you use this technique with older children, ask them to tell the story from a third person point of view—as if it was happening to someone else. This helps children analyze the situation from another perspective.

Planning Time—This technique helps children use their problem-solving skills to resolve conflicts. It works well for minor disagreements, but is not effective when children are angry or upset. When children ask you to help them solve a problem direct them to a quiet spot and give them three minutes to work out the problem themselves. After three minutes ask the children if they have worked out a solution. If so, praise them and ask what it is. If not, use mediation, reflective listening, or another technique to help the children resolve the situation. In the overview section of the module, Ricky and Brad used planning time to solve their problem.

Role Playing—This technique allows children to reenact a situation in front of an audience so they can better understand their behavior. Begin by defining the conflict: give the time, describe the place, provide relevant background information, and state who was involved. Have the children involved, or volunteers, act out the conflict. If they get stuck, ask leading questions. Keep this part of the role play brief. At the point of the conflict freeze the action. Ask the audience to suggest ways to resolve the conflict. Have the players incorporate the suggestions they prefer and wrap up the role play. Discuss what happened, how the conflict could

Try these conflict resolution techniques.

have been prevented, how the players felt, and other possible solutions.

You also can teach children this technique using sample conflicts, rather than real ones. Once they learn to role play, they can use the technique to resolve differences. Some children will not want to participate. Others may be willing to role play privately, but not with an audience.

Role Reversals—This technique helps children see a situation from another person's point of view. Begin the role play as described above by "setting the stage." Start the role play, then freeze it. Ask children to change roles and do the role play again, this time assuming the role of the other person. Stop the role play when the children seem to understand the other person's perspective. Discuss the role play and possible solutions.

Another popular technique for conflict resolution is described by Elizabeth Crary.[3] Known as SIGEP, this technique follows the six steps described below:

1. **Stop**. Have everyone involved in the conflict stop to regain composure and self-control so they can discuss the situation.

2. **Identify**. Encourage children to talk about why are upset. Ask questions such as:

   What was happening before your disagreement?

   How do you feel?

   What do you want to happen?

   What do you think the other people want?

   Ask children to be as specific as possible, "She gave herself extra money when she was banker," rather than, "She's a cheater." Observe children's body language and listen to their words.

3. **Generate**. Give everyone a chance to brainstorm possible solutions to the problem. Accept all ideas, without rejecting any as being too hard to implement, or too far fetched. Encourage children to use their creativity. Let them exhaust their suggestions before offering any of your own.

4. **Evaluate**. Consider the usefulness of all of the ideas generated by the children and staff. Have children think about whether an idea would work, is fair, and what might happen if they tried it. The children should agree to try one of the ideas. The others can be saved in case the first one doesn't solve the problem.

[3] Based with permission on Elizabeth Crary, *Kids Can Cooperate* (Seattle, WA: Parenting Press, 1984), pp. 41-45.

5. **Plan**. Discuss how to carry out the decision. What needs to happen first? Can the children do it without adult help? How will they know if their decision worked?

Teaching children how to resolve conflicts is an important part of your job. Children will use these skills throughout their lives in a variety of school, family, work, and social situations. By teaching conflict resolution skills, you can help make the program a more peaceful place. Children will learn to consider the views and feelings of others.

Conflict resolution skills are used throughout our lives.

Applying Your Knowledge

During the next week conflicts are likely to arise at your program. When they do, use one or more of the conflict resolution techniques described in this learning activity to help children resolve their problem. After the situation is resolved describe the conflict and answer the questions on the form that follows. An example is provided.

Using Conflict Resolution Techniques
(Example)

The Conflict

Children involved/ages: *Polly (7 years) and Margo (8 years).*

What happened to cause the conflict?

Last week Margo let Polly use her pencil with the soccer ball eraser. Today Polly took the pencil out of Margo's cubby without asking permission.

How did the children handle (or mishandle) the conflict?

Margo saw Polly using the pencil. When she snatched the pencil from Polly, it broke in half.

The Technique

Describe the technique you used or taught to the children.

We used SIGEP to discuss and resolve the problem.

How did the children respond?

It helped defuse the situation. The girls were able to discuss their feelings and why they each felt justified. Polly said she thought it was okay to take the pencil without permission because last week Margo said they could take turns using it. Margo said she has a pencil collection and she likes to keep them in good condition, so she doesn't like other people using them. After solving the problem the girls made a poster so others could learn about SIGEP.

How was the conflict resolved?

Polly apologized to Margo and vice versa. Margo agreed to leave her special pencils at home or in her backpack because they are very important to her. Polly agreed to pay for half of a new pencil. She also promised to not take things from Margo's cubby in the future.

Would you use this technique with other children? Explain why or why not.

Yes. I plan to introduce it at a group meeting using a story about two children having a conflict. Then children can use it themselves if they find it helpful.

Using Conflict Resolution Techniques

The Conflict

Children involved/ages: _____

What happened to cause the conflict?

_____

_____

How did the children handle (or mishandle) the conflict?

_____

_____

_____

The Technique

Describe the technique you used or taught to the children.

_____

_____

How did the children respond?

_____

_____

_____

_____

_____

How was the conflict resolved?

_____

_____

_____

Would you use this technique with other children? Explain why or why not.

_____

_____

_____

Discuss this activity with your trainer and your colleagues. Plan ways to use conflict resolution techniques as a regular part of your program.

Learning Activity V.
Involving Children in Setting Rules and Limits

IN THIS ACTIVITY YOU WILL LEARN TO:

- involve the children in setting clear, simple rules and limits;

- communicate rules clearly to children; and

- enforce rules consistently.

It's easier to follow rules that are stated positively.

Rules and limits help both children and staff agree on what behaviors are acceptable. Both adults and children are more likely to accept and follow rules when they are stated in positive terms that describe what to do, rather than what not to do. For example, your program might have a rule about staff use of the telephone. How do the following two statements make you feel?

- You **may not** use the telephone for personal calls while on duty.

- You **may** use the telephone on breaks and for emergencies.

Most people would prefer the second statement because it tells you what you may do, rather than what you may not do. Human nature is such that we are more willing to comply with rules that are stated positively. When rules are stated negatively, we are likely to feel as though we have been accused. For example, upon hearing "You may not use the telephone for personal calls while on duty," someone might think, "Of course I wouldn't do that. I know it's not right to leave the children while I'm on duty. Whoever wrote this rule doesn't have any respect for me or my colleagues." Upon hearing, "You may use the phone on breaks and for emergencies," someone might think, "That's a reasonable rule. It gives a time when I can use the phone and acknowledges I wouldn't leave the children while I placed a personal call."

Simple rules tell children what they should do.

Children also need simple rules that tell them what they should do, rather than what they should not do. For example, "walk inside so you don't hurt yourself" rather than "don't run inside" tells children what they can do and why. There are many times during the day when you must remind children of the rules and limits. Children are more likely to internalize the rules when your reminders are worded positively and delivered in a brief and firm manner. For example:

- "Only one person can speak at a time" instead of "You can't all talk at once."

- "Use your words to tell others how you feel" instead of "No fighting."

- "Walk indoors" instead of "No running indoors."

Children feel safer when they know adults will enforce rules and limits consistently. These feelings of security tend to make children feel freer to explore and experiment.

Children are likely to respect rules when they understand the reasons behind them. They also are more likely to follow rules they help create. When involving children in setting rules, talk to them about the consequences of actions. "What might happen if you go to the art room without signing out?" Children could come up with answers and also think of a rule. "Sign out when going to another room in the building. We need to know where you are in case something happens to you. You might get hurt and no one could help because they wouldn't know where to find you."

Children can help create rules.

It's important to have just enough rules to keep the program functioning smoothly. When there are too many rules, children can't remember what to do. Too few rules might mean the children aren't safe and the environment is disorderly.

As children grow and mature, they can handle more freedom, more activities, and more responsibility. You need to observe carefully to see when individual children or the whole group can handle greater freedom. There is a fine line between keeping children safe and keeping them from having chances to grow and be independent. The limits set at the beginning of the year may need to be adjusted in a few months' time. It may be appropriate to have different rules depending on children's ages and abilities. For example, perhaps the younger children must be escorted back indoors from the playground, whereas older children can tell a staff member, then go in by themselves.

Review and revise rules as children grow and mature.

Applying Your Knowledge

In this learning activity you use positive phrases to list your program's rules. Then you answer some questions about one of the rules. First read the example on the next page and then complete the blank forms that follow.

Rules for the School-Age Program
(Example)

Staying healthy and safe:

Wear a batting helmet when it's your turn at bat. Wash your hands before and after eating.

Respecting the rights of others:

Ask for permission before using other people's belongings. When you want to be alone, you can go to the quiet area.

Not hurting yourself or others:

Use your words to tell others how you feel. Climb the ladder to the loft one at a time.

Caring for the equipment and materials:

Use the arts and crafts materials in areas with washable floors.

Now select one of the rules or limits you listed and answer the following questions.

Rule: *Everyone helps at clean-up time*

Why do you have this rule?

Our program is set up so children can get materials themselves and put them back when they are finished. They like doing things on their own and learn self-discipline.

How do you make sure all adults apply the rule in the same way?

Adults and children work together at clean-up time. If there are problems with consistency, we talk about them after the children leave for school in the morning.

How do you follow through and support your words with actions?

If a child doesn't respond to the reminder, I walk over to the child. Then I get on the child's level and repeat the reminder: "It's clean-up time."

Give an example of a simple, clear statement that states the rule positively.

"There are five minutes until clean-up time. Finish your work, then start putting things away."

What might you say to respect and acknowledge a child's feelings?

"I know you aren't finished with your drawing. You can put it in your cubby until tomorrow."

How do you act with authority and show confidence?

I always give a ten-minute, then a five-minute warning. I never apologize when I announce it's clean-up time. When a child is slow to stop playing, I just say, "It's clean-up time."

Rules for the School-Age Program

Staying healthy and safe:

_____

_____

_____

_____

_____

Respecting the rights of others:

_____

_____

_____

_____

_____

Not hurting yourself or others:

_____

_____

_____

_____

_____

Caring for our equipment and materials:

_____

_____

_____

_____

_____

Discuss these rules with a colleague who also works in your program.

Now select one of the rules or limits you listed and answer the following questions.

Rule: _____

Why do you have this rule?

_____

_____

_____

How do you make sure all adults apply the rule in the same way?

_____

_____

_____

How do you follow through and support your words with actions?

_____

_____

_____

Give an example of a simple, clear statement that states the rule positively.

_____

_____

_____

What might you say to respect and acknowledge a child's feelings?

_____

_____

How do you act with authority and show confidence?

_____

_____

Discuss your answers with your trainer.

Learning Activity VI.
Responding to Challenging Behaviors

IN THIS ACTIVITY YOU WILL LEARN TO:

- look for the reasons behind a child's challenging behavior; and

- develop a plan for responding to a challenging behavior.

Challenging behaviors, such as repeatedly talking back to staff or being overly aggressive, are likely to occur again and again. This may mean something in the child's life is disturbing. The child doesn't know how to express his or her feelings appropriately, so he or she acts out.

Challenging behaviors occur again and again.

It's important to remember that, in most cases, there is a reason for the child's behavior. Perhaps a situation at home or at school is causing the child to be upset or frustrated; perhaps it's the environment at the school-age program. The program schedule, activities, or expectations may be inappropriate for this child. Some possible causes of challenging behaviors include the following:[4]

There are usually reasons for children's behavior.

Children need more attention than they are getting. Children need to feel important and valued. Sometimes, when children don't receive enough positive attention, they act out to get negative attention. Their need for attention is so great they "misbehave" because it will get adults to notice them and spend time with them. Unfortunately, once they are successful in getting attention by misbehaving, they are likely to continue the unacceptable behavior until the cycle is broken.

They are affected by a physical condition. Health problems and conditions such as illness, allergies, disabilities, lack of sleep, poor nutrition, or hunger can contribute to children's misbehavior. Learning disabilities and conditions such as attention deficit disorder (ADD) can cause a child to have both academic and behavior problems. When a child frequently or consistently has difficulty behaving appropriately, the possibility of physical causes should be considered. Staff can discuss examples of the child's behavior with the parents and request the child be evaluated by the family physician.

---

[4] Based with permission on Project ETC, Greater Minneapolis Day Care Association and Portage Project, *Special Training for Special Needs; Module 5: Program Implementation* (Minneapolis: Portage Project, 1989).

They are feeling bored or confined. No matter how interesting and varied the activities are at the program, some children will be bored and feel like they would rather be somewhere else. It helps to make an extra effort to include such a child when planning program activities and starting new clubs.

They are seeking more control of the situation. Sometimes children have very few opportunities to make decisions or have control over their lives. Perhaps between home, school, and the school-age program there are too many rules and too few opportunities for children to choose what they want to do, what materials they want to use, and who they would like to play with. When children are able to make decisions they feel as though they have some control over their lives and they begin to develop self-discipline. For example, Kyle might not be allowed to decide whether or not he goes to the school-age program; however, he can choose what to do while at the program.

When a child repeatedly exhibits a challenging behavior over a long period of time, all the adults who care for the child need to discuss the possible causes of the problem. You can reassure the child's parents there are times when some children behave this way, but the behavior cannot be allowed at the school-age program. You can then agree on a plan for consistent responses to the behavior. It is very important to let the child know he or she is still loved and cared for, even if he or she has a challenging behavior.

Applying Your Knowledge

In this learning activity you first think of a child in your program who has a challenging behavior. Describe the child's behavior and your response. Next, ask the child's parents if they would be willing to participate in this activity. Describe the activity and the behavior you will be observing. Stress that observation notes are always confidential. Then, talk with the parents to learn about the child's behavior at home and at school. Jointly develop a plan for responding to the behavior. Review the example on the next page, then complete the blank form that follows.

Responding to Challenging Behaviors
(Example)

Child: *Emily*   **Age:** *9 years*   **Date:** *October 16*

What behavior is challenging?
Emily has been stealing small items from the staff and from other children.

How often does this occur? How long has it been going on? When does it happen?
About once or twice a week. For two weeks. It seems to happen when Emily is angry or disappointed because she was left out of an activity.

How do you respond now?
We talk to Emily about the consequences of her actions—staff won't trust her, the other children won't want to play with her, she won't be able to participate in favorite activities.

How does the child respond?
She seems genuinely sorry for her behavior, and very embarrassed. She cries and says she knows it's wrong to steal. She promises she won't do it again.

Did something happen at the program that might have upset the child?
Recently Emily tried out for the lead in the play we are doing and didn't get it. She was very disappointed and kept asking why she wasn't chosen. She had a hard time understanding that the girl who was chosen gave a better performance during auditions. She was offered another part, but said she didn't want to be in the play after all.

Did something happen at home that might have upset the child?
Her parents can't think of anything, but Emily has stolen several small items from her older sister in the past few weeks. They thought Emily was going through a stage of normal sibling rivalry, even though Emily and her sister have always gotten along well.

Did something happen at school that might have upset the child?
Her parents checked with her teacher who said Emily has stolen a few items at school— an eraser from his desk, and a troll from another child. Each time Emily was confronted about stealing she returned the items and apologized.

Conclusion:
Emily may be retaliating for not being chosen for the lead in the play.

Plans for responding to this behavior:
I discussed the situation with my colleague who is helping the Drama Club with their play. He and I will meet with Emily to invite her to think again about taking another part in the play. Her parents and the staff at the program will continue to talk weekly to discuss her progress. We'll continue to use positive guidance techniques to guide her behavior. We will make it a point to give her a lot of positive reinforcement.

What happened when you tried out your plans? Has the behavior changed or gone away?
Emily agreed to take another part in the play. Her behavior has improved dramatically. Her parents say she has been talking about the play a lot and is having fewer problems in school.

Responding to Challenging Behaviors

Child: _____   Age: _____   Date: _____

What behavior is challenging?

_____

_____

How often does this occur?   How long has it been going on? When does it happen?

_____

_____

_____

How do you respond now?

_____

_____

How does the child respond?

_____

_____

Did something happen at the program that might have upset the child?

_____

_____

_____

Did something happen at home that might have upset the child?

_____

_____

_____

Did something happen at school that might have upset the child?

_____

_____

_____

Conclusion:

_____

_____

_____

_____

Plans for responding to this behavior:

_____

_____

_____

_____

What happened when you tried out your plans? Has the behavior changed or gone away?

_____

_____

_____

_____

Discuss this activity with your trainer.

SUMMARIZING YOUR PROGRESS

You have now completed all the learning activities for this module. Whether you are an experienced school-age staff member or a new one, this module has probably helped you develop new skills for guiding children's behavior. Before you go on, take a few minutes to summarize what you've learned.

• Turn back to Learning Activity I, Using Your Knowledge of Child Development to Guide Behavior, and add specific examples of what you learned about helping children develop self-discipline while you were working on this module to the charts. Compare your ideas to those in the completed charts at the end of the module.

• Next, review your responses to the pre-training assessment for this module. Write a summary of what you learned, and list the skills you developed or improved.

_____

_____

_____

_____

_____

_____

_____

_____

_____

_____

_____

_____

_____

_____

_____

If there are topics you would like to know more about, you will find recommended readings listed in the Orientation in Volume I.

Your final step in this module is to complete the knowledge and competency assessments. Let your trainer know when you are ready to schedule the assessments. After you have successfully completed them, you will be ready to start a new module. Congratulations on your progress so far, and good luck with your next module.

ANSWER SHEETS

Guiding Children's Behavior

1. How did Ms. Mingus demonstrate respect for the children?

   a. She gave Katy an opportunity to explain why she thought the program needed new games.

   b. She handled the situation as a "storage problem" rather than accusing the children of being careless with the games.

2. How did Ms. Mingus encourage children's self-discipline?

   a. She asked for volunteers to help organize the games.

   b. She asked the children what supplies they needed, then told them where to find them.

   c. She asked the children to think of better ways to store the games.

Providing an Environment That Encourages Children's Self-Discipline

1. How did Ms. Anton know Kendall was upset?

   a. She knew it was unusual for Kendall to be the last off the bus.

   b. She heard Kendall complaining to herself about the cubbies.

   c. She knew it was unusual for Kendall to be quiet during a club meeting.

2. How did Ms. Anton's guidance help Kendall learn self-discipline?

   a. She accepted Kendall's feelings.

   b. She offered to work with Kendall to plan a homework schedule.

   c. She taught Kendall a skill—doing a schedule—the child can use in the future without adult assistance.

Using Positive Methods to Guide Individual Children

235

Helping Children Understand and Express Their Feelings in Acceptable Ways

1. Why did Mr. Franklin suggest the boys sit down on the couch to discuss their problem?

   Sitting on the couch removed the boys from the source of their problem so they could discuss it more calmly.

2. How did Mr. Franklin help the boys express their feelings in acceptable ways?

   a. He taught them a conflict resolution technique they could use to solve this problem and other problems that might arise in the future.

   b. He let them know he was confident they could solve their own problem, but would help if he was needed.

Understanding and Responding to 5- to 7-Year-Old Children

What 5- to 7-Year-Old Children Are Like	How Staff Can Use This Information to Promote Self-Discipline
They can think through problems in their minds.	*When children disagree, encourage them to use their thinking skills to resolve their differences. Ask open-ended questions to extend their thinking—"What might happen if...?" "What other ways could you do that...?" Give children plenty of time to think through problems on their own. For example, when two children decide to play a board game, watch as they discuss the rules rather than stepping in to explain them.*
They may still have difficulty sharing and taking turns.	*Provide duplicates of popular items and materials so children don't have to wait too long to join in a favorite activity. Set up systems for taking turns and help children find something to do while waiting.*
They may have difficulty controlling their behavior in group situations.	*Have appropriate expectations for the amount of time children of this age can spend in large groups. Offer opportunities for children to participate in activities in small groups—for example, two or three children can play catch rather than joining a large group playing softball. Observe to see when children need to leave the group to spend time alone or just with a few others.*
They like teamwork and following rules. They may disagree about what rules say and what is "fair." They may make up games with rules and routines.	*Stock up on a variety of board games such as Connect Four, Boggle, Pictionary, and Scrabble for Juniors. Introduce new games by reading the directions out loud with the children. Offer to play the game with the children the first time. If they accept the offer, stop frequently to ask the children if you are following the rules. Provide materials children can use to make games, have them write down rules they have agreed on or dictate them to an older child or staff member. Respect their invented games, rules, and routines as long as they are safe and don't hurt anyone's feelings.*
They become more and more independent.	*Involve children in the program's routines, according to their abilities. Give children increasing responsibility and more difficult tasks as they develop new skills. Allow children to do as much as possible for themselves—making snacks, selecting activities, storing their belongings.*
They may hide their feelings, fears, and worries from adults.	*Encourage children to express their feelings through writing, dramatic play, and art work. Provide books about feelings, fears, and worries and use them as discussion starters. Be available to listen when children are ready to share with you.*

Understanding and Responding to 8- to 10-Year-Old Children

What 8- to 10-Year-Old Children Are Like	How Staff Can Use This Information to Promote Self-Discipline
They expand and use their reasoning skills to solve problems, negotiate, and compromise with peers.	*Teach children to use conflict resolution as a way to work through problems. When children try to get you to solve their differences, encourage them to assume responsibility for resolving their differences. Model techniques such as negotiation and compromise as you work with children.*
They develop their own games with complicated rules and may fight when they think someone has broken the rules.	*Provide materials for making up board games. To avoid misunderstandings, suggest they write down the rules. When children make up an outdoor game, ask them to explain the game and the rules to you. This may help if you are later asked to mediate a disagreement. Suggest children make up new ways to play popular games.*
They learn to express their anger and frustration in acceptable ways.	*Praise children when they use self-control. Provide outlets—clay, art materials, a quiet place to get away, soft music and earphones—for reducing stress, so children don't become overwhelmed by anger and frustration.*
They learn to use good judgment.	*Compliment children when you notice them using good judgment. "That was a good idea to put the gerbil back in his cage when he started squirming. It would have been difficult to catch him if he wiggled out of your hands."*
They learn to accept responsibility for their actions.	*Encourage children to pick up after themselves and clean up spills. Also, when their behavior hurts another child (either physically or emotionally), talk about how they might behave differently in the future. Encourage children to make amends for their actions.*
They do more and more on their own, without adult supervision and direction.	*Encourage children to make choices, form clubs, and lead meetings. Recognize and value what makes them unique—special talents, skills, achievements. Let them know the special things about them you value—the way they include a younger child in their play or their perseverance when they are having trouble with a homework assignment. Respect their need to keep some "secrets" from adults.*

Understanding and Responding to 11- to 12-Year-Old Children

What 11- to 12-Year-Old Children Are Like	How Staff Can Use This Information to Promote Self-Discipline
They are able to negotiate, compromise, and solve problems.	*Teach children how to present and support their opinions when they differ with those of a friend. Help them learn to listen to another person's point of view.*
They may test program rules and adult authority and talk back to staff members.	*Recognize it is normal for children in this age group to test rules and challenge adults. When they do break program rules, discuss the incident with them and help them accept the consequences.*
They want to be accepted by their peers, to be a member of the group.	*Encourage children to recognize their own values and stick to them even when their peers want them to do something different.*
They may be in a hurry to grow up and may mimic teenage behaviors.	*Help children feel good about themselves at their current age. Allow them plenty of responsibility and independence so they don't feel like little kids. Try to accept the harmless imitations and ignore those that can be annoying at times, such as using slang or talking about music all the time.*
They may have their judgment tested by strong peer group influences.	*Discuss with children how they feel when pressured by their peers to do things they know are not appropriate, such as using drugs or alcohol. Help children practice responses that express their feelings: "I want to keep my body in good health because I am an athlete." "I know a kid who tried that once and it made her really sick so I don't want to do it." "No thanks."*
They may use "swear" words to be "cool." These words are generally used in daily conversations with peers rather than in anger.	*Make it very clear that swearing is not allowed at the program, and specify the consequences. Remember children of this age use swear words to feel like a part of their peer group, not because they are "bad."*
They may test the limits of their physical skills.	*Be sure the equipment and materials used by the younger children is sturdy enough to support the older ones. Agree on rules to keep everyone safe. For example, the loft may be reserved for older children at certain times and younger ones other times. Make sure the program's equipment is sized appropriately for older children.*
They are beginning to think in abstract terms; they can think about the consequences of their actions.	*Encourage children to think through their plans before carrying them out. Ask open-ended questions such as "What might happen if you do that?" "Is there another way you could handle that situation?"*

Creating an Environment That Promotes Self-Discipline

Children's Behavior	Possible Problems in the Environment	How You Might Change the Environment
Children accuse each other of cheating when playing board games.	*The games are too difficult or children don't know how to play them. The written rules are lost. Staff or other children may give too much attention to the "winners."*	*Ask for volunteers to make sure there are copies of the rules for each board game. Play the games with children until they understand the rules. Ask children to explain the rules to you to make sure they know how to play the game. Suggest changing the rules if needed to make the game easier to play. Avoid focusing on winning the game.*
Children get into fights when they can't use a material or piece of equipment.	*There are not duplicates of favorite items—particularly those that are popular with the younger children. There is no system for taking turns or sharing limited resources.*	*Ask the program to purchase extras of popular items. Work with children to set up a system for taking turns and to restrict use of resources in limited supply. For example, children can cut the tissue paper in half when they need only a small piece. Make a note to order a larger supply of resources that are used up quickly or are most popular.*
Children begin projects but do not finish them.	*The projects are not really of interest to children. They are bored with the interest areas and other activities.*	*Assess children's interests through conversations, a written survey, or several small group meetings. Involve children in creating new interest areas that respond to the survey results.*

Creating an Environment That Promotes Self-Discipline
(continued)

Children's Behavior	Possible Problems in the Environment	How You Might Change the Environment
Children make fun of others because something about them is different.	*Children have not learned to value what makes each person unique. The program atmosphere may emphasize competitiveness rather than cooperation.*	*Provide materials—books, games, pictures, records—that reflect the children's diverse ethnic and cultural backgrounds. Provide opportunities for children to share their special hobbies and interests—what makes each person unique. Keep track of the times competition is a part of program activities. Strive to minimize competition and include more opportunities for children to cooperate as they play a game or complete a project.*
Children can't find their belongings when it's time to go home.	*Children don't have individual cubbies, or they are located too far from the entrance. Children are not expected to help take care of the program's materials.*	*Provide individual cubbies or storage areas for each child located near the entrance. Let children know they are expected to care for the program's materials and their own belongings. Store materials in labeled containers and make sure children can reach the shelves or cupboards.*

GLOSSARY

Challenging behavior   Behavior such as talking back to adults, swearing, or being overly aggressive that occurs again and again and is often difficult to handle.

Consequence   The natural or logical result of a behavior.

Discipline   The actions that adults take to guide and direct children toward acceptable behavior.

Limits and rules   Guidelines set jointly by staff members and children as to what are acceptable behaviors.

Positive guidance   Techniques that help children learn to behave in acceptable ways. These methods help children develop self-discipline.

Punishment   Control of children's behavior by use of fear.

Self-discipline   The ability to control one's own behavior.

Module 11:

FAMILIES

OVERVIEW

WORKING WITH FAMILIES INVOLVES:

- communicating with parents often to exchange information about their child at home and at the program;

- offering a variety of ways for parents to participate in their child's life at the program; and

- providing support to families.

Recent studies have shown that the most effective programs for children are those which actively promote and encourage the involvement of families. School-age staff are in a unique position with children and families. Like teachers, you see children daily and have ready access to their parents. Over a period of time you are likely to have more contacts with families than any other professional. Your position allows you to support families and help children and their parents maintain close relationships. Good working relationships with families enable school-age staff to be more responsive to each child's needs. When parents* and staff work as a team, they can share information and discuss ways to provide consistent care at home and at the program.

No matter how much time children spend outside their homes—at school, at the school-age program, playing sports, or engaged in other activities—their parents are the most important people in their lives. Parents can teach you a lot about their children—what they like to do, what they don't enjoy, things they do well, skills they are developing. It is important to share similar information with parents on a regular basis. In this way parents can feel connected to their children's lives at the program and become knowledgeable consumers who value the quality of your program.

Some parents may not show any interest in becoming involved in the program. They may feel uncomfortable with you and the other staff, or they may simply be too busy. Parents who are already actively involved in their children's school and community activities, may not have additional time to devote to the school-age program. You may be able to think of some innovative ways to

School-age staff and parents work as a team.

---

* In this module, "parents" refers to the adult members of a household who nurture and care for a child.

involve these families; however, there will always be some families who prefer to keep their involvement to a minimum.

Most parents are interested in their children's activities.

Working with families is often a very rewarding part of your job. Most parents are concerned about their children and want to do what's best for them. Let them know you share their concern and want to provide a program that meets children's needs and allows them to grow and learn. Make sure they know you enjoy working with their child and share their excitement when their child cooks dinner, learns to play chess, receives a sports award, or is recognized for school achievement.

School-age staff work with families in a variety of ways. Conversations with parents are opportunities to get to know each other and to exchange information about a child's activities at home and at the program. Parents should always be welcome at the program. For those who cannot visit during the day, you can provide a variety of other ways for them to participate.

Often parents have questions about what their child does at the program and who he or she plays with most often. They may ask you about a stage their child is going through or how to respond to a frustrating or confusing behavior. You can respond to these requests by drawing on your own experience, or you can refer parents to books or other resources on school-age children.

Listed below are examples of how school-age staff demonstrate their competence in working with families.

Communicating With Parents Often to Exchange Information About Their Child at Home and at the Program

Encourage parents to drop in at the program at any time. "We're looking forward to your visit tomorrow afternoon, Mr. Kendricks. We're all eager to see the slides you took on our camping trip."

Learn each parent's name and something about them as a way to build trust. "I thought of you last night, Mr. Parker, when I watched the television special on New Mexico. That's where your family lives, isn't it?"

Share interesting, positive information about children's activities at the program, verbally or in writing. "Dear Ms. Stanon: Jared learned how to weave this week. He's making a scarf using lots of colors and a unique pattern he created."

Ask parents about their children's interests and use the information to individualize the program. "This magazine has an article about ice dancing. Your mom told me you really like to watch the skaters on television."

Give parents information about a younger child's routines. "Mary wasn't very hungry at snack. She said she ate a big lunch at kindergarten. She may be extra hungry at dinner tonight."

Respond to parents' questions and concerns. "If you think Graham needs more physical activity we can encourage him to play group games or try running with the Jogging Club."

Share information about yourself with parents to help them get to know you. "I'm taking courses so I can be a physical education teacher one day. In the meantime I share my love for sports with the children at the program."

Hold regular parent-staff conferences to share information about children's progress and to plan for the future. "Ms. Wendell, it's been six months since our last conference, so it's time to schedule another one. Here's a planning form to help you think about what you want to discuss. Tomorrow you can give me some times that would be good for both you and your partner."

Use a variety of communication strategies such as newsletters, bulletin boards, handbooks, message centers, phone calls, and notes home. "Hello, Ms. Stratton. This is Jennie from the school-age program. Is this a convenient time to talk?"

Suggest ways to coordinate a child's program and home experiences. "Mark has been very interested in our cooking activities. He might want to prepare a special dish at home so the whole family can enjoy one of his creations."

Offering a Variety of Ways for Parents to Participate in Their Child's Life at the Program

Let parents know their contributions and visits are appreciated. "Ms. Nelson, we're pleased you came by today. It was a nice surprise for Jimmy when you spent an hour with the group."

Give parents opportunities to make decisions about their child's activities. "Daniel seems really interested in learning to skate. Do you think he'd like us to offer an opportunity to go ice skating?"

Survey parents' needs and offer appropriate workshops and resources. "Many of the parents want to know more about how to help children express their feelings without losing their tempers, so we're having a workshop next month."

Offer a variety of parent involvement options to accommodate different schedules, interests, and skills. "Thanks so much for typing this month's newsletter for us, Ms. Peterson."

Hold regularly scheduled parent meetings and informal family events at times that are convenient for most parents. "Ms. Hanes, you'll be pleased to know that most of the other parents also preferred to have our next meeting on a Saturday. We'll arrange to have parking available. I think we'll get a large turnout."

Provide an orientation for new parents so they can get to know staff and learn what children do at the program. "First, we're going to see a slide show created by the children to show parents what they do here. We think it really captures the spirit of this program. Then we'll introduce the staff and answer your questions."

Involve parents in making decisions about the program. "Dear Parents: It's time for our annual program planning process. Please join us for a pizza dinner and planning meeting next Wednesday, right after the program closes for the day. Your children are welcome to join us, too."

Providing Support to Families

Maintain confidentiality about children and families. "Thank you for sharing this information with me. With your permission I will share it with the director. You can be assured we will not let it go any further."

Provide information on child development to help parents understand what behaviors are typical of school-age children. "Like many six-year-olds, Jody prefers playing non-competitive games that don't have winners or losers."

Work with parents to help them develop their own strategies for handling a difficult behavior. "Thanks for letting us know about Jimmy's tendency to get into arguments with his grandfather. Many preadolescents go through a stage when they like to argue with adults about what's fair. How can we work together to help Jimmy express his views without being disrespectful?"

Recognize when families are under stress and offer additional support. "It's often hard to meet children's needs when one parent is in the hospital. We'll help Sherrie as much as we can at the program."

Introduce parents to others who live in the same neighborhood or have children of similar ages. "Ms. Marcetti, I'm glad to see you. I want to introduce you to the Purnells. They live near you and your children spend a lot of time together at the program."

Make an effort to get to know all the parents in the program. "David has been coming to the program for three weeks, but I still haven't met his grandmother. She drops him off in the morning before I arrive and he takes the bus home. Tomorrow I'm going to come a little early so I can be sure to meet her."

Notify a supervisor when it seems a parent needs professional help. "Ms. Grimaldi, do you have a few minutes to talk? I've had several disturbing conversations with Mr. Jackson and need to discuss them with you."

Working With Families

In the following situations, school-age staff are working with families. As you read them, think about what the staff are doing and why. Then answer the questions that follow.

Communicating with Parents Often to Exchange Information About Their Child at Home and at the Program

Nine-year-old Molly joined the program a month ago. She is a bit shy and has spent much of her time at the program working and playing by herself. Ms. Kee and Molly's parents, the Morans, have been sharing information about Molly's progress in making new friends. Molly loves to write stories and plays at home. Last week she told Ms. Kee she had finished writing a play and wanted to put on a show for others at the program. Ms. Kee helped her find several children who wanted to work on the play. The children met several times this week to practice. Molly seemed happy her play was being performed and that she was making new friends. Ms. Kee knew the Morans would be pleased with their child's progress. She decided not to say anything directly about Molly's accomplishments. Instead, she invited Ms. Moran to come a few minutes early one afternoon so she could see Molly in action. Today, Ms. Moran arrives in time to watch the last half of the rehearsal. She smiles at Ms. Kee and says, "What a relief to see Molly having such a good time with the other children!" Ms. Kee nods in agreement and says, "Yes, Molly has made some good friends. I'll keep looking for ways to help her stay actively involved in the program."

1. **Why did Ms. Kee think it was important for Molly's mother to visit the program?**

   _____

   _____

   _____

2. **What other kinds of information will Ms. Kee and the Morans need to share, now that Molly is making friends?**

   _____

   _____

   _____

When Mr. Bradley comes to pick up six-year-old Jerry at the end of the day, he approaches Ms. Williams and asks, "How can I be more involved in the program? I've had to work a late shift recently, so I've missed the family nights. Jerry seems very disappointed that I don't know what's going on at the program. Can you think of something I could do so Jerry will know I'm interested in what he does here?" Ms. Williams asks Mr. Bradley several questions about his work and other interests. Then she says, "Jerry and the other children who come here after kindergarten have been asking when they can play with the wooden trucks again. The trucks are broken, and we haven't had time to get them fixed. From what you tell me, it sounds as if you're really good at fixing things. You could take them home, and you and Jerry could repair them together and then bring them back. Every time Jerry and his friends play with the trucks, they will be reminded you made them work again." After looking over the trucks Mr. Bradley says, "This is an easy fix-it job. And it would be great to include Jerry in doing something for the program. Thanks for the idea. We'll take the trucks home today and have them back soon." As Ms. Williams helps Jerry and his dad collect the trucks she says, "I'm sure there are other parents who've missed our family nights because they had to work. We have to schedule meetings at different times so more parents can attend."

Offering a Variety of Ways for Parents to Participate in Their Child's Life at the Program

1. **How did Ms. Williams help Mr. Bradley think of a way to be involved with the program and show Jerry he was interested?**

_____

_____

_____

2. **What did Ms. Williams learn from Mr. Bradley?**

_____

_____

_____

Providing Support to Families

"I just don't know what to do," says Ms. Thomas when she drops off 11-year-old Maria one morning. "Maria says she's too old to come here and wants me to let her stay home by herself. She doesn't want to be around the little kids and wants to spend more time painting. She takes a class every Saturday and doesn't have time in between to practice what she's learned. I'm not sure she's ready to be home alone. Do you have any suggestions?" Mr. Lopez says, "I'm glad you shared that with me. Lately, Maria has seemed ready for more independence. I had planned to talk with her today about what she would like to do at the program. I understand your concern about having Maria stay home alone. We'll try to make some adjustments to give her more opportunities to work on her special interests at the program." Ms. Thomas is relieved and says, "I'm glad you're willing to make some changes to help Maria feel better about coming here. Can we talk again in a few days to see how you think she's responding to the changes?" Mr. Lopez thinks this is a good idea and says, "Why don't we meet next week? We can share some ideas about ways to help Maria feel good about herself at home and here as she becomes more independent." Ms. Thomas nods in agreement and leaves looking a lot less concerned.

1. What did Mr. Lopez do to help Ms. Thomas understand Maria's behavior?

    _____

    _____

    _____

2. What does Mr. Lopez plan to do to help Ms. Thomas understand and respond to Maria's growing need for independence?

    _____

    _____

    _____

Compare your answers with those on the answer sheet at the end of this module. If your answers are different, discuss them with your trainer. There can be more than one good answer.

Your Own Family Experiences

School-age staff bring many firsthand experiences to their role in working with families. Most of us grew up in a family. Some of us are now raising families of our own or have grown children. Our own experiences influence how we view families, what we think a family should look like, and how parents should raise their children.

What is a family?

Think for a moment about what the word "family" means to you. Do you think of a mother and father and one or more children living together? Or, do you think of different kinds of family relationships?

The families of the children you work with may resemble your own, or they may be very different. Children may be growing up with a single mother or father or with a stepparent. They may live with several relatives—their mother, a grandmother, an aunt and her children—or they may live with a grandparent who has legal custody. A family might include children, a parent, and his or her partner—of the same or different gender. In short, the traditional view of a family does not always hold true today.

Parenting can be a difficult job.

In addition to families "looking" different, many families today are experiencing multiple sources of stress that can make parenting a very difficult job. In "family-friendly" communities, resources are dedicated to services such as parks and recreation, housing, public transportation, health care, adult education, and job training. In less affluent communities these services may be unavailable or inadequate. Families must make do with substandard housing, limited transportation, and health care systems that do not meet their needs. This lack of supportive services, accompanied by stressors such as violence, drug and alcohol abuse, and poverty, can challenge the innate resources of any family.

It is not uncommon for staff to blame parents when their children are having problems. This is especially true when staff see parents who don't behave toward their children as the staff think they should. If you have difficulty accepting the behaviors and life-style of some of the children and families in your program, it would be helpful to examine the source of your negative reactions. Are you comparing families to your own? Do you think "good" parents manage their lives so someone will be home with their school-age children? Do you expect children's families to conform to your own personal values? Are you willing to learn about different parenting styles? It may help to remember that all parents want the best for their children, and they are probably trying as hard as they can to be good parents. They too are guided by their own experiences growing up in a family.

Before you begin the learning activities in this module, spend a few minutes thinking of how your own views and experiences may affect the way you work with families. Consider the following questions:

Whom do you consider to be part of the family in which you grew up?

_____

_____

_____

_____

_____

How are the families of the children in your program different from your own family?

_____

_____

_____

_____

_____

What pressures do parents have today that your parents didn't experience?

_____

_____

_____

_____

_____

What pressures are the same?

_____

_____

_____

_____

_____

How do you think your own views and experiences as a family member affect your work with other families?

_____

_____

_____

_____

_____

_____

_____

_____

When you have finished this overview section, you should complete the pre-training assessment. There is no glossary for this module.

PRE-TRAINING ASSESSMENT

Listed below are the skills school-age staff use in their work with families. Think about whether you do these things regularly, sometimes, or not enough. Place a check in one of the boxes on the right for each skill listed. Then discuss your answers with your trainer.

Communicating With Parents Often to Exchange Information About Their Child at Home and at the Program

	I Do This		
	Regularly	Sometimes	Not Enough
1. Learning the names of all parents and something about them to build trust.	☐	☐	☐
2. Sharing information about yourself with parents to help them get to know you.	☐	☐	☐
3. Sharing interesting, positive information about children's activities at the program.	☐	☐	☐
4. Encouraging parents to visit the program at any time.	☐	☐	☐
5. Suggesting ways to coordinate the child's program and home experiences.	☐	☐	☐
6. Asking parents to share information about their child's interests and using this information to individualize the program.	☐	☐	☐
7. Holding parent-staff conferences to share information about each child's progress and to make plans for the future.	☐	☐	☐
8. Using a variety of communication strategies, for example, newsletters, bulletin boards, handbooks, message centers, phone calls, and notes home.	☐	☐	☐
9. Responding to parents' questions and concerns.	☐	☐	☐
10. Giving parents information about a younger child's routines (eating, toileting, resting).	☐	☐	☐

Offering a Variety of Ways for Parents to Participate in Their Child's Life at the Program

	I Do This		
	Regularly	Sometimes	Not Enough
11. Involving parents in making decisions about their child's activities at the program.	☐	☐	☐
12. Letting parents know their contributions are appreciated.	☐	☐	☐
13. Surveying parents' needs and interests and providing appropriate workshops and resources.	☐	☐	☐
14. Offering a variety of ways to participate in the program to accommodate parents' varied schedules, interests, and unique skills.	☐	☐	☐
15. Holding regularly scheduled parent meetings and informal family events at times that are convenient for most parents.	☐	☐	☐
16. Providing an orientation for new parents so they can get to know staff and learn what children do each day.	☐	☐	☐

Providing Support to Families

17. Maintaining confidentiality about all children and families.	☐	☐	☐
18. Providing information on child development to help parents understand what behaviors are typical of school-age children.	☐	☐	☐
19. Working with parents to help them develop their own strategies for handling a difficult behavior.	☐	☐	☐
20. Recognizing when families are under stress and offering additional support.	☐	☐	☐
21. Introducing parents to others who live in the same neighborhood or have children of similar ages.	☐	☐	☐
22. Making an effort to get to know all the parents in the program.	☐	☐	☐
23. Notifying a supervisor when it seems parents need professional help.	☐	☐	☐

Review your responses, then list three to five skills you would like to improve or topics you would like to learn more about. When you finish this module, you can list examples of your new or improved knowledge and skills.

_____

_____

_____

_____

_____

Begin the learning activities for Module 11, Families.

LEARNING ACTIVITIES

Learning Activity I:
Developing a Partnership with Parents

IN THIS ACTIVITY YOU WILL LEARN TO:

- work with parents to share information about each child; and

- develop and maintain a partnership with parents.

High-quality school-age programs depend on a strong partnership between staff and parents. This partnership must be based on respect, trust, and the understanding that the child's experiences will be enhanced when all the adults who care for him or her work together.

Strong partnerships benefit everyone.

A strong partnership between parents and staff benefits everyone involved. Parents feel reassured about their parenting skills. Staff also feel confident about their role, and they learn more about providing a program based on their own and the parents' understanding of the child. Children feel more secure knowing that both their parents and the school-age staff are people who care about them and are supportive.

Developing a partnership may take a lot of work. Sometimes staff members and parents have different views on childrearing. They may even have different ideas about the child's strengths, interests, and needs. Parents and staff may not always understand each other's point of view and may disagree about how to solve a problem. What they almost always have in common, though, is genuine concern for the child's well-being.

Although both staff and parents know a lot about a particular child, this knowledge and information needs to be combined to create a total picture. Here are some examples of the kinds of information each half of the partnership can provide.

Parents have information about the following areas in a child's life:

Parents have a lot of information to share.

Health history. "If you need any more information about Ben's asthma, please let us know. We want to work with you to protect his health and provide an appropriate level of activities."

Relationships with other family members. "Carla really enjoys being with her older brother. Every morning they eat together and talk about their plans for the day."

Ways the child likes to relax. "When Yancey is tired, he likes to sit by himself and read."

Foods the child enjoys. "Kristin made her own pizza last night. She sure has some creative ideas about toppings!"

Foods the child can or cannot eat. "Drew is allergic to all kinds of nuts."

The child's reaction to new people and situations. "Marsha has always been very outgoing. She can be a little overwhelming until you get to know her."

The child's reaction to changes in routines. "Sonia gets very upset if I ask her to dress before breakfast. She likes to eat first, then get dressed."

The child's activity level. "Leah has lots of energy and likes to participate in games where she can keep moving. But if she doesn't take a break once in a while, she can get over excited."

The child's reaction when things aren't going well. "Jason loves gymnastics, but sometimes he gets frustrated easily and may lose his temper if he makes a mistake."

The child's sensitivity to his or her environment. "Ben gets upset when there's a lot going on around him; he can't concentrate on what he's doing."

The child's favorite activities at home. "Travis spends hours shooting baskets outdoors on the weekends. He hates having to come in when it's too dark to see the hoop."

The child's fears. "Darrell is afraid of heights. We're not sure why, but he refuses to use climbers and slides because he thinks he will fall."

What the child did last night, over the weekend, or on vacation. "We went to the beach for our vacation. Haki collected buckets full of shells."

Who the child plays with at home. "Our 13-year-old neighbor and Roxanne like to play together. Roxanne idolizes her and wants to act and dress just like her."

The family's lifestyle. "We like to get outdoors as much as possible. Peter likes to go hiking in the mountains."

How the child "used to be" as well as how the child is now. "When Julie was 8, she really enjoyed doing art projects. Now that she's 9, she just wants to be with her friends, no matter what they are doing."

School-age staff have information about the following areas in a child's life:

Staff know about the child's experiences at the program.

Favorite play materials and activities. "When Tanya arrives each morning, she goes right to the blocks. She has fun making complicated buildings with turrets and balconies."

Which games and materials are too frustrating. "Jamal isn't ready to play chess yet, but he enjoys checkers and did well in the program's tournament."

What challenges the child enjoys. "Arnie is really excited about making paper airplanes. He used the paper airplane design book to make one that flies longer distances."

How the child plays with others. "Janna likes to watch for a while before she joins in with the other children."

How the child reacts to changes in the environment. "When we put out new tapes and CDs, Elena is usually the first to listen to them."

How the child tells others what he or she is feeling. "When Carmela is angry with another child, she says, 'I don't like you. You're not my friend.'"

What the child talks about at the program. "Today, Carlos talked about going to see his cousin, Louis. He's very excited about it."

What the child does upon arrival at the program after school. Jorge goes over to watch the gerbils when he comes in after school. He likes to have some quiet time by himself when he arrives."

Establishing the Partnership

Your relationship with a child's parents begins when their child first enters the program. Although the parents probably don't know you, you are the person who will be with their child for several hours each day, five days a week. It is natural for them to want to learn as much as they can about you, the program, the other children, and the program's activities. Share this information and tell them something about yourself. Let them know what you are like and why you enjoy working with children. Describe a typical day, both before and after school, and give parents a copy of the daily and weekly schedules. You might want to create a "get acquainted" bulletin board featuring pictures of the staff along with brief descriptions of their backgrounds, interests, and special skills.

Begin to get to know the parents, too. Find out their interests, what kind of work they do, how they feel about their child attending the program, and what stress they may be handling. Let them know how you will work with them to share information about their child. Explain that their involvement is welcomed as you make decisions about the child's activities at the program.

Let parents know you appreciate and respect their child.

At first, you and the parents will get to know each other through brief conversations at the program, or perhaps on the phone. Be friendly and respectful; always greet each parent by name. Share interesting, positive information about their child's experiences. Let them know by your attitude and tone of voice that their child is appreciated and well-supervised: "Sean had an active day today. He and his friends practiced a song for the talent show, he read a story to some of the younger children, and he played basketball in the gym." These communications build trust and acceptance, which will lead to a stronger partnership.

If parents don't respond to your efforts to establish a partnership, try to put yourself in their place. Try to understand their feelings about leaving their child at the program. Some parents are concerned about not spending as much time with their children as they would like. It's helpful to think about your own feelings about the parents and how you may be conveying these through your tone of voice, facial expressions, or the kinds of information you share.

Although you do many things with children that parents also do (such as providing guidance or making snack), your role is not the same as that of the parents. Always remember parents need your support, but they don't need you to take over their role.

Maintaining a Strong Relationship

Once a trusting relationship has been established, you need to continue to involve parents in their children's experiences at the program. The partnership is strengthened by continued communication and appreciation for each partner's role in encouraging the child's learning and development. The partnership also grows when both parents and staff can see how the child benefits from their teamwork. "Janine seems to enjoy the whole afternoon much more since she started eating snack as soon as she arrives. Thank you for letting us know her stomach starts to growl like clockwork at 3:30! It's hard for anyone to get involved if they're really hungry."

Some suggestions for maintaining a strong partnership follow.

Try these suggestions.

Respond to parents' concerns or questions even though they may seem trivial. Such concerns are important to the parents and therefore should be acknowledged. "I know you want Sam to do well in school. Perhaps we could sit down with him and agree on a plan for when he will do his homework. Some of the children do their homework as soon as they arrive, but others need to take a break first. They actually find it easier to focus and do a better job on their assignments after they have done something physical or creative. The staff help the children remember when it's time to get started."

Help parents focus on their child's accomplishments instead of comparing their child to others the same age. "Denise is really good at heading off arguments among her friends. All the staff are impressed by her negotiating skills."

Help children and parents feel good about belonging to the same family. "Ms. Bradley, Jerry was really pleased you came on our field trip to the science museum. He really liked it when the other kids talked about being in your group."

Wait until you are asked before offering advice. When you are asked, be clear about what is fact and what is opinion. "At the training session I went to last week, I learned about how important it is for 10- and 11-year-olds to spend time with their friends. The social skills they develop by hanging out with their buddies help them throughout their lives."

Share problems when you need to work together to help the child. "Erica frequently lashes out at children when she gets angry and says things that are hurtful. When can we meet to discuss ways to help her deal with her feelings?"

Acknowledge events and transitions in the families' lives. "Congratulations on your promotion! Lavonne told me the whole family had a party to celebrate."

Be sensitive to normal guilt feelings parents may have about the time their children spend at the program. Be careful not to make assumptions about parents or judge them because their lifestyle is different from yours.

Keep in touch when the child is absent or ill. "Hello, Ms. Carson, how is Paula feeling today?"

Help families cope when one parent is away. Suggest sending art, photographs, letters, tapes, or stories to the parent who is away. Remind children that their parents are thinking about them even when they are gone.

Maintain confidentiality when parents share something private with you. "I'm glad you told me about this. It will help me work with Brian. Don't worry about my telling someone else. I understand this is confidential."

Applying Your Knowledge

In this learning activity you focus on strengthening your partnership with the parents of one of the children in the program. Select a family with whom you feel comfortable but whom you would like to know better. Let the parents know you have selected them, and ask for their written permission to participate in this learning activity. Then, for two weeks, record your daily communications—any information you each share. At the same time, look for any changes in how you respond to this child. Read the shortened example that follows; then begin the activity.

Parent-Staff Communication Record
(Example)

Child/age: _Michael, 9 years_   **Length of enrollment:** _3 months_

Parents: _Karen Parker and Frank Anderson_

Dates: _November 6-20_

Day One

A.M.   *Greeted Ms. Parker and reminded her I was starting this activity. She told me Michael is excited about using the new woodworking tools.*

P.M.   *Mr. Anderson came to pick up Michael. I told him Michael and his friend Joel used the new woodworking tools. They're trying to think of something to build together. He asked me about this learning activity (Michael's mother had described it) and wished me luck.*

Day Two

A.M.   *When Mr. Anderson brought Michael, he said carpentry was his hobby and he and Michael had spent the evening drawing plans for a bird feeder the boys could build. He offered to pick up some wood and bring it tomorrow morning. I thanked him and told him several children were interested in observing birds. It would be great to have a bird feeder to encourage the birds to gather near our windows. Father and son both seemed pleased.*

P.M.   *Ms. Parker picked up Michael. She told me Michael would be leaving early on Friday because they are picking up his Uncle Dennis at the airport. Michael is excited about seeing his uncle, who is a scuba diver. He often brings slides of unusual underwater creatures he has seen on his dives. I asked if she thought Michael might be interested in learning more about marine life before his uncle came to visit. She said, "Yes, I think he would like to impress Uncle Dennis!" I told her about Dolphin Log, a magazine on underwater life the program gets. I said Michael might like to borrow the latest issue for a few days. She asked Michael if he would like to borrow the magazine. He smiled and nodded his head. Ms. Parker thanked me while Michael signed out the magazine.*

First Weekly Summary
(Example)

Information you shared:

I'm doing this learning activity.

Michael and his friend Joel have been trying out the new woodworking tools.

Michael and Joel want to make something together.

Some of the other children are interested in birdwatching, and it would help to have a birdfeeder.

We subscribe to a magazine about marine life Michael might enjoy reading.

Information parents shared:

Mr. Anderson's hobby is carpentry, and he helps Michael design woodworking projects.

Michael is excited because his uncle, a scuba diver, is coming to visit.

Michael wants to learn more about underwater life.

How has the partnership helped you work with this child?

I know about Michael's interests.

I can suggest things for his parents to do with him at home.

Mr. Anderson helped Michael develop a plan for a birdfeeder and offered to bring in some wood for the project.

I suggested a magazine to help Michael learn more about underwater life so he could share this interest with his uncle.

Parent-Staff Communication Record

Child/age: _____   **Length of enrollment:** _____

Parents: _____

Dates: _____

Day One

A.M. _____

_____

_____

_____

P.M. _____

_____

_____

_____

Day Two

A.M. _____

_____

_____

_____

P.M. _____

_____

_____

_____

Day Three

A.M. _____

_____

_____

_____

P.M. _____

_____

_____

_____

Day Four

A.M. _____

_____

_____

_____

P.M. _____

_____

_____

_____

Day Five

A.M. _____

_____

_____

_____

P.M. _____

_____

_____

_____

First Weekly Summary
(Complete after five days.)

Information you shared:

_____

_____

_____

_____

_____

_____

_____

_____

_____

_____

_____

_____

_____

Information parents shared:

_____

_____

_____

_____

_____

_____

_____

_____

_____

_____

_____

_____

_____

Day Six

A.M. _____

_____

_____

_____

_____

P.M. _____

_____

_____

_____

Day Seven

A.M. _____

_____

_____

_____

_____

P.M. _____

_____

_____

_____

Day Eight

A.M. _____

_____

_____

_____

_____

P.M. _____

_____

_____

_____

Day Nine

A.M. _____

_____

_____

_____

P.M. _____

_____

_____

_____

Day Ten

A.M. _____

_____

_____

_____

P.M. _____

_____

_____

_____

Second Weekly Summary
(Complete at the end of another five days.)

Information you shared:

_____

_____

_____

_____

_____

_____

_____

_____

_____

_____

_____

_____

_____

_____

Information parents shared:

_____

_____

_____

_____

_____

_____

_____

_____

_____

_____

_____

_____

_____

Review all your notes and answer the question on the next page.

How has the partnership helped you work with this child? (Give at least five examples.)

_____

_____

_____

_____

_____

_____

_____

_____

_____

_____

Discuss this activity with the child's parents and your trainer.

Learning Activity II.
Keeping Parents Informed About the Program

IN THIS ACTIVITY YOU WILL LEARN TO:

- keep parents informed about the program; and

- improve parent-program communication.

Parents feel more involved in the program when they know what's happening.

One of your most important responsibilities is to work with the director and other staff to keep parents up to date on activities at the school-age program. Parents feel more involved in the program when they know specific things that are happening. For example, they might like to know there's a new piece of equipment on the playground, the staff are attending a training workshop, the children will be making pumpkin bread for snack, one of the staff will be on vacation next week, and this month's parent meeting will focus on encouraging children's independence. Some of this information is passed from staff to parents during the times when children are picked up or dropped off. These times, however, are usually too brief to keep all the parents informed about everything that goes on at the program. Also, in some programs children arrive and leave by bus, so staff don't see parents everyday. The school-age program needs to use a variety of communication techniques to keep all parents informed about current activities and future plans.

Use newsletters to keep parents informed.

One of the most common ways to keep parents informed about the school-age program is through newsletters distributed to all parents. They contain general information that affects all families and, for large programs, specific information about each room. Often one person is responsible for putting the newsletter together; however, all staff contribute news. Parents and children also can be involved in gathering information, writing articles, or typing an issue. In addition to news about past and coming events, the newsletter also can include the month's menus, suggested activities for parents and children to do at home, information on community events of interest to families, and reviews of children's books or books on parenting or related topics. The newsletter can include space for parents to make suggestions for future issues or provide news, information, or a favorite recipe. This reinforces the partnership between parents and staff and lets parents know the newsletter is a useful result.

A parent might volunteer to work with children who are interested in contributing to the newsletter. Ideally, the volunteer would arrange his or her schedule to meet with the children during program hours. Children can prepare some of the items, such as a report on a poll of favorite activities, original jokes or poems, staff interviews, or a children's "opinion" column.

Parent handbooks are another way to inform parents. The handbook can present the program's policies and procedures and list opportunities for parents to become involved. It can be organized by topic (calendar, holidays) or alphabetically. Give a copy to each family and provide updates whenever necessary.

The following alphabetical list will give you some idea of the information provided in a parent handbook:[1]

Include a variety of information in the parent handbook.

Absences
Activities
Advisory committee
Calendar
Communication between program and home
Conferences/Meetings
Discipline and guidance
Dropping out of the program
Early dismissal days
Emergencies/Illness
Emergency closings
Enrollment/Fees
Field trips
Holidays/Vacations
Hours
Meals and snacks
Parent involvement
Personal belongings
Program philosophy
Release of children
Rights and responsibilities of children and parents
Staffing
Telephone numbers
Transportation

[1] From Lincoln, Sunny Hollow, and Neill Adventure Club Programs, *Adventure Club Parents' Manual* (Robbinsdale, MN: Community Education and Services, Independent School District 281, Robbinsdale Area Schools, 1978).

Try these suggestions.

Here are some other suggestions for keeping parents informed:

Establish a message center where each family has a "mailbox." Shoe bags with multiple pockets work well for this purpose. These can be used to provide parents with general news and information.

Set up a parent bulletin board in the lobby or some other area through which all parents must pass. Post articles, a calendar of events, reminders of upcoming meetings, the week's menus, and other items of general interest.

Create a family photo board to help parents learn more about other children and families. Each family can provide a recent photograph (including pets, if they have any). You might also ask parents to complete a brief questionnaire about their favorite foods, sports, recreation activities, hobbies, and places to visit. You can post the responses next to each family's photo. When new families enroll, add their photos to the board. You could set aside one section to announce family news, such as the birth of a new baby, or to display postcards from families that are traveling.

Sponsor a family evening featuring a play or other production written, acted, directed, and produced by the children—complete with costumes, props, playbills, and refreshments. Use this as an opportunity to discuss other activities taking place at the program.

Applying Your Knowledge

In this learning activity you answer some questions about a communication technique your program uses to keep parents informed. First review the abbreviated example that follows. Then select a communication technique, suggest ways to improve it, implement your suggestions, and report on the results.

Communicating With Parents
(Example)

Communication technique: *Program newsletter*

What information is included?

Upcoming field trips, birthdays, new games and magazines, special interest clubs for the month, best riddle of the week (selected by children), and activities parents and children might want to do together.

How often is the information shared or updated?

Bi-weekly

What is the role of the staff?

We take turns coordinating the writing, proofing, and making copies.

What is the role of the children?

They make suggestions about things their parents would like to know about the program.

How could they be more involved?

They could do some of the writing—articles, jokes, stories, poems. They could illustrate the newsletter, conduct surveys and polls, and help reproduce and collate the finished newsletters.

What is the role of the parents?

They read it.

How could they be more involved?

Parents could help produce the newsletter. They could provide us with information or articles. We could ask for volunteers to work with the children on a regular basis to help them produce the newsletter.

After trying out your ideas, what were the results?

I sent home a questionnaire asking parents for suggested items and for help in preparing the newsletter. I got lots of suggestions, and two parents offered to help. They worked on the latest issue. We included some parent-written articles, including one about a new park. One parent came in and worked with the children who were interested in producing the newsletter. These children conducted several polls about favorite snacks and activities. For the next issue they are sponsoring a joke exchange; jokes submitted by children will appear in the newsletter.

Communicating With Parents

Communication technique: _____

What information is included?

_____

_____

_____

How often is the information shared or updated?

_____

_____

_____

What is the role of the staff?

_____

_____

_____

What is the role of the children?

_____

_____

_____

How could they be more involved?

_____

_____

_____

What is the role of the parents?

_____

_____

_____

How could they be more involved?

_____

_____

_____

After trying out your ideas, what were the results?

_____

_____

_____

_____

_____

_____

Discuss this activity with your trainer.

Learning Activity III.
Providing Ways for Parents to Be Involved

IN THIS ACTIVITY YOU WILL LEARN TO:

- use techniques for parent involvement; and

- plan and implement a parent involvement strategy.

Create a variety of options for parent involvement.

Most parents would like to be involved in their child's life at the program, but they may not know about all the different ways they can contribute. Sometimes parents can arrange their work schedules so they can eat breakfast at the program once a month, go on a field trip, or attend a special program. Such activities benefit both parent and child. However, many parents are not able to participate in this way. It's important to offer a variety of options for parent involvement that match parents' interests, skills, and schedules. When parents register their children for the program, you can have them complete a brief questionnaire about how they would like to be involved in the program.

In addition to matching parents' interests with several options for involvement, you can let parents know how much their participation benefits the program. Parents who come on field trips may enjoy themselves so much they don't need much encouragement to offer to do it again. The parent who sews new curtains for the children's puppet theater, however, may never see the theater in action. In such a case, be sure to write a personal thank-you note. You could enclose a copy of the play the children wrote and produced and a photo of the puppet theater in action. Similarly, the parent who types the newsletter should be listed in every issue as the person who makes it possible for the news to get out to the other families.

Try these suggestions.

Here are some suggestions for helping parents become involved in your program.

Hold an orientation for new parents several times a year. Because families come and go during the year, you need to provide more than one orientation.

Involve parents in building or landscaping projects that can be worked on over a period of time. When a project is completed, hold a celebration party.

Keep a job jar in the room containing index cards with program-related jobs you never get around to doing that a parent could do without coming to the program. Parents can select a job from the jar, then see you for further instructions. Jobs might include repairing broken materials, creating science and nature kits or shopping at yard sales for cooking utensils or costumes.

Organize a family breakfast or dinner when parents can eat at the program on their way to work or home. Breakfast can be something simple—juice and bagels, for example. Dinner might be a meal planned and prepared by the children.

Invite parents to share their interests and talents. Parents might loan items for display, such as paintings, photographs, collections of artifacts, woodworking projects, or photo albums. Some parents might be willing to bring a slide show or video of their travels to share with the children.

Hold a family movie night, planned and hosted by the parents. The program could sell popcorn and drinks to raise funds for extra materials or field trips.

Schedule a "fix-it" night or a Saturday when children and parents can work together to spruce up the program facility, paint walls, give all the bicycles tune-ups, or prepare a plot of ground for a garden.

Open the program for one evening or on a weekend afternoon when children come to the program as though it were a regular day. Parents can also come and participate in games and sports activities, make a collage, join in a dance class, or sit back and observe how their child enjoys the program's activities.

Set up a parent corner. Include books, magazines, brochures, and other resources of interest to parents. If possible, provide comfortable chairs and refreshments.

Ask a parent to organize a photo album about the program. You can provide the pictures and the book; parents and children can put it together. Display the photo album in the reception area. Include a cover page thanking the family that organized the album.

Provide copies of a frequently updated wish list of resource materials and people you would like to have at the program. Parents might make contributions themselves, or they could help by putting you in touch with businesses, community organizations, or individuals who be willing to contribute time, talents, and materials.

Organize a series of parent workshops on topics related to raising school-age children. You can survey parents to find out what topics would be of most interest to them.

Applying Your Knowledge

In this learning activity you try out a parent involvement strategy. Select from those mentioned earlier, or make up one of your own. Discuss your selection with the director and other staff. Ask for their ideas about implementing this strategy. First read the example; then complete the chart that follows to describe the strategy you chose and how it helped parents become involved.

Involving Parents

(Example)

Strategy:

The staff will sponsor a family games afternoon and early dinner.

Plans:

We will ask for parent volunteers to help us plan the event. The children can pick games they think their parents would enjoy. Younger and older siblings will be invited, too. We will charge a small fee per family to offset the costs involved. After the games we will have an early dinner—pizza, salad, and carrot cake. Everyone—parents, children, and staff—will help clean up.

Results:

Four parents volunteered to help us plan and set up on the day of the event. The children were very excited about sharing their favorite games with their parents and siblings. They chose volleyball, Ultimate Frisbee, and Capture the Flag as the games to play. We set up volleyball in the gym, and the other two games outdoors. We offered some other activities outdoors for the younger siblings. About half of the families attended. The parents got very involved with the games and seemed to really enjoy playing with their children. Dinner was very relaxing because we had the pizzas delivered and used paper plates. Cleanup was a breeze with everyone pitching in.

Follow-up Plans:

We decided to make this a regular activity offered once in the spring and once in the fall. Already the parents who did not attend, but heard how much fun it was, are asking when the next event will be. We'll encourage the parents to do more of the planning next time.

Involving Parents

Strategy:

_____
_____
_____
_____
_____

Plans:

_____
_____
_____
_____
_____

Results:

_____
_____
_____
_____
_____

Follow-up Plans:

_____
_____
_____
_____
_____

Discuss this activity with your trainer and your colleagues.

Learning Activity IV.
Planning and Participating in Parent-Staff Conferences

IN THIS ACTIVITY YOU WILL LEARN TO:

- prepare for a conference by reviewing information about a child's development; and

- participate in a parent-staff conference.

At least twice a year, parents and school-age staff need to meet to review how the child is progressing in all areas of development and to set goals for continued growth and learning. You may not think conferences are necessary in school-age programs because the children are not there all day. However, if a child attends both before and after school, this adds up to a large part of the day. A lot of growth and learning takes place in your program, and this needs to be shared with parents.

Parent-staff conferences are opportunities for in-depth discussions.

Parent-staff conferences are opportunities to focus on one child and family without any distractions or interruptions. They are opportunities to explain the program's goals and reaffirm your partnership with parents. Although much information about the child is shared throughout the day, conferences are times when you and the parents can discuss the child in depth and reaffirm your trust in each other.

Usually a conference has no single goal; it can meet a number of different needs. Here's what some specialists have said about their goals for parent conferences.[2]

> "To make the parents aware of how their child is developing, at what level she/he is functioning, and if she/he is in need of any special help." Janet Rogers, Lycoming Child Day Care, Williamsport, PA.

> "To give the parent confidence in the staff; to establish a social relationship between parent and staff." Margaret Fredrickson, Northedge School, Sudbury, MA.

---

[2] Adapted with permission from "Ideas for Effective Parent Conferences," *Child Care Information Exchange* (Exchange Press, PO Box 2890, Redmond, WA 98073, November 1979), pp. 26-27.

CARING FOR CHILDREN IN SCHOOL-AGE PROGRAMS

"To discuss the child's development; to identify future goals." Shelly Brick, Kensington-Kingstowne Child Care Program, Philadelphia, PA.

"To get to know the parents enough to feel comfortable with them and them with me; and to better understand the child through the parent." Lois Grigsby, Kendal Lab Child Care, Evanston, IL.

"To foster greater awareness of the importance the environment plays in a child's development—to educate the parents." Jan Lucas, Westend Day Care, Portage la Prairie, Manitoba, Canada.

"To provide support for working parents by supplying information on child development, available social services, etc." Tracy Neri, The Day Care Program Facility, Norwich, VT.

Parents also have goals for the conference. They may have a specific concern they would like to discuss or a suggestion for how they would like you to work with their child. They may have a complaint about something the program does or doesn't do. Often parents want to be reassured you like their child, are competent, and think they are doing a good job raising their child.

Planning for Conferences

Explain to parents when they enroll their child how often conferences take place, their purpose, and what is discussed. When it's time to schedule a conference, ask parents what time would be most convenient for them to attend. Offer several options and provide enough lead time so parents can make plans. Allow enough time so you and the parents don't feel rushed. Ask them to think of any questions they might have and topics they want to cover. You might want to develop a planning form parents could use to prepare for the conference. Tell them you hope to learn more about the child's life away from the program— at home, at school, and in the community—so you can better support the child's growth and learning.

To make the best use of the time set aside for the conference, it's important to do some planning. You will need to think about what points you want to cover. Review your observation notes, anecdotal records, and any other written materials that provide objective information about the child. You can also collect samples of the child's art, stories, or other creations. Organize your notes to make sure you have covered all areas of development—physical, cognitive, and socio-emotional. If you have any concerns about the child's health (for example, if you suspect the child might need glasses), these should be written down. Ask your colleagues to share any information they have about this child.

Many parents are interested in how their child interacts and gets along in a group setting with his or her peers. They want to know as much as possible about what their child does while at the program—for example, with whom the child plays, whether the child is more likely to initiate group activities or follow another child's lead, the activities and materials that really spark the child's interest, and how the child handles disagreements. Make sure your notes include examples that will help parents picture and understand what their child does at the program.

Sometimes staff members feel a little uneasy before a conference. It may help to role-play with your supervisor or a colleague. You can practice sharing your observations and answering the kinds of questions the parents are likely to ask.

At the start of the conference, try to establish a relaxed and comfortable tone. Older children can be included in the conference if parents think it is appropriate. Anticipate at least five minutes of social conversation before the more serious discussions begin. Before the conference, decide who will take the lead in the conference. (Usually this is the staff member with primary responsibility for this child.) This person should begin by explaining how the conference will proceed: "I'm so glad you could come today. Let me tell you how we'll proceed. We'll talk about a typical day for Karen, both before and after school. First, I'll provide information based on our observations at the program. Next, you can let us know what Karen likes to do at home and in school. . ." This is a good time to stress that the conference is a time for sharing information and is not in any way an evaluation of their child's performance.

During the conference, be sure there are many opportunities for parents to provide input and ask questions. After discussing all areas of the child's development, the next step is to set goals and develop strategies for continuing to promote the child's growth and learning. These strategies will be implemented at home and at the program. You and the parents can determine the best way to share the goals and strategies with the child. (Older children can

Participating in the Conference

be included in the planning process.) The goals and strategies will serve as the framework for discussions at the next conference.

Try these suggestions.

Here are some other suggestions for conducting successful conferences.

Begin and end the conference with a positive statement about your relationship with the child. "We really enjoy A.J.'s sense of humor. He seems to have an endless supply of new jokes and is able to see the humor in every situation."

Ask parents an open-ended question if they seem uncertain or reluctant to talk about their concerns. "What else about Rebecca or the program would you like to discuss?"

Invite parents to work with you by asking questions and seeking their advice. Stress the importance of consistency between home and the program. "It's very helpful to hear that Paul responds well to praise. We'll remember to let him know we value his efforts."

Listen carefully to what parents have to say, without interrupting or rushing them. Accept their feelings even if they are different from your own. Restate their comments and suggestions to make sure you have heard them correctly. "You would like us to encourage Shauna to get involved in a greater variety of physical activities."

Share problems using factual and objective information. Avoid preaching, blaming, criticizing, or judging. "We have noticed on several occasions Kirsten has exaggerated about small things that happen at the program. Have you noticed similar behavior at home?"

Pay attention to parents' reactions by maintaining eye contact and being aware of body language that may indicate the parent is feeling tense, hurt, disappointed, or angry.

Summarize your discussion at the end of the conference, emphasizing what actions you each have agreed to take and how you will follow up. "We agree Laura is ready for more independence. We can find ways for her to assume more responsibility at the program. At home she can have more freedom to plan her weekend outings with friends. We'll talk next month to review these strategies." Add a positive statement about the child.

Take notes during the conference, especially if you are discussing a complex or difficult situation. Explain to parents your notes will help you follow up on their concerns.

Offer more than one suggestion when parents ask you for advice about handling a specific situation. If you don't know the answer to a question, tell the parents you will look into it and get back in touch. Encourage them to think about what would be best for their child. "Some parents find it helpful to ignore their child's interest in the latest fads in dress because these interests pass quickly. Other parents think it's important to set guidelines about appropriate clothes to wear in different situations—school, place of worship, shopping, or going out with the family."

Applying Your Knowledge

In this learning activity you develop a plan for holding a conference with the parents of one of the children in the program. Include information from your own observations and those of other staff. Conduct the conference, then answer the evaluation questions.

Planning a Conference

Child: _____   Parents: _____

Age: _____   Age at last conference: _____

Date of conference: _____   Date of last conference: _____

Describe a typical day at the program for this child:

_____
_____
_____
_____
_____
_____
_____

What sparks this child's interests?

_____
_____
_____
_____
_____
_____

How does this child handle disagreements?

_____
_____
_____
_____
_____
_____

With whom does this child play, and in what ways?

_____
_____
_____
_____
_____

Anecdotes to share:

_____

_____

_____

_____

_____

_____

Any concerns:

_____

_____

_____

_____

_____

_____

Developmental Summary

Use this form to summarize the child's progress in all areas of development. List the goals set at the last conference (if there has been one). For each area of development, provide specific examples of what the child does (for example, participates in gymnastics, offers to assist younger children, remembers rules, writes stories and plays).

Area of Development	Goals
Physical (for example, participation in sports, active games, movement, and dance, and use of fine motor skills: crafts, constructions, and puzzles)	
Cognitive (for example, use of thinking and reasoning skills to solve problems, explore math, read, write, do research, and plan and carry out ideas)	
Socio-Emotional (for example, interactions with children and adults, use of self-discipline, and ability to follow rules and respect rights of others)	

Suggested Goals

Use this chart to list some suggested goals for the next six months. You will also use the chart to prepare for the next conference—six months from now.

Area of Development	Goals
Physical (for example, participation in sports, active games, movement, and dance, and use of fine motor skills: crafts, constructions, and puzzles)	
Cognitive (for example, use of thinking and reasoning skills to solve problems, explore math, read, write, do research, and plan and carry out ideas)	
Socio-Emotional (for example, interactions with children and adults, use of self-discipline, and ability to follow rules and respect rights of others)	

Now hold your conference with the parents. Ask for their ideas on suggested goals and add them to the list above if you all agree. Complete the conference evaluation on the next page.

Conference Evaluation

After the conference, think about what happened and answer these questions:

How did you establish a relaxed tone?

_____

_____

_____

_____

How did you start the conference?

_____

_____

_____

_____

How did you provide for parent input?

_____

_____

_____

_____

Were you asked for advice? If so, how did you give it?

_____

_____

_____

_____

What anecdotes did you tell about the child's participation in the program?

_____

_____

_____

_____

How did you summarize the conference?

_____

_____

_____

_____

How did you end the conference?

_____

_____

_____

_____

What would you do differently next time?

_____

_____

_____

_____

Discuss this learning activity with your trainer.

Learning Activity V.
Reaching Out to Families

IN THIS ACTIVITY YOU WILL LEARN TO:

- recognize signs that families are under stress; and

- provide support to families under stress.

School-age staff can lend a helping hand.

Parents are often under stress. Balancing the demands of a job and family, trying to be involved in their child's school and the school-age program, and not understanding changes in their child's behavior can leave parents feeling overwhelmed. You are in an excellent position to lend a helping hand. Some parents will feel comfortable sharing their worries and seeking advice; others will not. Regardless of whether parents approach you or you approach them, keep in mind that supporting parents means enhancing their sense of competence by helping them find their own answers.

You can reach out to parents by providing support and information. In particular, you can:

- recognize when families are under stress;

- help parents locate appropriate resources; and

- give parents information and guidance on school-age children's development.

Recognizing When Families Are Under Stress[3]

Stress is a normal part of daily life for most families. Parents try to cope with typical frustrations and tension, and not let stress interfere with their work and home activities. Some families, however, are affected over a long period of time by significant sources of stress such as community violence, homelessness, substance abuse, or lack of basic necessities. The stresses are not caused by single events such as divorce or a car accident. Rather, they are routine, unrelenting, and woven into daily life. They are

---

[3] Adapted with permission from Derry Koralek, *Responding to Children Under Stress* (Washington, DC: Head Start Bureau, 1993), pp. 40-42.

a result of societal conditions and pressures that are beyond the control of individual families.

The following are examples of sources of long-term significant stress that might be experienced by the children and families in your program. There may be other sources that are specific to your community.

- Unemployment.

- Lack of necessities such as food, clothing, shelter, medical care.

- Lack of transportation to work, job training, or a health clinic.

- Exposure to violence in the home or in the community.

- Living in a shelter or other temporary housing situation.

- Living in overcrowded or inadequate housing.

- Chronic illness or disability of a child or other family member, accompanied by lack of access to needed services and support.

- Substance abuse in the household or in the community at large.

- Abuse and neglect of a child, spouse, or other family member.

- Depression or other mental illness of a child or adult family member.

- Learning a new language and adapting to a new culture.

Regardless of what is causing the high levels of stress in their lives, families tend to have similar concerns, needs, and behaviors. Some families have the skills and strength needed to cope with their stress in positive ways. However, some families are overwhelmed by their stressful environment. They may experience effects such as the following:

High levels of stress can overwhelm families.

- A sense that life is unpredictable, unstable, and chaotic. If families move frequently, children must change schools and adjust to new teachers and classmates. Children may have difficulty focusing on schoolwork and lack a sense of order and discipline in their lives.

- Inability to give their children affection and attention. Children become independent too soon.

- Unmet health and nutrition needs of children and family members. Families may not have access to needed health care, including immunizations, dental checkups, and counseling.

- Inconsistent, overly punitive, or nonexistent parental discipline.

Know the signs of stress.

When a family is under stress, the parents may seem disorganized, frequently forgetting things such as permission slips for a field trip or an upcoming school holiday. A parent might seem frustrated when a child is slow to get ready to go home, or the parent might state he or she doesn't know how to handle the child's growing independence: "It seems like all we ever do these days is fight." Parents under stress might be unwilling to accept help, or they might be more interested in talking about their own problems than their child's.

When you see signs of stress, it is important to not add to them. You can discuss the child's inappropriate behavior or the program's vacation schedule on another day. However, you will want to share information about their child that will help them get through a difficult evening. For example, letting a parent know their child has been tired and cranky all afternoon allows you to discuss whether the child might be coming down with the flu. Because the parent knows the reasons for the child's behavior, he or she is less likely to be frustrated or angered by the crankiness and more likely to comfort the child. When parents feel less stress, they are more likely to interact positively with their children and less likely to lose control.

Get to know all the parents.

Make an effort to really get to know the parents of the children in your program. Invite them into the room when they bring their children in the morning and when they pick them up. Place a suggestion box in a prominent place and draw attention to it. Encourage parents to visit often and make them welcome. Remember that you, the program, and the parents are part of a team working for each child's good.

Always notify your supervisor when you think parents may need professional help. Never make recommendations to parents without first clearing them with your supervisor. Your job is to help parents get the support they need, not to provide it yourself.

When parents do confide in you, it's essential to maintain complete confidentiality. This means you should not discuss a child with anyone other than your colleagues or the child's parents. This holds true for information about families as well. In addition, you should not share records with anyone who does not have a "need to know," and not hold discussions about children or families when other children are present. Ask your director about your program's guidelines for maintaining confidentiality.

Parents often need information on where they can get help for themselves, their child, or the family. Your director and trainer can give you information about parent education opportunities. Here are some things you can do to help.

- Encourage parents to connect with one another by introducing them to families that live in their neighborhood or have children of the same age.

- Develop a parent exchange list that helps parents support one another through the sharing of responsibilities and errands such as carpooling, grocery shopping, meal preparation, and car repairs.

- Call parents' attention to resources, newspaper or magazine articles, workshops, and television or radio shows on stages of child development, positive guidance, and family life.

- Display books on topics of interest to parents—step-parenting, juggling home and work responsibilities, fast and healthy meals—and invite parents to check out these resources.

- Tell parents about services and special programs provided by organizations in the community.

- Provide names, phone numbers, locations, and hours of operation when you suggest a program or event.

- Offer reluctant parents help in contacting other resources.

Helping Parents Locate Resources

Parents sometimes do not know as much as they want to about the typical development of children in the school-age years. Many books on child development do not cover middle childhood, and often parent education courses focus on infants through preschoolers. As a result, parents may expect too much or too little of a particular child at a particular age. Here are some things you can do to help.

- With the parents, observe a child, asking yourselves, "What is he or she experiencing?" to help parents see the world through the eyes of their child.

- Tell parents about workshops on sibling rivalry, independence, characteristics of early adolescents, and other topics of interest.

- Include information on child development in the program's newsletters and on the parent bulletin board.

- Invite parents to attend staff workshops.

Giving Parents Information and Guidance on Developmental Stages of School-Age Children

- Lend books or videotapes from the program's resource library.

- Schedule conferences to discuss particular problems.

Model appropriate ways to interact with children.

One of the best ways to provide information and guidance to parents on child development is during drop-off and pick-up times and in longer visits during the day. Without any extra effort or planning, you can model for parents appropriate ways to interact with children. For example, at pick-up time parents might see the following exchanges between a staff member and several children:

> Ms. Danforth encourages James to go back outside to help bring in the balls and sports equipment from the playground, laughs and talks with Julianna as she untangles a knot in her crocheting project, and asks Nat a question about his water color painting—"Tell me how you made the different colors blend together."

> These children's parents might comment, "I can't get James to put his things away at home." "Julianna's so impatient and frustrated when we crochet together at home that I gave up trying to teach her new stitches." "All Nat's paintings look the same to me."

> Ms. Danforth can use these comments to open conversations about promoting children's self-help skills, using learning situations as opportunities for relaxed talks with children, and supporting creativity by asking about children's artistic endeavors.

When you demonstrate positive ways of working with children, you do a lot to help parents improve their interactions with their children.

Applying Your Knowledge

In this learning activity you keep records of times when you reach out to parents in response to their requests or because you notice they need your support. Over the next few weeks, make a note of what you do. Write down the problem, what the parent asks for or what you see is needed, how you respond, and what the outcome is. Be sure to maintain confidentiality about these events. Begin by reading the example on the next page.

Reaching Out to Families
(Example)

Child: _Larry_   **Age:** _10 years_   **Date:** _October 23_

Problem:

Larry's been very quiet at home. He's usually very outgoing. He goes to his room after dinner and doesn't come out again until the morning. When asked if he's okay, he tells his parents, "I'm fine, leave me alone."

What parents asked for or what I saw was needed:

Larry's parents asked me if I had observed any changes in Larry's behavior. They asked me what he's been doing at the program.

My response:

I shared some comments Larry recently made about his upcoming move to a new home with his mother and younger sister. His parents said they are separating and that Larry's father would remain in their present home while his mother and the children moved to a new one. I asked them if they knew how Larry felt about the changes in their lives. They said they had not discussed it with the children yet. They didn't realize Larry knew what was going on. I said that I thought that Larry's quiet behavior might be because he is worried about the changes. I offered to ask the director for information about counseling services in the community. They said they would welcome the information. Also, we agreed to encourage Larry to participate in program activities.

The outcome:

The parents say the counseling has been very helpful. Larry seems more relaxed and is willing to talk about his feelings. At the program he's been an active member of several clubs. His parents and I talk about once a week to keep each other up to date on Larry's situation.

Reaching Out to Families

Child: _____   Age: _____   Date: _____

Problem:

_____

_____

_____

_____

What parents asked for or what I saw was needed:

_____

_____

_____

_____

My response:

_____

_____

_____

_____

The outcome:

_____

_____

_____

_____

Reaching Out to Families

Child: _____   Age: _____   Date: _____

Problem:

_____

_____

_____

_____

What parents asked for or what I saw was needed:

_____

_____

_____

_____

My response:

_____

_____

_____

_____

The outcome:

_____

_____

_____

_____

Reaching Out to Families

Child: _____ **Age:** _____ **Date:** _____

Problem:

_____

_____

_____

_____

What parents asked for or what I saw was needed:

_____

_____

_____

_____

My response:

_____

_____

_____

_____

The outcome:

_____

_____

_____

_____

Discuss your responses with your trainer.

SUMMARIZING YOUR PROGRESS

You have now completed all the learning activities for this module. Whether you are an experienced school-age staff member or a new one, this module has probably helped you develop new skills in working with families. Before you go on, take a few minutes to review your responses to the pre-training assessment for this module. Write a summary of what you learned, and list the skills you developed or improved.

If there are topics you would like to know more about, you will find recommended readings listed in the Orientation in Volume I.

Your final step in this module is to complete the knowledge and competency assessments. Let your trainer know when you are ready to schedule the assessments. After you have successfully completed them, you will be ready to start a new module. Congratulations on your progress so far, and good luck with your next module.

ANSWER SHEETS

Working With Families

Communicating With Parents Often to Exchange Information About Their Child at Home and at the Program

1. **Why did Ms. Kee think it was important for Molly's mother to visit the program?**

   a. Although Molly writes plays at home, Ms. Kee knew Ms. Moran would feel more reassured about Molly's new friendships if she actually saw her with the other children.

   b. She thought Ms. Moran would like to meet Molly's new friends; the Morans might want to encourage the children to visit each other on the weekends.

   c. She wanted Ms. Moran to see for herself that the program is a place where Molly finds it easy to make friends.

2. **What other kinds of information will Ms. Kee and the Morans need to share now that Molly is making friends?**

   a. What other interests, talents, and skills Molly is developing.

   b. How they can help her find ways to share her interests with other children at the program.

Offering a Variety of Ways for Parents to Participate in Their Child's Life at the Program

1. **How did Ms. Williams help Mr. Bradley think of a way to be involved in the program and show Jerry he was interested?**

   a. She asked him about his work and interests.

   b. She told him she'd noticed he was good at fixing things.

   c. She suggested that he and Jerry could repair the toy trucks for the program.

2. **What did Ms. Williams learn from Mr. Bradley?**

a. Parents who do not attend family nights are still interested in their children and may want to be involved in the program.

b. Parent meetings should be scheduled at different times to accommodate more families.

Providing Support for Families

1. **What did Mr. Lopez do to help Ms. Thomas understand Maria's behavior?**

a. He told her he had noticed Maria was ready to be more independent.

b. He said he had planned to talk to Maria about ways to make the program more interesting for her.

c. He said he would make some adjustments in the program to accommodate Maria's new interests.

2. **What does Mr. Lopez plan to do to help Ms. Thomas understand and respond to Maria's growing need for independence?**

a. He suggested they meet in a week to talk about how Maria responds to the changes at the program.

b. He offered to share suggestions about how they could both help Maria feel better about herself as she grows toward independence.

Module 12:

PROGRAM MANAGEMENT

OVERVIEW

MANAGING A SCHOOL-AGE PROGRAM INVOLVES:

- observing and recording information about each child's growth and development;

- working as a member of a team to plan an individualized program; and

- following administrative policies and procedures.

School-age staff play many roles. Your most important role is to develop a positive relationship with each child and provide children with a safe and interesting program. But, as you know, working in a school-age program involves much more. You encourage children's exploration and learning. You support families and help parents balance their conflicting work and home responsibilities. And, you and your colleagues use management skills to ensure the smooth operation of the program.

Your management role includes planning, conducting, and evaluating the program.

You and your colleagues may not see yourselves as managers. Most likely your program has a director who performs a variety of management tasks. The director develops budgets, makes hiring decisions, develops schedules, supervises staff, and provides training. Yet you and your colleagues are also managers. You work as a team to plan, conduct, and evaluate the program. Performing these managerial tasks allows you to create an effective environment, guide children's growth and learning, encourage their independence, and handle other responsibilities.

One of the best ways to contribute to program management is to use a systematic approach to observing children. Observing children and recording what they say and do, gives you useful information. You can then share that information with other staff and work as a team to plan a program that matches the skills and interests of individuals and the group.

School-age programs need policies and procedures that tell everyone—parents, children, staff, and volunteers—how the program typically operates. For example, a program policy might state that staff can allow children to leave the program with someone other than their parents when written permission is on file. Program procedures in this situation might include reviewing the permission form to make sure it is up-to-date and lists the person who is picking up the child, checking the individual's identification, and asking him or her to sign out the child on the daily attendance record. Upholding policies, following procedures, and maintaining appropriate records, help to keep the program running smoothly. They are part of your management role in the school-age program.

Listed below are examples of how school-age staff demonstrate their competence in managing a program.

Observing and Recording Information About Each Child's Growth and Development

Use a system to observe and record information that is objective, accurate, and avoids labeling. "Candice sat under a tree drawing circles in the dirt with a twig."

Observe children in different settings and at different times of the day. "Yesterday I observed Danielle while she and Terrence played with the sock puppets. The next time I'd like to observe her during a group activity."

Conduct observations for a specific reason: for example, to assess social skills, evaluate the environment, or identify the role a child assumes within the group. "Joey has a lot of good ideas, but he seems to have difficulty communicating them during activities and club meetings. I need to conduct some observations to see how he interacts with others and how they respond to him."

Record many instances of a child's actions before drawing conclusions about that child's abilities and needs. "I reviewed our observation recordings for Yancey. He uses a wide range of art materials, explores different techniques, and is willing to take risks and start over if his ideas don't work out.

Work with colleagues to develop a schedule for conducting regular observations of all the children in the program. "First, let's discuss how often we'd like to observe each child, then we can develop a schedule."

Conduct joint observations with a colleague to check the accuracy of the information collected. "Our observation recordings are so different we may need to ask a third person to conduct an observation with us."

Participate in staff meetings regularly to evaluate the program and to develop plans. "Next week we're going to the dress rehearsal for *Grease*. Let's think of some ways to extend the children's enjoyment of the musical. We can get a tape of the Broadway production and maybe some clothes from the 'fifties.'"

Share with colleagues information gathered from observing children and use it to plan for each child and for the group. "Dawn and Vinnie have been drawing cartoon characters all week. Maybe they would like to do a comic strip for our newsletter. If so, we can ask them what supplies they need."

Share information collected through observations with parents and encourage them to promote their children's growth and development. "Zach really likes playing board games, but sometimes he has a hard time following the rules. Would you have time to play games with him at home?"

Involve children in the planning process. "At Friday's group meeting we evaluate the week's activities and share our ideas for the coming week."

Conduct enrollment and periodic surveys of children and parents to collect information on skills, needs, and interests and to encourage feedback and suggestions. "When I reviewed the children's surveys I noticed hardly anyone is using the woodworking area any more. We need to take a closer look at this area."

Use creative thinking skills such as problem solving and brainstorming in planning and to handle problems and challenges. "We want to set up a variety of interest areas every day, but it takes a lot of time and work to do it. Maybe the children could help us set up. We would save a lot of time, and we could learn more about what they like to do."

Help children form clubs that allow them to explore their shared interests. "When I reviewed the children's surveys, I noticed we have enough interested children to start a Photography Club. I can meet with the interested children tomorrow afternoon."

Plan changes to the environment, materials, interest areas, and activities to address the cultures, abilities, and interests of individual children. "Gina is not a strong reader, but she really enjoys science fiction. She might like some of Daniel Pinkwater's books. They're interesting and not too difficult."

Appreciate and use the strengths of other team members, including parents, volunteers, and colleagues. "Every year Mrs. Parker volunteers to take the group on a late winter hike. She loves

Working as a Member of a Team to Plan an Individualized Program

nature—even during cold weather—and she shows us signs that spring is coming."

Plan some activities and events in conjunction with community resources. "The community police officer agreed to help us plan a 'safe biking rodeo.' Children can bring their bikes to the program and have them checked for safety."

Following Administrative Policies and Procedures

Review program policies before starting a new task. "I need to find out how we arrange for a field trip."

Complete management tasks according to a schedule. "Before the end of the month, I'll review the parent surveys so we can address their concerns and incorporate appropriate suggestions."

Use the program's system for recordkeeping. "Can you keep an eye on the children while I fill out the accident report for Paul's skinned knee?"

Keep informed about job responsibilities. "I've heard that new regulations for reporting child abuse are being developed. Will we have a staff meeting to discuss them?"

Provide substitute staff with adequate information on weekly plans and program practices. "When an outdoor game is canceled due to bad weather, refer to the list of back-up games on the bulletin board. Next to each one are the names of children who know how to lead it."

Share ideas related to program policies and procedures with colleagues and the supervisor. "Last fall it seemed important to gather the children for a daily meeting when they arrived. Now they seem bored during the meetings. Perhaps we should stop using the meetings for announcements, or maybe we don't need regular meetings anymore. I suggest we ask the children what they think."

Answer parents' questions about program operations and refer them to the supervisor if appropriate. "Mr. Wheeler, we need written permission for Brent to walk to his karate class. You can complete this form and return it at the end of the day. As soon as the form is on file, Brent can sign out to walk to his class."

Being an Effective Manager

In the following situations, school-age staff are managing a program. As you read them, think about what the staff are doing and why. Then answer the questions that follow.

Graham pours water into eight glasses on the science table. He reaches for a spoon. Mr. Munson kneels beside him and watches. Index cards and a pen are in his pocket. "It looks like you're ready to start. Do you think you'll be able to play a tune when you tap the glasses with a spoon?" "I'm not sure," says Graham, "but I like experimenting." Graham taps several glasses with the spoon. He looks at Mr. Munson and says, "Did you hear that? When there's less water, the sound gets lower. When there's more, it gets higher." He gently taps each glass. "It sounds like two glasses sound the same," says Mr. Munson. Graham responds, "That's because they have the same amount of water. I don't need two that are the same. I'll pour a little out of that one so I can have eight different sounds. I'm going to line the glasses up, starting with the ones with the least water. Then it'll sound like do-re-mi!" Graham arranges the glasses and begins making up a melody. Mr. Munson jots down on an index card: Graham likes to experiment, he arranged the glasses from less to more full to make the sound go from low to high, and he began to make up his own tune.

Observing and Recording Information About Each Child's Growth and Development

1. **How did Mr. Munson use a regular activity to gather objective and accurate information about Graham?**

   _____

   _____

   _____

   _____

2. **What did Mr. Munson learn about Graham?**

   _____

   _____

   _____

Working as a Member of a Team to Plan an Individualized Program

On Monday Ms. Wang asks the staff to spend time this week collecting information on how children use the quiet area. "I've noticed that this area is used less and less by children. At Friday's planning meeting, I'd like to discuss what we can do to make this area more inviting." During the week staff take turns conducting observations in the quiet area. They record how children use the homework table, listening corner, and reading nook. Staff also ask children what materials they'd like to have in the area and what changes they think are needed. Telma says, "The headphones don't always work. I really like to listen to music, but it's frustrating when it cuts on and off." Darnell says, "Sometimes, I like to do homework, but I can't find the supplies I need." During drop-off and pick-up times the staff asks parents for their input. Mr. Trenton responds, "Could you order some new magazines? Marcus says he's too old for the ones you subscribe to." On Friday the staff share what they have learned—the children would like the area to have homework supplies such as staplers and rulers, the program's magazines don't appeal to a wide age range, and the headphones may need to be replaced. They plan to make the following improvements: add a magazine shelf and subscribe to five new magazines, chosen with input from the older children; provide a plastic tote organizer stocked with pens, pencils, erasers, staplers, rulers, and other supplies suggested by the children; repair or replace the broken headphones.

1. **How did Ms. Wang and the staff use a team approach to planning?**

_____

_____

_____

_____

2. **How will the staff use the information they collected to plan an individualized program?**

_____

_____

_____

_____

Ms. Jacobs is reviewing the Staff Handbook on her break. "Even though I've been working here for a while," she tells Ms. Gaines, "I need to review our policies now and then. I have a volunteer coming in to work with me starting next week. Do you know where I can find the guidelines for supervising volunteers?" Ms. Gaines replies, "There's a brief overview in the section on staffing requirements in the Staff Handbook. You might also read the Volunteer Handbook. I had a volunteer work with me in the art area once a week all summer. Even though she wasn't allowed to be alone with the children, it was very helpful to have her do special projects on a regular basis. The Volunteer Handbook describes the kinds of things volunteers can do." Ms. Jacobs reads the section on staffing requirements and reviews the Volunteer Handbook. Later in the week she meets with a new volunteer to discuss the kinds of activities he would like to lead and to review policies about the role of volunteers at the program.

Following Administrative Policies and Procedures

1. **How does Ms. Jacobs stay informed about administrative policies and procedures?**

_____

_____

_____

_____

2. **What tasks did Ms. Jacobs complete according to the program's policies?**

_____

_____

_____

_____

Compare your answers with those on the answer sheet at the end of this module. If your answers are different, discuss them with your trainer. There can be more than one good answer.

Managing Your Own Life

Managing your home life can be challenging.

Many of the things you do at home contribute to your performance as a manager. You may pay bills, buy food and clothing, decide on major purchases such as a car or furniture, or plan a vacation or weekend outings. Management skills such as observing, individualizing, and planning are used in home and work settings. When you make a grocery list, for example, you consider how many people will be eating each meal, what foods each person likes, and what ingredients you need for each recipe. You can do this because you observe each member of your household, include them in planning balanced meals, and follow recipes—the "policies and procedures" for food preparation.

The more orderly and efficient you are in managing your life outside of work, the more time you have to do things other than chores. The more planning you do as a team, the more likely it is you and your family will enjoy spending time together. Think about times when careful management encourages efficient use of your time.

- You plan your errands so you can do them all at once rather than making several trips.

- You make sure you have all the tools and materials you need before starting a project, such as painting the kitchen cupboards or repairing a bicycle.

- You keep records of all bills and file receipts promptly.

- You keep emergency numbers posted beside the telephone.

- You plan outings or vacations that are of interest to everyone.

- You borrow a folding table and extra chairs from a neighbor when you are having a crowd over for a holiday meal.

- You make a "to do list" including what you must do today (having your car inspected), what you'd like to do (get a haircut), and what you can wait to do later (shop for a new bathing suit for next month's vacation).

- You remember the importance of relaxation and make time to exercise and talk with friends and family members.

Organizing your time and your environment to work **for** you (rather than **against** you) helps you manage more effectively. Use the chart on the following page to record something you've already done to manage your life more effectively, and to plan a strategy for solving a frustrating situation.

Frustrating Situation	What I Did
I used to spend time practically every day searching for my keys.	*I put a hook on the inside wall by the door. Now, I hang my keys there every day when I get home.*

Frustrating Situation	What I Could Do

When you have finished this overview section, you should complete the pre-training assessment. Refer to the glossary at the end of this module if you need definitions of the terms used.

PRE-TRAINING ASSESSMENT

Listed below are the skills used by school-age staff who are effective managers. Think about whether you do these things regularly, sometimes, or not enough. Place a check in one of the boxes on the right for each skill listed. Then discuss your answers with your trainer.

Observing and Recording Information About Each Child's Growth and Development	**I Do This**		
	Regularly	Sometimes	Not Enough
1. Using a system to observe and record what children say and do in an objective, accurate way that avoids the use of labels.	☐	☐	☐
2. Observing children in different settings and at different times of the day.	☐	☐	☐
3. Conducting observations for a specific reason: for example, to identify skills and interests, to evaluate the environment, or to measure progress.	☐	☐	☐
4. Recording many instances of a child's actions before drawing conclusions about that child's abilities and needs.	☐	☐	☐
5. Developing an observation schedule with colleagues so every child is observed on a regular basis.	☐	☐	☐
6. Conducting periodic joint observations with another staff member to check the accuracy of information collected; then comparing the recordings.	☐	☐	☐

Working as a Member of a Team to Plan an Individualized Program

	Regularly	Sometimes	Not Enough
7. Participating in regular staff meetings to evaluate program effectiveness and to develop weekly plans that incorporate the "lessons learned."	☐	☐	☐
8. Discussing observation recordings with other staff and using the information to plan for each child and for the group.	☐	☐	☐
9. Using parent surveys and open-ended questionnaires to collect information on children's interests and needs and to evaluate program effectiveness.	☐	☐	☐

Working as a Member of a Team to Plan an Individualized Program (continued)

	I Do This		
	Regularly	Sometimes	Not Enough
10. Involving children in the planning process.	☐	☐	☐
11. Sharing observation information with parents and encouraging them to help their children grow and develop.	☐	☐	☐
12. Changing the environment, offering new materials, and planning specific activities to address the culture needs, abilities, and interests of individual children.	☐	☐	☐
13. Conducting periodic children's surveys to identify their interests and encourage them to evaluate the program.	☐	☐	☐
14. Identifying topics of interest to several children and helping them form clubs to pursue these interests.	☐	☐	☐
15. Appreciating and using the strengths of other team members (colleagues, parents, and volunteers).	☐	☐	☐
16. Coordinating with social services, health, safety, and education resources in the community.	☐	☐	☐
17. Using creative thinking skills to plan and to address problems and challenges.	☐	☐	☐

Following Administrative Policies and Procedures

	Regularly	Sometimes	Not Enough
18. Meeting and talking with colleagues and the supervisor to provide input on program issues.	☐	☐	☐
19. Keeping informed about job responsibilities and program policies and procedures.	☐	☐	☐
20. Reviewing program policies before starting a new ta	☐	☐	☐
21. Completing management tasks according to a schedule.	☐	☐	☐

Following Administrative Policies and Procedures (continued)	**I Do This**		
	Regularly	Sometimes	Not Enough
22. Following the program's system for accurate and timely recordkeeping.	☐	☐	☐
23. Providing substitute staff with adequate information on weekly plans and program practices.	☐	☐	☐
24. Answering parents' questions about program policies and procedures and referring them to the supervisor when appropriate.	☐	☐	☐

Review your responses, then list three to five skills you would like to improve or topics you would like to learn more about. When you finish this module, you can list examples of your new or improved knowledge and skills.

_____

_____

_____

_____

_____

_____

_____

_____

Begin the learning activities for Module 12, Program Management.

LEARNING ACTIVITIES

Learning Activity I.
Using a Systematic Approach to Observing and Recording

IN THIS ACTIVITY YOU WILL LEARN TO:

- identify reasons for making observations in a school-age program; and

- develop a system for regularly observing and recording children's behavior.

Observing children is an ongoing process for people with children in their lives. They watch infants play and thrill at seeing them respond to others with cooing, smiles, and laughter. They watch toddlers and marvel at their first words and expanding physical skills. They watch preschoolers as they learn to play with others cooperatively. And they observe school-age children as they become independent individuals with unique personalities.

Why Observing Children Is Important

Observations are a useful way to get to know individual children—what they like to do, what skills they are developing, who they like to be with. It helps to have a reason for the observation, for example, to find out the role a child typically assumes during small group activities.

School-age staff observe children for a variety of reasons.

To determine each child's interests, skills, and needs. "Michael likes to read sports magazines. He keeps track of the 'stats' for his favorite college basketball teams."

To plan a program based on the interests, skills, and needs of each child. "There's been a lot of interest in recycling lately. Let's talk about using an environmental theme in several interest areas next week."

To measure each child's progress. "I've recorded the new volleyball skills Carla developed during outdoor play this month."

To resolve particular problems a child might have. "I reviewed my notes, and it seems Josh leaves games and activities when the atmosphere is very competitive."

To report children's progress to parents and colleagues. "Mrs. White, I'm glad to see you. Jasmine has been practicing for weeks, and today she mastered doing a forward flip on the trampoline. She wants you to watch the gymnastics class for a minute so she can show you."

To evaluate the effects of the environment and the program's activities. "Please bring your observations of this month's outdoor activities to Friday's meeting so we can discuss what went well and what we want to do differently next month."

Staff use the information gained through observations to provide a quality program that meets individual and developmental needs. They share the information with colleagues and parents, use it to plan activities, add new materials, and guide their interactions with children.

How to Observe

To undertake these and other tasks, you need to observe children carefully and systematically. This involves watching, listening to, and writing down what children do and say as it happens, according to a particular method. The information you write down is called a recording.

To be complete, recordings must include several facts. These are:

- the child's name and age;
- the observer's name;
- the date of the observation;
- the behavior (what the child you are observing does and says); and
- the setting (where the activity is taking place and who is involved—for example, "Debby and Ron sit on the floor in the quiet area looking at magazines").

Use these tips for recording observations of children.

Here are some suggestions for recording your observations of children:[1]

- Write what you see, not what you think is happening.
- Jot notes frequently. Carry a pad or index cards and pencil with you.
- Use short phrases instead of complete sentences, to save time.
- Try to abbreviate and shorten what a child said—don't try to write all the words, but get the gist of what is said.
- Describe *how* a child is doing or saying something.
- Develop a system of abbreviations or initials; for instance, for areas of the room, use dr-drama, qu-quiet, and so on.
- Use arrows to indicate movement.

[1] Adapted from materials developed by the Head Start Resource and Training Center (College Park, MD: University of Maryland, 1975).

- Make diagrams of the environment showing the child in relation to the setting, other children in the room, and adults.

- Underline words to indicate a particular intensity (for instance, "said loudly").

A single observation cannot provide a complete picture of a child. Children, like adults, do not behave in the same ways all the time. Illness, reactions to events at home, school, or the program, and other things affect what children do and say. Several brief (five- to ten-minute) observations can provide the information needed to determine a child's interests, skills, and needs. They should take place over a period of time. You can observe during indoor and outdoor activities and as children clean up, move from one activity to another, arrive and leave the program, and interact with peers and other staff. Children's abilities, interests, and needs change over time; therefore, observation is an ongoing process.

Observation is an ongoing process.

When you have collected several recordings on a child, you can make comments such as the following:

- "Wendy likes to work on puzzles with lots of pieces."

- "Justin can make a potholder on the loom."

- "Leo gets frustrated when we talk about colors. Today he said he can't tell the difference between brown and green; they look the same to him."

To draw conclusions such as these, you must be sure your recordings are both objective and accurate. Objective and accurate recordings include only the full facts about what is seen and heard. They do not include labels or judgments. Compare the following excerpts from an observation of two 6-year-old children playing in the block area.

Example 1: Objective and Accurate

Behavior: *Jake places block on top of tall tower. Bill nearby, building house. Bill moves back, looks at house. Bumps into Jake's tower. Tower falls, loud noise. Jake says, "Look what you did." Bill turns around quickly, laughs.*

Example 1 is an objective recording. It includes only the facts:

- what Jake does ("places block on top of tall tower");
- what Bill does ("moves back, looks at house" and "Bumps into Jake's tower");
- what happened ("Tower falls, loud noise");
- what Jake says to Bill ("Look what you did."); and
- how Bill responds ("turns around quickly, laughs").

Accurate recordings include **all** the facts about what a child (or children) does and says in the order they happen. Information is not omitted or recorded out of order. Read the following two examples of recordings that do not include all the facts and are not objective.

Example 2: Not Objective

Behavior: *Bill bumps into Jake's tower on purpose. Laughs—thinks it's funny that Jake has to start over. Is mean to Jake.*

Example 2 is not an objective recording. A label ("mean") is used and judgments are made ("Bill bumps into Jake's tower on purpose," "thinks it's funny"). Given what the staff member saw, he or she could not know what Bill was laughing at or whether he is "mean." A recording that he was "mean" does not tell anything useful about his behavior, since "mean" is a word that signifies different things to different people.

Example 3: Not Accurate

Behavior: *Bill looks behind him, sees Jake building tower. Moves back, makes tower fall. Bill laughs and Jake says, "Look what you did."*

In Example 3 a fact is added that has not been observed ("looks behind him, sees Jake building tower"). A fact is omitted ("Moves back, looks at house"). And facts are written out of order ("Bill laughs and Jake says, 'Look what you did.'").

Making an objective and accurate recording such as Example 1 requires practice. This skill can be developed during regular program activities. For example, as a staff member plays cards with a child, he or she may gain valuable information. A skilled individual takes the time to step back from his or her interactions to record that information. Opportunities for taking brief notes are present throughout the day. With practice, staff can complete recordings as they play with, interact with, and supervise children. Here are some examples.

Developing observation skills takes practice.

Child:	*Theresa*	**Age:**	*9 years*	**Date:**	*March 10*

Setting: *Drama area; Theresa and Erica are sitting near the puppet stage.*

Behavior: *Theresa holds up notepad. Says to Erica (7 years), "Yesterday I wrote a play about leprechauns. "I'll read it to you and then we can act it out." Erica sits and listens. Theresa reads play. Theresa looks in puppet box. Erica pulls out several puppets. Theresa says, "I want my play to be a puppet show, but there aren't any that look like leprechauns. Let's get some green stuff from the art area to make new puppets."*

Child:	*Nathan*	**Age:**	*6 years*	**Date:**	*September 9*

Setting: *Near the entrance, in cubby area, at morning arrival time.*

Behavior: *Nathan and mother enter. He wears baseball hat, carries lunch box. Mother says, "Put your hat and lunch box in your cubby. Before I go to work you can introduce me to Gabriel." Nathan smiles. Puts things in cubby. Waves and calls out to Gabriel at game table. "Look, Gabriel. This is my mom." They walk to game table.*

Child:	*Andy*	**Age:**	*12 years*	**Date:**	*May 10*

Setting: *Outdoors; Andy sitting under tree. On ground is sketch pad, pencil.*

Behavior: *Andy watches soccer game. Picks up pad, pencil, begins drawing. Jody walks by, says, "What are you drawing?" Andy says nothing. Jody comes closer. Andy holds up pad, says, "I'm drawing Eric dribbling the soccer ball. It's hard because I don't know how to make it look like he's moving."*

Child: *Lucas*   **Age:** *8 years*   **Date:** *October 3*

Setting: *Table set for self-service snack.*

Behavior: *Ms. Cafritz sets baskets of crackers next to juice pitcher and cups. Lucas grabs one, says, "I'm really hungry." Turns to Ms. Cafritz, says, "What can we put on the crackers? I'm starving." Ms. Cafritz points to peanut butter and cheese spread. Lucas reaches for peanut butter. Picks up knife, spreads peanut butter on crackers. Eats. "Now I'm thirsty. Peanut butter makes me thirsty." Pours juice in cup. Drinks juice in one swallow.*

Child: *Julie*   **Age:** *5 years*   **Date:** *February 14*

Setting: *Game table; Julie at table with parquetry blocks and patterns.*

Behavior: *Julie dumps blocks out of basket. Takes pattern card. Looks at card, puts it down. Moves blocks, picks up red diamond, places it on matching shape on card. Selects blocks to complete pattern, moves from upper left to lower right of card.*

Child: *Janet*   **Age:** *7 years*   **Date:** *February 17*

Setting: *Science area; Janet looking at box of sea shells.*

Behavior: *Janet takes all shells out. Hums. Sorts by size. Looks at shells on table. Picks up several small and two large that look alike. Puts together. Calls to Ms. Mason, "Look at this, I made a seashell family."*

Record your observations during program hours.

Some staff feel recording observations will take away from their time with children. At the end of the day, they try to jot down the things that happened. It is impossible, however, to remember accurately everything that took place: what each child did and said, or new skills children attempted. It is best to record observations during program hours as you interact with children or as soon as possible after the observation. You might ask a colleague to help cover an activity while you record children's interactions and behaviors. Work with your colleagues to develop a system and schedule for conducting regular observations of all the children in the program.

Here are some examples of staff completing recordings:

- Mr. Abrams joins Peter, Kia, and Carson on the outdoor basketball court. The children take turns practicing shots from the free throw line. After a few minutes, he suggests the children play a game of "Horse." Kim hasn't played before, so Mr. Abrams explains the rules. He steps aside and as the game progresses, he pulls a few index cards from his shirt pocket. He records the names of the players and a few notes on each child's skills.

- Ms. Donovan is helping Marisa set up a hand loom for a weaving project. Marisa looks for a yarn strong enough to use as a background. As Marisa sets up the loom, she makes sure the yarn isn't too loose or too tight. Several times she starts over. While the children put their materials and projects on the shelf, Ms. Donovan records on a note pad how Marisa persevered to set up the loom.

Checking Out Your Observations

In addition to recording in an objective and accurate way, staff members must be sure they see and hear what others see and hear. People often perceive the same situation differently. Eyewitness accounts of an accident show how several people, seeing the same event, can tell different stories.

For example, one person sees Barbara encourage Suzanne to be in the talent show and offer to teach her some new dance steps. Another, watching the same children, observes Barbara angrily tell Suzanne that unless she dances the way Barbara tells her to, she can't be in the show. Knowledge of what a child has done in the past, your feelings about a certain type of behavior, tone of voice, and many other factors influence what you observe and record.

It is useful to compare your recordings about a child with a colleague's observation information. If they are similar, an accurate record of a child's growth and development is being maintained. If they are very different, the information collected may not be useful. Two persons with different perceptions of a child's behavior should observe the child together over a short period of time. After each observation they can compare their recordings and discuss what they have seen. This method helps ensure accurate recordings. If the recordings still differ greatly, the program director or trainer can assist in solving the problem.

Applying Your Knowledge

In this learning activity you practice observing and recording. You can use the form on the following page, or one of your own design. Select a child to observe over a one-week period. Observe the child for five to ten minutes, once per day. Ask your program director, a colleague, or your trainer to observe the same child at the same time as you, on at least two occasions. Compare your recordings after each joint observation and at the end of the week.

Make several copies of this form before recording your observations.

Observation Form

Child: _____   **Age:** _____

Observer: _____   **Date:** _____

Setting: _____

Behavior: _____

_____

_____

_____

_____

_____

_____

_____

_____

_____

_____

_____

_____

_____

_____

_____

If your recordings are objective, accurate, and similar to those of your co-observer, begin the next learning activity. If your recordings differ and are not objective and accurate, select another child to observe and repeat this learning activity. Ask your trainer to observe with you again and record information about the same child. Then discuss your recordings with your trainer and begin the next learning activity.

Learning Activity II.
Individualizing the Program

IN THIS ACTIVITY YOU WILL LEARN TO:

- use information gained through observation to define each child's interests, skills, and needs; and

- plan appropriate activities for each child.

High-quality school-age programs reflect and respond to stages of development and individual needs.

High quality school-age programs are based on two kinds of knowledge: the characteristics of children at this stage of development and the interests, skills, and needs of individual children. The environment, materials, activities, and interactions in such programs reflect children's developmental levels and respond to what makes each child a unique person. For example:

> The staff of the Horizon House School-Age Program know that most children enjoy being creative, making "real" things, and choosing what materials to use and how to use them. They apply this knowledge by stocking the art area with a wide variety of materials. In addition, they provide specific items that respond to individual children. For example, knowing that Carlos likes to draw cartoons, they include charcoal and colored pencils in the art area and books that show step-by-step techniques for drawing familiar cartoon figures. They also know Carlos is a "perfectionist" so there are erasers to use with different kinds of pencils and papers.

Including Children with Disabilities[2]

Getting to know a child with disabilities and that child's family is the first step toward meeting the child's needs. Planning for children with disabilities requires careful thought and often the assistance of specialists.

An individual child's development may vary greatly across domains, revealing greater or lesser degrees of skill in different

---

[2]Adapted with permission from Toni S. Bickart, Judy R. Jablon, and Diane Trister Dodge, *Building the Primary Classroom* (Washington, DC: Teaching Strategies, Inc., Portsmouth, NH: Heinemann, 1999), pp. 32-33.

areas. Within every category of disability, individual children will develop differently and the span of development will be even wider than in children who are not disabled. A nine-year-old child with Down's Syndrome may be very verbal, social, and able to read on a first grade level, or the child may be rarely verbal, or social, and unable to match picture cards.

It is very important to know the child's learning styles, likes, and dislikes, and how the specific disability may or may not affect the child's involvement in the program. The following steps will help you and your colleagues plan how to include a child with a diagnosed disability.

- **Consult with the child.** Find out whether the child would rather talk with you alone, or with a family member present. Ask what has helped in the past and how you can best support the child now.

- **Consult with the family.** While this is important for all children, families of children with special needs may have extra information to communicate as well as specific suggestions to share.

- **Consult with the child's teacher.** You might do this through the child's family or contact the teacher directly, with the parent's permission. It is important to learn what approach the school uses, what services the child receives, what accommodations are provided, the goals set for the child, progress made and so on. In addition, you will need to set up an ongoing system for sharing information that will allow the school and program to provide the most appropriate activities for the child.

- **Consult with a specialist.** Although the strategies for working with different disabilities may overlap, it is essential for you to have specific guidance on each type of disability. Seek advice from specialists to learn the most up-to-date instructional approaches.

- **Gather resources.** You can find or create the resources you need to mainstream and include all children. Resources range from a special education assistant hired to work in the program, to finding articles about special strategies to support the child's involvement in activities. Attending a workshop or asking your director to provide an inservice event might help you to acquire new skills to meet a child's special needs. You are not expected to address every child's needs without support and resources.

These steps can help you plan for successful inclusion.

Learning About Individual Children

One of the most effective ways to get to know children, as described in the previous learning activity, is by using a system for observing and recording information. When you and your colleagues share information gained through observation you can confirm your impressions and create a total picture of each child. Parents can also help you learn about their children through informal conversations, interest surveys and questionnaires, and periodic parent-staff conferences. Of course, children themselves are also sources of information. Almost every interaction is an opportunity to learn more about a child. Children's skills and interests are constantly changing and growing—keeping in touch with each child is an ongoing part of your job.

Individualizing the program does not mean you have to provide separate materials and activities for each child.

Individualizing the program does not mean you have to provide a separate inventory of materials or plan special activities for each child in the program. Instead, you can respond to individual children during your regular planning process. Team members should review their observation notes and summarize children's skills, interests, and needs. As you plan for the coming week, think about what individual children might enjoy and plan ways to encourage their involvement in activities. For example:

> Mr. Addams says he has observed that Wanda always wins at checkers. His colleagues agree—they, too have noticed her skill. They think she might be ready for the more complex game of chess. However, they also know that Wanda is sometimes reluctant to try new things. She likes to win and it might take some time for her to be as good at chess as she is at checkers! Mr. Addams offers to give chess lessons to a small group. He will explain to Wanda that she might enjoy the challenge of learning to play chess. She can decide for herself whether to participate in the lessons.

Inventory should reflect children's current abilities and interests.

You can individualize the program through the materials and equipment you provide. In a typical school-age program, each interest area and the outdoors is stocked with a "basic" inventory. Throughout the year, as children grow, learn, gain skills, and develop new interests, the inventory changes to reflect current abilities and "passions." Some items are stored; new ones are added. Some examples follow:

- Luiz and his family recently moved here from El Salvador. He's learning to speak, read, and write, English. Ms. Logan added a Spanish-English dictionary to the quiet area.

- When the football season started, tag football became the favorite outdoor activity. To accommodate all the interested children, extra footballs were brought out of storage.

- Six-year-old Shanna is in the hospital having her tonsils out. Mr. Unger made sure there's plenty of paper and markers in the art area for children who want to make cards. He also brought out the health clinic prop box—several of the younger children want to play "hospital."

- Last week Justine tie-dyed an over-sized T-shirt. Several girls liked Justine's shirt so much they wanted to make their own. They brought in their own shirts and the tie-dye materials were left in place in the art area for an extra week.

Another way to individualize is to offer open-ended materials and activities that appeal to children at a wide range of skill levels. Children can choose the materials they want to use and decide how they want to use them. Different children can participate in different ways. For example, if you are going to make pizzas for snack one day, turn it into an open-ended activity. Each child can make a single-serving pizza, decide what shape to make the dough, what toppings to use, which seasonings to add, and so on. Another strategy that accommodates different skill levels is to plan an activity that has both basic and advanced elements. Some children can complete the basics while others pursue more advanced techniques. For example, one windy day you might decide to provide materials and instructions for making kites. Children could make plastic bag kites (a relatively simple project) or box kites (a more complex undertaking).

School-age staff play many different roles as they interact with children in the program. These roles vary according to what you are doing and the individual children with whom you are interacting. The support and guidance you provide to each child is individualized. It is based on what you know about a child and what that child needs from you. For example, when giving instructions to a child who is easily distracted, you might sit close to the child, stop frequently to ask the child to repeat what you said, and ask if he or she has any questions. Giving instructions to a child who can focus with ease might be more direct—this is what you do, do you have any questions?

School-age staff play many roles.

Each school-age program has a look and feel that matches the staff and children enrolled. You and your colleagues can individualize your program by getting to know individual children and using this knowledge to plan activities, select materials, and provide appropriate guidance and encouragement.

Applying Your Knowledge

In this learning activity you practice your observation skills again by conducting periodic observations of three children for a week. Your recordings should include at least the information asked for on the form provided in Learning Activity I. You can use copies of that form, a notepad, or index cards.

Select three children to observe, one from each age group (5 to 7, 8 to 10, and 11 to 12). If you do not have children in each of these age groups enrolled in your program, select three children with as much difference in age as possible.

Observe each child for a five- to ten-minute period at least once a day. At the end of the week review your recordings to see what you learned about these children.

On the next page is an example of an "Individualization Summary Form." It shows what was learned from observations of three children and how the information was used. Read this example, then use your own recordings to complete the blank Individualization Summary Form.

Summary Form for Individualizing
(Example)

Child: *Ray* **Age:** *11 years* **Date:** *April 12*

How does this child usually play (alone, with several friends, in a group)?

Inside, he spends time alone doing homework, using the computer, or designing paper airplanes. He also joins in group art activities such as tie-dying. Outside, he joins in large group games and sometimes does things on his own.

What does this child like to do (favorite games, play materials, activities)?

He likes to get some of his homework done first, then he reads or works on his paper airplane designs. He likes special art projects that allow for creative expression. He likes organized sports, especially softball.

What kinds of activities does this child start, join in, or ask others to join in?

He likes to do most indoor activities alone. Outdoors, he often takes the lead and organizes the softball games.

What skills has this child acquired?

Ray has good reading comprehension (he likes to re-tell a story's plot for anyone who is interested) and can read for long periods of time. He follows written instructions well (like those in the paper airplane book). He applies his creative skills in airplane designs and in art projects (he has invented a number of unique knots for tie-dye). He uses leadership skills to organize softball games. He is a very accurate pitcher.

What can you do to build on the child's interests and skills?

I can suggest he write book reviews to post on the bulletin board in the quiet area where other children can read them. Also, I can provide additional books on a slightly more challenging level.

I can ask him if he would like to start a Paper Airplane Club and hold an airplane festival outside.

He might like to try rice paper dying, which is similar to tie-dying.

I can encourage him to help other children learn how to pitch.

Summary Form for Individualizing

Child: _____ **Age:** _____ **Date:** _____

How does this child usually play (alone, with several friends, in a group)?

_____
_____
_____
_____

What does this child like to do (favorite games, play materials, activities)?

_____
_____
_____
_____

What kinds of activities does this child start, join in, or ask others to join in?

_____
_____
_____
_____

What skills has this child acquired?

_____
_____
_____
_____

What can you do to build on the child's interest and skills?

_____
_____
_____
_____

Summary Form for Individualizing

Child: _____ **Age:** _____ **Date:** _____

How does this child usually play (alone, with several friends, in a group)?

_____

_____

_____

_____

What does this child like to do (favorite games, play materials, activities)?

_____

_____

_____

_____

What kinds of activities does this child start, join in, or ask others to join in?

_____

_____

_____

_____

What skills has this child acquired?

_____

_____

_____

What can you do to build on the child's interest and skills?

_____

_____

_____

_____

Summary Form for Individualizing

Child: _____ Age: _____ Date: _____

How does this child usually play (alone, with several friends, in a group)?

_____
_____
_____
_____

What does this child like to do (favorite games, play materials, activities)?

_____
_____
_____
_____

What kinds of activities does this child start, join in, or ask others to join in?

_____
_____
_____
_____

What skills has this child acquired?

_____
_____
_____
_____

What can you do to build on the child's interest and skills?

_____
_____
_____
_____

Discuss your observation recordings and your plans for these three children with your trainer. If you found it difficult to complete your recordings, discuss why that was so, and try to find ways to record observations on a regular basis.

Learning Activity III.
Involving Parents and Children in Program Planning

IN THIS ACTIVITY YOU WILL LEARN TO:

- use interest surveys to collect information about children's interests, skills, and needs;

- address survey results in program planning; and

- help children establish clubs that allow them to build on their interests and skills.

School-age children are constantly growing, changing, and developing new interests and skills. It is important for staff to stay in tune with children's changing needs in order to offer an interesting and dynamic program. Surveys, completed by both parents and children, provide information you can use to determine whether changes in the program are needed.

Parent Surveys

Generally, parents know their children better than anyone else. They have valuable insights into their children's strengths and needs, likes and dislikes, talents, abilities, and interests. Informal discussions at drop-off and pick-up times are an ongoing source of information about children. You can also gather information systematically through parent surveys. Surveys can alert you to areas where individual children need special help and guidance. They can help you stay in touch with new ideas, skills, and abilities children are developing through home, school, and community activities. At times, your perspective may differ from the parent's—you see the child in a group setting rather than in a home and family. Sharing these different perspectives helps parents and staff to work together to understand and guide each child more successfully. Parent surveys can also identify common interests, talents, and needs. The program can respond to these by revising the schedule, starting new clubs, or otherwise tailoring the program structure so it is appropriate for the children enrolled.

Here are examples of what you can learn about children through parent surveys:

- Bonnie is looking forward to summer camp. She'll miss the school-age program, but she'll have fun with her "camp" friends.

- Simon loves listening to his dad's stories about wild animals at bedtime. Together, they have filled several scrap books with pictures from magazines.

- Hannah gets frustrated when she tries to learn something new. When she doesn't succeed immediately she says, "Who cares about this anyway?" and walks away.

- Matthew is on a basketball team. He would like the chance to practice his skills.

- Liam, Jasmine, and Kendra are all pet lovers. Liam and Jasmine have cats, Kendra has a dog, and all three children wish they had more pets to care for.

Use open-ended questionnaires to solicit parent input.

Parent surveys can be conducted at the beginning of the program year and periodically as needed. The "Pre-Attendance Parent Information Survey" on the next page could be a part of the program's enrollment process. In addition, you can use open-ended questionnaires to solicit input from parents at appropriate points throughout the year. Here are some suggested questions:

- What do you like best about the program?

- In what ways is the program meeting your child's needs?

- In what ways is the program not meeting your child's needs?

- What would you like to change about the program, if anything?

Keep these questionnaires brief, ideally no more than one page. Parents are more likely to respond if the questionnaire can be completed quickly.

Pre-Attendance Parent Information Survey

Dear Parents:

We are looking forward to having your child in our program. In order to plan an exciting program of activities, we would like to know more about each individual child. Please take a few minutes to answer the questions below. You may want to discuss this with your child.

Parent's Name: _____ **Date:** _____

Child's Name: _____ **Nickname (if applicable):** _____

Age: _____ **Grade:** _____ **School:** _____

Family's Primary Language: _____ **Child's Primary Language:** _____

Mother's Phone Number: (home)_____ **(work)**_____

Father's Phone Number: (home)_____ **(work)**_____

These are my child's favorite activities:

☐ **Sports and Games**
Which ones?

_____

☐ **Arts and Crafts**
Which ones?

_____

☐ **Music and Dance**
List special interests and talents and types enjoyed.

_____

☐ **Reading**
List types of books enjoyed, magazines and journals, special topics.

_____

☐ **Plays and Drama**
List special interests and talents and activities enjoyed (i.e., puppetry, charades):

_____

☐ **Building Things**
What kinds? (i.e., block building, Legos and similar construction materials, woodworking)

_____

☐ **Nature**
What kinds?

_____

☐ **Science**
What kinds?

_____

☐ **Hobbies or Other Interests**
List any that are current.

_____

What new skills or interests would your child like to develop?

_____

_____

How would you describe your child's temperament?

_____

_____

What do you think are your child's best qualities?

_____

_____

How does your child react and adjust to new situations and new people?

_____

_____

Please describe your child's strong dislikes or fears (if applicable).

_____

_____

Please indicate what kinds of extra help or support your child may need.

_____

_____

What else would you like us to know about your child?

_____

_____

Gathering Information From Children

The most valuable sources of information about children's skills and interests are the children themselves. You can encourage children to offer input on the kinds of things they like to do and how the program should be operated (schedule, rules, how snack is served, new materials). In addition, watching, talking, and listening to children will help you learn about children's interests and about what they think needs to be changed.

The program can conduct periodic surveys to find out how well children's needs and interests are being met and what adjustments might be needed. Surveys can be a part of the enrollment process or conducted periodically during the year. If written surveys are used, keep in mind that older children may enjoy completing these on their own, but younger children may need assistance from a staff member or an older child. Older children might also use the survey to "poll" other children in the program and prepare a report on the results. Staff members could use the survey format to conduct "focus groups" with children, concentrating on a few questions or program areas each day. Or staff could use the survey to interview individual children.

Survey results can help you identify topics of special interest to children that might lead to planning and establishing clubs. Clubs are excellent vehicles for encouraging school-age children to explore a topic of interest. They give them the chance to develop and use new skills, and allow them to discover their individual talents. Clubs can be organized around almost anything that interests a small group of children in the program. They may meet several times a week for a month or more. If interest is high, they may continue for several months before children have fulfilled their goals and are ready to move on to something else. For example:

Clubs let children explore special interests and skills.

> When Ms. Benson reviews the results of a recent survey, she identifies a small group of children who are interested in comedians, clowns, and acting. Ms. Benson offers to help them form a club to learn more about clowning and perhaps to perform as clowns. Galen, who takes acting classes and performs in children's theater, helps lead the meetings. Ms. Benson provides books and other resources, invites a volunteer from the community theater group to talk with the children about clowning, and responds to the children's requests for costumes, make-up, and props. Over the course of six weeks, the children discuss different clowning styles, create their own costumes and make-up, and write and perform skits for the rest of the children.

349

The children in your program might like one of these clubs.

Clubs that are often successful with school-age children include:

cartoons	dancing	cooking
acting	chess	pet care
magic	mystery solving	card collecting
paper airplane design	kite flying	calligraphy
newspaper	inventors	gardening
environment	current events	weaving

An example of a survey used to find out what children like to do appears on the following pages.

Applying Your Knowledge

In this learning activity you survey the children in the program to determine their current needs and interests. You can use the questions on "What's Fun, What's Fabulous," or the "Planning Survey," or make up ones relevant to your program. Ask children to respond in writing, in small group meetings, or during one-on-one interviews. If you serve a wide age range use a combination of approaches—older children can respond in writing and younger ones in interviews with you or an older child.

Next, use the survey results to help children plan and start a club. After the club has been meeting for two weeks, answer questions about what happened.

What's Fun?   What's Fabulous?[3]

1.   If you could do anything you want out of school, what would you do? Describe it, or draw a picture of yourself doing it.

2.   What activity in the whole world would you most like to do?

3.   What is your favorite thing to do out of school?

4.   What is your least favorite thing to do out of school?

5.   When you are not in school, what do your friends do that you wish you could do?

6.   What are you good at?

7.   What do you wish you could do better?

8.   What do you wish you could do that you don't know how to do?

9.   What do you like to do at school? Is there anything you don't like to do at school?

10. What do you do at school that you would like to do out of school?

11. What do you like to do around the house?

12. What do you like to do with your family?

13. What are your favorite things to do each season (winter, spring, summer, fall)?

14. What places (other than home and school) would you like to visit more often?

15. What's your best time of day and why?

16. What's your worst time of day and why?

[3]Adapted with permission from Joan Bergstrom, *School's Out* (Berkeley, CA: Ten Speed Press, 1990), p. 39.

Club Planning Survey

1. What activity in the whole world would you most like to do?

   _____

   _____

2. Describe your least favorite thing to do when you are at home.

   _____

   _____

3. What do you do at school that you would like to do out of school?

   _____

   _____

4. What do you do well?

   _____

   _____

5. What do you wish you could do better?

   _____

   _____

6. What would you like to learn how to do?

   _____

   _____

7. Is there something you would like to teach other children to do?

   _____

   _____

Plan for a New Club

Focus: _____

Potential Club Members and Ages:

_____

_____

Purpose:

_____

_____

_____

Activities:

_____

_____

_____

_____

Schedule:

_____

Leader(s):

_____

Resources:

_____

_____

_____

Community Volunteers (if any):

_____

_____

Staff Responsibilities:

_____

_____

_____

_____

Over the next two weeks, use the plan to help children establish their club. Then answer the following questions.

Club: _____

How did the children respond to the club activities?

_____
_____
_____
_____

Did the club activities help children build on the interests they expressed in the survey?

_____
_____
_____
_____

What changes did you make to the original club plan?

_____
_____
_____
_____

What would you do differently if you offered this club again?

_____
_____
_____
_____

How could you work with the children to expand or extend the activities of this club?

_____
_____
_____
_____

Discuss your experiences helping children plan and implement a club with your colleagues and your trainer.

Learning Activity IV.
Working as a Team for Long-Range and Weekly Planning

IN THIS ACTIVITY YOU WILL LEARN TO:

- develop weekly plans; and

- evaluate the effectiveness of your plan.

Planning involves thinking about what you want to do and how you will do it. It means taking time to consider what activities to offer, what materials are needed, and how to support individual children. It also means each staff member must assume responsibility for carrying out the plans.

Planning helps you be well-prepared for each day.

When you plan, you are better prepared. You have sufficient materials and children are involved in activities suited to their skills and interests. As a result, the program runs more smoothly.

All members of the team—staff, parents, volunteers, and children—can contribute to program plans. The more involved in planning everyone is, the more likely they are to realize the important role everyone plays in carrying out the plans.

In the planning process, there is a place for each team member's particular strengths, interests, and talents. Each member may have valuable observations, ideas, or concerns to contribute. An attitude of trust and respect enables each team member to communicate problems and to recognize and appreciate successes.

Two types of planning are useful for school-age programs: long-range planning and weekly planning. Long-range planning involves thinking ahead to the coming year. It includes an annual budget, planning for equipment purchases, and planning a variety of activities for each month of the year. For example, you know that the weather in May is warm, and children are likely to spend long periods of time outdoors. Therefore, you can think ahead to make sure you have sufficient equipment for sports and games and to plan outdoor activities that provide a wide range of choices. By planning ahead, you will be ready with the materials and equipment you need. Long-range planning also is necessary if you want to arrange a special event, such as a trip or a party. It is the best way to ensure that special events really happen.

Long-range planning covers the coming year.

School-age staff contribute to weekly plans.

Weekly plans are more detailed than long-range plans. Weekly planning does not need to be a lengthy process. In many programs, planning meetings take place before children arrive or after they leave. Staff members who work together need to plan together. In addition, it is important to invite children to participate in both planning and leading activities and to involve parents as much as possible. A planning form can be very helpful. In your program there may be a form everyone uses. You can use or adapt the form provided in this module.

Consider these planning categories.

The following planning categories may be useful for your program:

Special focus—a theme or topic emphasized during a given week that guides planning of materials and activities. For example, for the theme "traveling by airplane," staff could turn the drama area into a cockpit and passenger section; place books and brochures on air travel in the quiet area; encourage children to design, build, and decorate model airplanes in the art area; feature posters displaying the history of man and flight in the science area; and schedule a field trip to an airport.

Meetings—times to gather the children together to plan activities, sing songs, give performances, play games, solve problems, discuss issues; and scheduled club meetings.

Special activities—events planned for a small group of children or the whole group. Staff might plan a visit to a nature center or organize a wacky Olympics festival.

Outdoor activities—the choices offered to children in the program's outdoor space. Including the outdoors as a separate category encourages you to plan for outdoor activities as thoughtfully as you do for indoor ones.

Changes to the environment—the addition of new equipment or materials, or changes in the arrangement of indoor or outdoor space. For example, a display of pet care posters may be added to the nature area, or the easels might be moved to make room to set up a large net to be used for a weaving project.

Target children—those children who may have particular needs, skills, or interests you want to address during a given week. By targeting these children during the planning process, the team can design activities and materials to meet their needs. Target children may include a child whose parent will be away for several months. This child might need extra time with staff; books or pamphlets about the place where the parent will be; and an opportunity to tape a message, write a letter, or make a gift for the absent parent. To ensure confidentiality, it is best not to include this category in the written plan posted on the bulletin board.

Staff responsibilities—the assignment of specific tasks to each staff member to ensure they get done. For example, if the plan is to have children start a vegetable garden, someone must get the supplies (seeds, plants, and fertilizer) and gather the tools. It is important to agree on who will do what and to post a list reminding people of their assignments.

School-age staff have many tools and strategies they can use to help them plan. First, they know what children are typically doing at a given age and stage of development. Second, staff have specific knowledge about each child. Information gathered through observations and recordings, from conversations with parents, and from surveys (of parents and children) is invaluable in the planning process. Knowing, for example, a child is going on a trip may lead staff to add suitcases and books about trips to the drama area.

Knowledge of children's developmental and individual needs guides the planning process.

Staff members use yet another strategy that guides the planning process: they carefully observe how children use the environment. Daily observations provide important clues as to what changes are needed. For example, if a display of items found on a nature walk has been in the science area for several weeks, staff members may note there is little interest in the area. Putting some things away, adding new ones, or even changing the location of some items can spark children's interest. Observations also let staff know when something planned is not working. For example, if children are mixing up the playing pieces from board games and leaving them scattered on the table, they may need help learning the rules. Or if the games are left sitting on the shelf, they may be too challenging. These observations tell staff the children need a different variety of board games.

Daily observations provide important clues.

Finally, staff consider what special activities they want to offer in a given week. These usually respond to the children's interests. For example, if a group of children is particularly interested in protecting the environment, staff might help them organize a recycling campaign. Others, who are more interested in singing and dancing, may enjoy producing their own video. Special activities may coincide with the time of year—in the fall, a trip to a pumpkin farm followed by cooking recipes that use pumpkin. They may also be related to local, national, or world news events—for example, reading about and watching the Olympics may lead to creating an Olympic festival. Staff also plan special activities they think children will enjoy—watching a magic performance, visiting a pottery studio, or making fresh pasta and

Special activities respond to children's interests.

sauce. The special interests or talents of staff members are valuable here. An adult's enthusiasm for music or cooking is quickly communicated to the children and can expand their interests.

Themes for special activities may be very focused—Chinese New Year, sports heroes, wire sculpture. Or, they can be open-ended, easily lending themselves to use in every interest area—What's Your Invention? (board game, recipe, sport, art technique); Going Places (food, music, crafts, dances, products, famous people); Making the News (school, program, world).

Evaluation is the last step in the planning process.

Evaluating the experiences you provide for children is an integral part of the planning process. After you have conducted activities, it is helpful to discuss the following questions:

What happened each day? What activities did children engage in? What did staff do to respond to children's questions, experiences, interactions? What activities did staff initiate? What activities did children initiate?

Which activities were successful and which were not? Which activities should be repeated? Which ones should be dropped? What might you do differently next time? Offer different materials? Provide more or less guidance?

What changes should be made in the environment? Should furniture and equipment be rearranged? Should new props, materials, equipment, and supplies be added?

How were children's individual skills, needs, and interests addressed? Did each child have many opportunities to choose materials and activities?

It is important to go through an evaluation such as this one during each planning meeting.

Applying Your Knowledge

In this learning activity you review a sample weekly planning form. Then, with a colleague and several children, you will develop a weekly plan for your program. After using the plan you evaluate its effectiveness. Begin by reviewing the example. Agree on a time to hold a planning meeting with your colleague and the children. You can use the blank form that appears after the example or one of your choosing. Finally, implement the plan, then answer the evaluation questions provided.

School-Age Program Weekly Plan
(Example)

Week of: _May 10-14_ **Special Focus:** _How Things Work_

	Monday	Tuesday	Wednesday	Thursday	Friday
Meetings	Group: Review week's events Jogging Club: 3:00-3:30 p.m. Drama Club: 3:30-4:30 p.m.	Jogging Club: 3:00-3:30 p.m. Magic Club: 3:30-4:30 p.m.	Group: New song, Marvelous Toy Jogging Club: 3:00-3:30 p.m.	Jogging Club: 3:00-3:30 p.m. Chess Club: 3:30-4:30 p.m.	Group: Speak Your Mind session
Special activities	Producing musical sounds (music student from college)	Making musical instruments	Bread baking	Behind-the-scenes tour of the building (with maintenance staff)	Use catalogues to plan garden, order seeds
Outdoor activities	Easel painting outdoors (with tempera, poster, water color paints)	Repairing your bike (cycling club volunteer)	Paper airplane flying contest	What to do in a lightning storm (Red Cross demonstration)	Draw layouts for garden (what will be planted in each row?)

Changes to the Environment

Drama Area	**House Corner**	**Math**
Auto mechanics prop box TV repair kit	No changes this week	Graph paper, drafting tools, blueprints

Blocks and Construction	**Board and Table Games**	**Quiet Area**
Supplies for building functional machines	Supplies for making up games	_3-2-1 Contact_ (new science magazine) _How Things Work_ (by David Macaulay) _Popular Mechanics_ (back issues)

Outdoors	**Music/Movement**	**Science and Nature**
Street hockey equipment	Rag-time tapes, scarves, hats	Pulleys, magnets, electric circuit, siphon

Woodworking	**Arts and Crafts**	**Miscellaneous**
Screwdrivers, pliers, wrenches Small machines and appliances (cords removed)	_How Paper Airplanes Fly_ (book) Different kinds of paper for airplanes	Seed catalogues Paper, envelopes, stamps (for ordering seeds)

School-Age Program Weekly Plan

Week of: _____   Special Focus: _____

	Monday	Tuesday	Wednesday	Thursday	Friday
Meetings					
Special activities					
Outdoor activities					

Changes to the Environment

Drama Area	House Corner	Math
Blocks and Construction	Board and Table Games	Quiet Area
Outdoors	Music/Movement	Science and Nature
Woodworking	Arts and Crafts	Miscellaneous

Evaluating Your Plan

How did you (staff and children) work as a team to develop the plan?

_____
_____
_____
_____

What happened each day?

_____
_____
_____
_____

Which activities were successful and which were not?

_____
_____
_____
_____

How did children respond to changes in the environment?

_____
_____
_____

How did the plan meet children's individual skills, interests, and needs?

_____
_____
_____
_____

What would you do differently next time?

_____
_____
_____

Discuss your plan and your experiences in using it with the colleague and children on your planning team.

Learning Activity V.
Following Administrative Policies and Procedures

IN THIS ACTIVITY YOU WILL LEARN TO:

- identify your program's administrative policies and procedures; and

- complete management tasks according to a schedule.

You are part of a large system.

As a school-age staff member, you are a part of a large system. Your role in this system includes coordinating with other staff, with parents, with your director, and possibly with schools and other agencies in the community. If you operate in shared space, you may also coordinate with a school principal, custodial staff, or other groups who also use the facility. You also need to know and follow the program's administrative policies and procedures. These policies and procedures usually address the following topics:

- hours of operation;

- acceptance/registration procedures;

- fees and service charges;

- safety requirements;

- medical and health requirements;

- fire prevention and evacuation procedures;

- policy on closing for bad weather;

- contingency plans for responding to emergencies;

- reporting accidents;

- using, ordering, and replacing consumable supplies;

- reporting suspected child abuse and neglect;

- reporting maintenance needs for furniture and equipment; and

- using positive guidance.

Policies and Procedures

All staff need to be aware of these policies and procedures so everyone follows the same regulations during the program's day-to-day operations. In addition, parents may seek answers to questions about discipline, accidents, or other issues. When staff know the procedures regarding such issues, they can provide parents with information or direct them to discuss an issue with a supervisor, when appropriate.

The program's policies and procedures also address your role in maintaining files. These records may include:

The program staff collect and maintain records and forms.

- child health examinations;

- observation recordings;

- daily attendance reports;

- parent contact forms;

- contagious disease exposure forms;

- medical emergency consent forms;

- weekly plan outlines;

- field trip permission forms;

- food service reports;

- inventory records;

- supply request forms;

- staff time sheets; and

- staff leave request forms.

To follow the program's procedures for reporting and recordkeeping, you may find it helpful to keep a list of necessary reports and the date each is due. Some reports are due daily or weekly. Others are completed when an incident occurs, such as an accident. Still others, such as inventory reports, are used once a month. Your role will vary according to the reporting task. Some information, such as observation recordings for children, may be collected and reviewed periodically by staff. Other reports, such as a summary of a parent-staff conference, may be completed by one staff member but kept on file in case other people need to review the information.

Your knowledge of individual children and awareness of appropriate practice for school-age programs, can be applied to issues related to the overall program. You can talk with colleagues and management staff about ways to improve the program as a whole. Suggestions on staffing patterns, enrollment policies, and other practices and procedures will be welcomed by administrators whose goal is to provide a high-quality program that meets the needs of children, parents, and staff.

Your input can help improve the program.

There are laws and regulations on including children with disabilities.[4]

The past several decades have seen a succession of federal, state, and local laws and regulations which require that children with disabilities be included in regular education settings. The landmark Education for All Handicapped Children Act of 1975 (P.L. 94-142), more recently amended and reauthorized as the Individuals with Disabilities Act (IDEA), calls for a "free and appropriate public education" in the "least restrictive environment" for children with disabilities. And the Americans with Disabilities Act (ADA) of 1990 extends the principles of non-discrimination to a wide variety of other settings with respect to people with disabilities, including school-age programs.

These legal provisions reflect the importance of "supplementary aids and services" (e.g., classroom aides, consultations, or resource services) to achieve the inclusion of children with disabilities in regular programs. The law requires state and local regulations to ensure that staff "are provided with the technical assistance and training necessary to assist them in this effort" (Individuals with Disabilities Education Act 1991). You should always seek the advice of specialists when addressing needs that may be beyond your expertise or experience.

When successfully executed, the inclusion of children with disabilities in a school-age program can be a very rewarding experience for everyone involved. Inclusion provides an environment in which all children can succeed. It helps children with disabilities to gain independence and autonomy; enables all children to develop comfortable, fair relationships with others; and teaches all children to resist stereotypes, name calling, and overcoming other barriers when they appear. Children with disabilities are children first. They thrive in an environment that accepts differences and where adults strive to meet each child's individual needs. For more information on this Act, contact the Department of Justice Hotline in Washington, DC, at (202) 514-0301 (voice) or (202) 514-0381 (TDD), or the Child Care Law Center in San Francisco, California, at (415) 495-5498.

Applying Your Knowledge

In this learning activity you review your program's administrative policies and procedures for completing various kinds of reports. Then you complete a schedule indicating when these reports are due and what your responsibilities are with regard to completing them. Begin by reading the example of a report schedule on the next page.

---

[4]Adapted with permission from Toni S. Bickart, Judy R. Jablon, and Diane Trister Dodge, *Building the Primary Classroom* (Washington, DC: Teaching Strategies, Inc., and Portsmouth, NH: Heinemann, 1999), pp. 31-32.

Report Schedule
(Example)

Report	Staff Responsibility	Date Due
Observation and recordings	Record observations according to schedule	Review with team members on last Friday of each month
Attendance	Record attendance for group	Every Friday
Time sheet	Fill in hours worked each day	Every Friday
Supply requisition	Request consumable supplies when inventory is low	15th of each month
Annual leave request	Request leave	Two weeks prior to date for which leave is requested
Contagious disease exposure	Complete form when parent notifies staff of child's illness	By 6:00 p.m. on the day parent notifies me of illness
Inventory	Record quantities of equipment, toys, and consumable supplies	May 30

Report Schedule

After reviewing your program's policies and procedures, list below the reports required, staff responsibilities for completing them, and when they are due.

Report	Staff Responsibility	Date Due

Discuss this schedule with your trainer. If you need additional space, duplicate this form. Review and follow your program's administrative policies and procedures throughout the year.

SUMMARIZING YOUR PROGRESS

You have now completed all the learning activities for this module. Whether you are an experienced school-age staff member or a new one, this module has probably helped you develop new managerial skills. Before you go on, take a few minutes to summarize what you've learned.

- Turn back to Learning Activity II, Individualizing Your Program. Review the recordings completed for the children in your group. Why are they examples of objective and accurate recordings? How did you use this information to individualize the program for these children? How did you use this information in your weekly plans?

_____

_____

_____

- Next, review your responses to the pre-training assessment for this module. Write a summary of what you learned, and list the skills you developed or improved.

_____

_____

_____

_____

_____

_____

_____

_____

If there are topics you would like to learn more about, you will find recommended readings listed in the Orientation in Volume I.

Your final step in this module is to complete the knowledge and competency assessments. Let your trainer know when you are ready to schedule the assessments. After you have successfully completed them, you will be ready to start a new module. Congratulations on your progress so far, and good luck with your next module.

ANSWER SHEETS

Being an Effective Manager

Observing and Recording Information About Each Child's Growth and Development

1. **How did Mr. Munson use a regular activity to gather objective and accurate information about Graham?**

   He recorded what Graham did and said during an experiment at the science table.

2. **What did Mr. Munson learn about Graham?**

   a. He likes to experiment.

   b. He can use his discoveries to make choices and decisions.

   c. He understands cause and effect.

   d. He can solve problems.

   e. He is independent and resourceful.

   f. He likes to make up tunes.

   g. He likes to talk about what he learns.

Working as a Member of a Team to Plan an Individualized Program

1. **How did Ms. Wang and the staff use a team approach to planning?**

   a. Ms. Wang asked staff members to gather information about how children use the quiet area.

   b. Staff collected information through observations and conversations with children and parents.

2. **How will the staff use the information they collected to plan an individualized program?**

   a. They will repair or replace the headphones so Telma and other children can listen to music.

   b. They will provide homework supplies needed by children such as Darnell.

   c. They will involve the older children in selecting new magazines that will address their interests.

1. **How does Ms. Jacobs stay informed about administrative policies and procedures?**

   a. She reviewed a chapter in the Staff Handbook and read the Volunteer Handbook.

   b. She discussed certain procedures with a colleague.

2. **What tasks did Ms. Jacobs complete according to the program's policies?**

   She met with the new volunteer to discuss the kinds of activities he might want to lead and to review policies on the role of volunteers at the program.

Following Administrative Policies, Practices, and Procedures

GLOSSARY

Administrative policies and procedures
Written descriptions of the program's systems for operations and the steps involved in completing all tasks.

Colleagues
The staff members with whom you work in the school-age program.

Individualized program
A program in which the environment, materials, activities, and interactions with children are suited to each child's interests, skills, and needs.

Objective recordings
Written information that includes only the facts about behaviors seen and heard.

Systematic observation
Consistent watching, listening to, and recording of what children say and do, according to a particular method.

Module 13:

PROFESSIONALISM

OVERVIEW

MAINTAINING A COMMITMENT TO PROFESSIONALISM MEANS:

- continually assessing one's own performance;

- continuing to learn about school-age children; and

- applying professional ethics at all times.

A professional is a person who uses specialized knowledge and skills to do a job or provide a service. As someone who guides the growth and learning of children during out-of-school hours, you are a member of an important profession. You work with children during the years when they are increasingly interested in exploring the world beyond home and family. You help them master new skills; learn to solve problems; build relationships with others; develop creativity; and become resourceful, responsible, and independent individuals. The care and guidance you provide affects how children feel about themselves. These experiences enable children to see themselves as competent individuals. They are then more likely to make good decisions and succeed in life.

School-age staff provide professional services.

Professionalism means applying what you know about school-age children to offer a diverse program of activities. Professionals take advantage of opportunities to learn more about children and to develop and continually improve new skills. They continually assess their work and are open to fresh ideas and new perspectives.

Professionals continue to learn and develop new skills.

As a professional in a school-age program, your role includes supporting families. When parents have confidence in the reliable, high-quality care you and your colleagues provide, they can feel better about themselves as parents. Their own job performance is also improved, because they know their children are participating in a safe, interesting, and challenging school-age program. And the information and insights you share with parents promote a sense of teamwork.

When you need a service (such as medical or legal advice, electrical repairs), you look for a professional business or individual who can meet your needs. You choose professionals because you want:

- the needed service;

- specialized knowledge;

- a commitment to quality;

- dependability; and

- effectiveness.

In all these areas, staff of school-age programs make unique professional contributions. They provide:

- the needed service—a high-quality out-of-school program;

- specialized knowledge—an understanding of what school-age children are like and how to meet their needs appropriately;

- a commitment to quality—a developmentally appropriate program in a safe and healthy environment;

- dependability—service on a regular basis; and

- effectiveness—a program that helps children learn more about the world, explore special interests, develop self-discipline, become independent, and gain lifelong skills.

Stages of Professional Development.[1]

Lilian Katz, an early childhood educator, has studied how teachers grow professionally. Her research suggests they pass through four different stages of professional development, each of which is briefly described below. Although you are not in the traditional role of a teacher, it is likely these stages apply to your professional development, too.

Stage One: Survival

Staff are new and often insecure. They devote most of their attention to learning the program's routines and performing tasks as assigned. If you are at this stage, you may have these feelings. Orientation, training, and experience will help you move to Stage Two, **consolidation.**

[1] Based on Lilian G. Katz, *Talks with Teachers of Young Children, A Collection* (Norwood, NJ: Ablex, 1995).

Stage Two: Consolidation

Staff become more confident and begin to look beyond simply completing the daily routines. They seek new ways to accomplish routine tasks and to handle problems. If you are at this stage, you will find it useful to exchange ideas with other school-age professionals, for example, at conferences and workshops. Conversations, staff meetings, training sessions, and open discussions will help you grow and move to Stage Three, **renewal.**

Stage Three: Renewal

After a year or two on the job, staff may begin to be bored with the day's routines. Their interest and enthusiasm may fall. If you are at this stage you may need new challenges. Try to attend conferences and workshops, participate in professional organizations, or pursue a special interest. These professional activities will provide needed stimulation and help you move to Stage Four, **maturity.**

Stage Four: Maturity

Staff at this stage are committed professionals. They understand the need to seek new ideas and skills and continue to grow professionally. If you are a mature school-age professional, you can be a model for new staff. You might also seek new challenges as a director or trainer.

You are part of a profession that requires many different kinds of skills. In your work you fulfill the roles of educator, child development specialist, recreation leader, health care advisor, and nutritionist. Your work is important to the children you care for, their families, and the community.

Maintaining a commitment to professionalism has several positive results. First, it builds your self-esteem. You feel proud when you learn new skills, acquire knowledge, and become more competent. The sense of success you experience as you become a competent school-age professional builds confidence and is rewarding and fulfilling.

Second, when you provide a professional program, you are helping children grow, learn, and develop to their full potential. And third, your professional behavior helps the field of school-age care. As you and your colleagues provide a high-quality program for children, you build respect for the profession, which can result in more recognition and support for the important service you provide.

Listed on the following pages are examples of how school-age staff maintain a commitment to professionalism.

Continually Assessing One's Own Performance

Identify areas where their own performance could be improved. "I've tried several strategies to help Jason express his feelings with words, instead of his fists, but they're not working. Maybe this article will give me some new ideas."

Review their own performance against written procedures and guidelines. "I know I should never leave the children unsupervised. I'll wait until Mr. Tansky returns before I go to the supply room."

Identify and apply their unique skills and experiences to their work. "I really enjoy my volunteer work at the animal shelter. I think I'll ask the children if they're interested in volunteering there, too."

Use professional standards as guides for providing high-quality care. "This publication describes the elements of a high-quality school-age program. We can use it to evaluate our program and to plan improvements."

Continuing to Learn About School-Age Children

Participate in professional organizations and training activities. "I'm going to attend this conference to learn more about how to meet individual needs in a group setting."

Keep current about procedures and guidelines concerning school-age children.

Read books and articles to keep informed about new programming ideas for school-age children. "I'd like to attend that workshop on community service opportunities for school-age children. Several children have expressed interest in volunteering."

Apply knowledge and skills on the job. "Helping Julie make friends was much easier after I read the article on building positive group interaction. The ideas in the article really worked."

Talk with and observe colleagues to learn more about working with school-age children. "I've arranged to observe how Ms. Baker runs a group meeting because I can't seem to keep my group together like she does."

Develop and follow short- and long-range plans for professional development. "I'm planning to finish this module by the end of the month. I'll finish all thirteen by the end of the year."

Maintain accurate, confidential records and keep information about children and their families confidential. "The files we keep on each child are confidential, Mrs. Gomez. Rudolpho's file will be kept in our locked cabinet. Only the program staff, you, and your husband are allowed to read his file."

Are honest, dependable and reliable in performing their duties and responsibilities. "Boy, I'm tired this morning, but I won't call in sick because I know the children are really looking forward to the Drama Club we're starting today."

Treat each child as an individual and show no bias because of culture, background, abilities, or gender. "Billy and Robert, you have been using the woodworking area for quite a while. Marcia wants to make a birdhouse, too, and it looks like there's room for all of you. Would you please share the tools with her?"

Speak out against practices that are not developmentally appropriate. "We don't want to force Sam to play softball if he doesn't want to. Many children prefer games that are less competitive."

Stand up for parts of the program they believe are appropriate for the children. "Mr. Davis, having the chance to make some choices about what she would like to do is important to Sarah. It allows her to explore and work on things that interest her and helps her develop a sense of responsibility for her own actions."

Support other staff when they need assistance. "I'd be happy to help you work with the older children to set up an area they can use as a stage, Mr. Bailey. Just let me know when you're ready."

Support parents and treat them with respect at all times. "You're right, it does seem like only yesterday that Kelley first started in the program. I think she may be ready for some more independence at the program and at home."

Model positive language and communication skills. "Spending every day with school-age children makes it hard not to pick up their slang. I try to model standard vocabulary, however, so they'll hear the language they're likely to use when they are adults."

Dress appropriately for the job. "I brought my boots so I could go outside with the children who want to go sledding."

Take care of their own physical, emotional, social, and intellectual needs. "Tonight I'm having dinner with a close friend. I always feel energized after being with her."

Applying Professional Ethics at All Times

377

Maintaining a Commitment to Professionalism

In the following situations school-age staff are maintaining a commitment to professionalism. As you read them, think about what the staff are doing and why. Then answer the questions that follow.

Continually Assessing One's Own Performance

As Ms. Chavez watches the children get on the school bus, ten-year old Julie pushes past Luther, a first-grader. Julie yells to her friends, "Save me a seat." Her push makes Luther lose his balance and step on Demian's foot. Ms. Chavez reacts without thinking. She gets on the bus yelling, "Julie, you're the most inconsiderate child I've ever seen. Get off the bus and go to the end of the line." The other children stare as Julie walks down the aisle. Ms. Chavez continues shouting. "You'll wait like everyone else. I'm sick and tired of you picking on younger children." By the time the bus leaves Ms. Chavez is hoarse and has a headache. She walks back inside, thinking to herself, "I really handled that poorly. Julie was out of line, but so was I. My response was out of control!" Knowing it won't help to feel sorry for herself, Ms. Chavez sits down to reflect on the situation. She says to herself, "Tomorrow I will apologize to Julie and the rest of the children. I'll make it clear that her behavior was inappropriate; but I'll also tell her I'm sorry I lost control." Ms. Chavez's reflections lead to several conclusions. She writes them down, along with her plans for change: "I'm tired at work because I don't get enough sleep. It's very late by the time I cook dinner, help Aseem with his homework, and get to bed. I will call a family meeting to talk about reorganizing our evenings so I'm not up so late. Also, as the youngest in my family, I was picked on frequently, so I'm very sensitive when I see similar behaviors. In the future, when older children are unkind to the younger ones, I'll use positive guidance to help children learn to treat each other with respect."

1. How did Ms. Chavez assess her own performance?

_____

_____

_____

_____

2. What did she decide to do with the results of her assessment?

_____

_____

_____

_____

Mr. Sullivan completes a self-assessment for school-age professionals, then meets with his supervisor, Ms. Abrams, to identify three areas where he could improve his skills. They discuss what might be reasonable goals. Mr. Sullivan decides to review a module on guidance (one of the three areas) during the following month and attend the in-service training session on the same topic. Ms. Abrams schedules a time to observe and offer suggestions for improving the way he provides guidance to children. They plan to meet again in a month to discuss progress on the plan and how Mr. Sullivan's skills improved.

Continuing to Learn About School-Age Children

1. How did Mr. Sullivan decide what knowledge and skills he should work to improve?

_____

_____

_____

_____

2. How did Mr. Sullivan plan to expand his existing knowledge and skills?

_____

_____

_____

_____

Applying Professional Ethics at All Times

Ms. Perkins arrives to pick up her child, Danny, at the end of the day. As she walks in, she glances disapprovingly at Billy, one of the children playing with her son. In a loud voice, she declares, "I've seen Billy wearing that old sweatshirt every day this week." Ms. Johnson walks over to Billy, puts her arm around his shoulder, and says, "This sweatshirt is Billy's favorite. It feels comfortable, like an old friend." Then Ms. Johnson turns to Ms. Perkins and says, "Ms. Perkins, come on over here for a minute and let me tell you about Danny's day."

1. How did Ms. Johnson maintain professional ethics in talking to Danny's mother?

_____

_____

_____

_____

2. How did Ms. Johnson interact with Billy in a positive manner?

_____

_____

_____

_____

Compare your answers with those on the answer sheet at the end of this module. If your answers are different, discuss them with your trainer. There may be more than one good answer.

School-Age Care and You

Each school-age professional, just like each child, is a unique person with special interests and strengths. You bring your own interests and skills to your profession, and you share them with the children in the program. Whether a person shares a love of music or a love of the outdoors, the children pick up on his or her enthusiasm and learn to appreciate something new. By using special interests on the job, you can make your work more satisfying and fun.

You also bring your unique personal style to your work. Some staff have boundless physical energy; others are calm and easygoing. Both styles are valuable. The important thing is to look at your own personal style and consider how it affects your interactions with the children in the program.

What are your special abilities and interests? What do you most enjoy? Which personal qualities enhance your work as a school-age professional? Which ones sometimes make your work more difficult? What do you like best about your job? What would you like to change? These are questions school-age professionals can ask themselves to identify what makes them unique and what special qualities they bring to the profession.

The reading that begins on the following page will help you think about yourself and the reasons why you became a school-age professional.

Each person has special interests and abilities.

Being Curious About Yourself[2]

Who are you? What do you care about? Why are you here? What interests you about school-age children? What gives you pleasure in being with them? Which of your interests do you enjoy sharing with them? How do you use your talents to contribute to their growth and development? What are your goals for them?

Does all this seem obvious—of course you know about yourself? In fact, most of us keep growing in self-understanding, and we learn in the same way we learn about other people—by observing ourselves and reflecting on our observations. Why did I get so mad when Kim accidentally turned up the volume on the stereo? Did it trigger something in me that had little to do with what happened? Why do I find it so hard to like Kim? I catch myself being almost mean to her—sarcastic, in a way that just isn't appropriate for someone who works with children. Why do I do that?

Sometimes a friend or colleague can help us think through our self-observations if we're willing to share them. It can be uncomfortable, learning more about ourselves, especially about the parts of ourselves we really don't like. Some people seek counseling to get help with this process. They want someone to listen thoughtfully to their question about themselves.

What do you like to do with children? Sing, cook, play sports and games, help them develop new skills and discover their talents, listen and talk with them about their ideas and concerns, watch them play and explore new interests, provide help and encouragement when they have problems? Do you get to do what you like to do on your job? If not, could you? As you spend each day with children, it's important to have many opportunities to make decisions, to say, "This is what I want to do next." Not at the children's expense, but in response to both your needs and theirs. If staff are contented and growing, children are more likely to be contented and growing, too.

Which describes you better: You like nurturing children; you like teaching children; you like playing with children? Competence in working with school-age children may be based on any of these preferences. Nurturing is being responsible, taking good care of children, appreciating their growth; if you're experienced as a parent, that may be the role you fall into naturally in this field. Teaching implies particular interest in children's thinking and problem solving, in what they know and understand—and in helping them learn. Playing with children implies being in touch with the child in yourself.

What kind of learner are you? How do you learn best? People learn in different ways—by reading, taking classes, observing children's behavior, discussing their experiences with colleagues and friends, going to conferences and workshops, trying things for themselves and seeing what happens. Which of these things work for you? Does your program encourage you to keep learning and give you credit for what you do? A school-age program is a *living place* for children and adults. It should be a good place to live together and learn about the world. What are you learning at your work? How are you continuing to grow? What risks are you taking?

---

[2] Adapted with permission from Elizabeth Jones, "The Elephant's Child as Caregiver," *Beginnings* (Redmond, WA: Exchange Press, 1986), p. 10.

Taking a Look at Yourself

Think about how you feel about your work. Take time to consider what you really want to say. Reflection is an important part of being a professional.

Now answer the questions that follow.

I think I'm really good at:

_____

_____

_____

_____

I really enjoy:

_____

_____

_____

_____

I can share my interests and skills with children in the following ways:

_____

_____

_____

_____

What I find most difficult about my work is:

_____

_____

_____

_____

I would like to be better at:

_____

_____

_____

_____

I would like to know more about:

_____

_____

_____

_____

Discuss your responses with two colleagues. Have they learned anything new about you? Do they see things you did not see? Use the space below to write what you learned from reflecting on your role as a school-age professional.

_____

_____

_____

_____

_____

_____

_____

_____

_____

_____

_____

_____

_____

_____

_____

_____

_____

When you have finished this overview section, you should complete the pre-training assessment. Refer to the glossary at the end of the module if you need definitions for the terms used.

PRE-TRAINING ASSESSMENT

Listed below are the skills school-age staff use to maintain their commitment to professionalism. Think about whether you do these things regularly, sometimes, or not enough. Place a check in one of the boxes on the right for each skill listed. Then, discuss your answers with your trainer.

I Do This

Continually Assessing One's Own Performance

	Regularly	Sometimes	Not Enough
1. Identifying areas where performance needs improvement.	☐	☐	☐
2. Reviewing performance against written procedures and guidelines.	☐	☐	☐
3. Identifying and applying personal skills and experiences in working with school-age children.	☐	☐	☐
4. Using professional standards as guides for providing high-quality care.	☐	☐	☐

Continuing to Learn About School-Age Children

5. Joining and participating in professional organizations and training activities for school-age staff.	☐	☐	☐
6. Reading books or articles on child development and appropriate programming for school-age children.	☐	☐	☐
7. Talking with and observing colleagues to learn more about working with school-age children.	☐	☐	☐
8. Applying knowledge and skills on the job.	☐	☐	☐
9. Keeping current about procedures and guidelines concerning school-age children.	☐	☐	☐
10. Developing and following short- and long-range plans for professional development.	☐	☐	☐

Applying Professional Ethics At All Times

	I Do This		
	Regularly	Sometimes	Not Enough

12. Maintaining accurate records and keeping information about children and their families confidential. ☐ ☐ ☐

13. Carrying out duties in an honest, dependable, and reliable way. ☐ ☐ ☐

14. Speaking out against practices that are not appropriate. ☐ ☐ ☐

15. Supporting program practices that are developmentally appropriate for school-age children. ☐ ☐ ☐

16. Showing no personal bias against any child enrolled in the program. ☐ ☐ ☐

17. Supporting colleagues when they need assistance. ☐ ☐ ☐

18. Supporting parents and treating them with respect at all times. ☐ ☐ ☐

19. Modeling positive language and communication skills. ☐ ☐ ☐

20. Dressing appropriately for the job. ☐ ☐ ☐

21. Taking care of your own physical, emotional, social, and intellectual needs. ☐ ☐ ☐

Review your responses, then list three to five skills you would like to improve or topics you would like to learn more about. When you finish this module, you can list examples of your new or improved knowledge and skills.

_____

_____

_____

_____

_____

Begin the learning activities for Module 13, Professionalism.

LEARNING ACTIVITIES

Learning Activity I.
Assessing Yourself

IN THIS ACTIVITY YOU WILL LEARN TO:

- recognize your own skills and abilities; and

- use national standards for quality school-age care to assess your own competence.

Every profession sets standards for performance. Your program has written statements of its philosophy, policies, and procedures. You should become familiar with these statements. These standards are not meant to restrict you, but rather to serve as guides. In using them, you, your colleagues, families, and children can confirm you are providing high-quality care.

The National School-Age Care Alliance and the National Institute on Out-of-School Time (NIOST) developed the *NSACA Standards for Quality School-Age Care*. The *Standards* are based on the self-study and improvement process, Advancing School-Age Quality (ASQ) developed by Susan O'Connor from NIOST. The new standards are the criteria used for NSACA's program improvement and accreditation system, the Advancing and Recognizing Quality (ARQ) System.

This training program allows school-age staff to gain the skills needed to plan and implement a program that meets the *NSACA Standards*. The *Standards* outline 36 keys of quality, organized under six categories.

1. **Human relationships** are addressed in all Modules, with extensive coverage in Module 7, Creative, Module 8, Self, Module 9, Social, Module 10, Guidance, Module 11, Families, and Module 12, Program Management.

2. **Indoor environment** is addressed in Module 3, Program Environment.

3. **Outdoor environment** is addressed in Module 3, Program Environment

4. **Activities** are addressed in Module 4, Physical, Module 5, Cognitive, Module 6, Communication, Module 7, Creative, and Module 12, Program Management,

Standards for Quality School-Age Programs

This training program supports the *NSACA Standards*.

There are three steps in the ARQ system.

5. **Safety, health, and nutrition** are addressed in Module 1, Safe, and Module 2, Healthy.

6. **Administration** is addressed in Modules 12, Program Management and 13, Professionalism.

Programs using the ARQ system complete the following three steps:

- **Determine readiness:** Review the *NSACA Standards*, discuss current program practices, focus on targeted improvements, and decide whether the program is ready for the full self-study process.

- **Complete the self-study:** Form a self-study team with families, children, staff, and the host of the program; review the results of surveys completed by children, families, staff, the director, and the host; observe program operations; summarize strengths and needs and set goals for improvement; and implement plans and review progress.

- **Seek accreditation:** Submit a self-study summary, program description, and fee to NSACA; open the program to two NSACA Endorsers who use the *NSACA Standards* to rate the program; receive accreditation, if criteria are met, along with a program report of strengths and areas for continued improvement.

Programs seeking accreditation can order a program improvement and accreditation kit from NSACA. Each kit includes manuals, agendas, questionnaires, a poster, and a video.

You can review all of the *NSACA Standards* at their web site—www.nsaca.org—or order a copy from the National School-Age Care Alliance, 1137 Washington Street, Boston, MA 02124. Reviewing the *Standards* and completing the pre-training assessments for each module should give you a comprehensive picture of your skills and capabilities. This review will also help you identify areas you need to know more about and skills you need to develop or improve.

Applying Your Knowledge

In this learning activity you read excerpts from the *NSACA Standards for Quality School-Age Care*. Next you discuss with a colleague how the standards apply to your program and your roles as school-age professionals.

NSACA Standards for Human Relationships

1. Staff relate to all children and youth in positive ways.

a) Staff treat children with respect and listen to what they say.

b) Staff make children feel welcome and comfortable.

c) Staff respond to children with acceptance and appreciation.

d) Staff are engaged with children.

2. Staff respond appropriately to individual needs of children and youth.

a) Staff know that each child has special interests and talents

b) Staff recognize the range of children's abilities.

c) Staff can relate to a child's cultural style & primary language

d) Staff respond to the range of children's feelings and temperaments.

3. Staff encourage children and youth to make choices and to become more responsible.

a) Staff offer assistance in a way that supports a child's initiative.

b) Staff assist children without taking control, and they encourage children to take leadership roles.

c) Staff give children many chances to choose what they will do, how they will do it, and with whom.

d) Staff help children make informed and responsible choices.

4. Staff interact with children and youth to help them learn.

a) Staff ask questions that encourage children to think for themselves.

b) Staff share skills and resources to help children gain information and solve problems.

c) Staff vary the approaches they use to help children learn.

d) Staff help children use language skills through frequent conversations.

NSACA Standards for Human Relationships: Discussion

Which *NSACA Standards* for human relationships are met by your program?

_____
_____
_____
_____
_____
_____
_____
_____

Which *NSACA Standards* for human relationships are not met by your program?

_____
_____
_____
_____
_____
_____
_____
_____

What can you and your colleagues do to improve human relationships in your program?

_____
_____
_____
_____
_____
_____
_____
_____

Meet with your trainer to discuss ways to implement the suggestions developed by you and your colleagues.

Learning Activity II.
Continuing to Learn About Working With School-Age Children

IN THIS ACTIVITY YOU WILL LEARN TO:

- continue to expand your knowledge and skills; and

- make short-and long-range professional development plans.

No matter how many years you've worked with school-age children or how much you already know, it is important to continue to learn more about your profession. This is true for a number of reasons.

Continual learning has many benefits.

There is always new information to be learned. All professionals need to keep up with the latest developments in their fields. Research and experience often lead to new, more effective strategies for working with children. Learning and growth are ongoing for the school-age professional.

Continual learning makes you an active, thinking person. School-age staff who are always learning new things are more interesting people. They have new ideas to bring to the program to inspire children. If you enjoy learning, you probably help children enjoy learning, too.

You care about children. Each article or book you read, every discussion you participate in, and every conference you attend, gives you new insights or helps you resolve nagging problems. Because you care about all children, you are always alert for new and helpful information relating to their development. Suppose, for example, a child with a disability joins your group. You may seek to learn new ways to include this child in the program's activities.

You want to grow professionally. A commitment to continue learning can lead to improved performance. Learning results in a greater confidence and may also lead to more responsibility, a promotion, and a salary increase.

Continual learning is affirming. You may rediscover ideas you'd tucked away. The process of learning tends to affirm the good work you've been doing and the knowledge you already have.

There are many ways to continue learning.

How can you continue growing and learning professionally? In addition to participating in this training program for school-age staff, there are many other ways you can continue learning. You might:

- join professional organizations;

- read books and articles;

- use the Internet;

- network with other professionals in the field;

- observe colleagues in action; and

- take advantage of training opportunities.

NSACA is your professional organization.

The National School-Age Care Alliance (NSACA) represents all of the public, private, and community-based organizations and individuals involved in out-of-school programs for children and youth. The mission of the alliance is to "build a profession that develops, supports, and promotes quality school-age care." NSACA is a voice for over 8,000 members—school-age policy-makers, directors, trainers, practitioners, and advocates—of 35 affiliates in 50 states.

As described in Learning Activity 1, NSACA, in conjunction with the National Institute on Out-of-School Time (NIOST), has developed and implemented the *NSACA Standards for Quality School-Age Care* and a system for school-age program improvement and accreditation, *Advancing and Recognizing Quality (ARQ)*. Programs in 36 states and overseas have completed the ARQ process and received NSACA accreditation.

NSACA holds an annual training conference and publishes a professional journal, *School-Age Review*. The journal features reports on research, articles on successful strategies for school-age staff, and reviews of books, media, computer software, and other resources. For more information, contact NSACA at::

National School-Age Care Alliance
1137 Washington Street
Boston, MA 02124
(617) 298-5012
www.nsaca.org

The following are other organizations that address issues of interest to school-age professionals.

Association for Childhood Education International (ACEI) *Latasha*
17904 Georgia Avenue, Suite 215
Olney, MD 20832
(800) 423-3563
~~www.udel.edu/bateman/acei~~ *www.acei.org*

ACEI, established in 1892, is represented in all 50 states and in many nations abroad. The association addresses the care and education of children from birth through adolescence. There is a separate division for Later Childhood/Early Adolescence. Publications include a newsletter, research journal, and numerous books. ACEI holds an annual national conference.

Center for the Child Care Workforce *Jimmy*
733 15th Street, NW, Suite 1037
Washington, DC 20005-2112
(202) 737-7700
www.ccw.org

This nonprofit advocacy organization, formerly the Child Care Employee Project, works to improve the wages, status, and working conditions of child care professionals. Organized in 1977 by child care workers, the center provides assistance to child care providers, parents, policymakers, and the media on issues that affect the child care workforce. A quarterly newsletter and a variety of materials on child care employee issues are available.

The Center for Youth Development and Policy Research *Armelis*
Academy for Educational Development
1825 Connecticut Avenue, N.W.
Washington, DC 20009-5721
(202) 884-8000
www.aed.org/us/cyd

Through a variety of initiatives and publications, the work of this organization is focused on youth development. Their goals include promoting good practice, increasing opportunities for youth involvement, building a youth development infrastructure, and increasing public support for positive youth development for all young people. Their *Promising Practices Bank of After-School Programs* initiative hopes to create a process for identifying and sharing information about effective school-age programs.

Andria

National Association for the Education of Young Children (NAEYC)
1509 16th Street, NW
Washington, DC 20036-1426
(202) 232-8777 or (800) 424-2460
www.naeyc.org

With more than 90,000 members, NAEYC is the largest early childhood professional organization in this country, providing resources and support for meeting the needs of children from birth through age 8. NAEYC publishes *Young Children* (a journal of ideas, findings, and issues concerning children) and a variety of books, posters, and other media materials. Their annual national conference offers professional training on a range of topics, including a track devoted to school-age care. Conference attendees can meet other school-age professionals as well as writers and researchers on child care and child development. NAEYC has 360 affiliate groups working locally, statewide, and regionally on behalf of young children. The national headquarters can provide information on local affiliates.

Nancy

National Black Child Development Institute (NBCDI)
1023 15th Street, NW, Suite 600
Washington, DC 20005
(202) 387-1281
www.nbcdi.org

NBCDI advocates on behalf of the growth and development of African-American children. It organizes and trains networks of members to voice concerns regarding policies that affect children and their families. NBCDI sponsors an annual conference focused on critical issues in child care development, education, foster care and adoption, and health. NBCDI also publishes *Black Child Advocate,* a quarterly newsletter.

Lorena

National Community Education Association (NCEA)
3929 Old Lee Highway, Suite 91A
Fairfax, VA 22042
(703) 359-8973
www.ncea.com

This non-profit membership association advances the idea that the educational resources of a community should be available to learners of all ages and educational backgrounds. The organization supports community involvement in public education and interagency cooperation to meet the learning and human service needs of community residents. The association's quarterly publication, *Community Education Journal*, focuses on the exchange of ideas and practices in community education. Read selected articles on the web site. Forty state community education associations are affiliate members of NCEA.

National Institute on Out-of-School Time (NIOST)*
Center for Research on Women, Wellesley College
106 Central Street
Wellesley, MA 02481
(781) 283-2547
www.niost.org

Linda

Since 1979, this group has conducted research, designed educational programs and conferences, and provided consultation and technical assistance. Services are used by individuals concerned with school-age child care: parents, employers, school personnel, elected officials, policymakers, researchers, program directors, and school-age staff. The NIOST is a source of books, technical papers, and videos for school-age professionals. Project staff also lead training workshops and provide technical assistance on all aspects of school-age care.

National Intramural-Recreational Sports Association (NIRSA)
4185 SW Research Way
Corvallis, OR 97333-1067
(541) 766-8211
www.nirsa.org

Nicole

The National Intramural-Recreational Sports Association is a nonprofit professional organization dedicated to the establishment and development of high-quality recreational sports programs and services. Representing thousands of individuals and organizations, NIRSA serves as the leading advocate for excellence in recreational sports. NIRSA provides access to educational resource materials as well as a professional network. Ensuring that those involved in recreational sports remain up to date is a prime concern for NIRSA. Through professional support materials and sponsored projects, NIRSA enhances the quality of campus and community recreation.

National Latino Children's Institute (NLCI)
1412 West Sixth Street
Austin, TX 78703-5139
(512) 472-9971
www.nlci.org

Claudia

---

* Formerly the School-Age Child Care Project (SACCProject)

NLCI advocates for the welfare and healthy development of Latino children. The organization conducts public education campaigns on issues of importance to the well-being of Latino children. NLCI also has a resource center with materials and information.

National Recreation and Park Association (NRPA)
22377 Belmont Ridge Road
Ashburn, VA 20148
(703) 858-0784
www.nrpa.org

This nonprofit service, research, and educational organization has membership opportunities for professionals, volunteers, students, and organizations through branch, state, and regional organizations. Services and publications are offered according to the branch of membership. Branch affiliations include:

- National Student Recreation and Park Society

- National Therapeutic Recreation Society

- Society of Park and Recreation Educators

- American Park and Recreation Society

- National Society for Park Resources

- Armed Forced Recreation Society

- Citizen and/or Board Member

- National Aquatic Section

- Leisure and Aging Section

Books and articles can help you expand your knowledge and skills. The bibliography in the Orientation section of Volume I provides an extensive list of books and other resources for school-age staff. The public library may have these titles. Check in the adult and/or children's collections.

Get to Know Your Way Around the Internet

If you have access to the Internet at home, through your program, or at the local library, a world of information is just a mouse click away. Most of the school-age and youth serving organizations have web sites, as do publishers of resources for school-age staff. Educational television shows and museums have companion web sites. Government agencies such as the Department of Education, the Department of Health and Human Services, and the Office of Juvenile Justice and Delinquency share publications for children, staff, and families on line. In addition, government-sponsored clearinghouses and projects offer research reports and practical strategies on line. Not to mention, every site has links to other sites, making on line sources of information virtually unlimited. If you are a novice, you will find helpful guidance on learning to use the Internet at the Community Learning Networks web site, **www.cln.org/guidebooks.html**. When you enter a site, go to the site map, which serves as a "table of contents."

Below are a few examples of useful sites for school-age staff.

You will find useful information at these web sites.

California Collaborative After-School/School-Age Project (www.gse.uci.edu/schoolage)
Sponsored by the California Department of Education, this site includes resources, online training videos and virtual reality cases, news, list serves, a chat room, and links to sites for recreation and learning activities, child and adolescent development, substance abuse prevention, and more.

National Network for Child Care (www.nncc.org/SACC/sacc.page.html)
Sponsored by the Cooperative Extension Service, this site includes a collection of articles on topics of interest to school-age staff and program directors.

Federal Support to Communities Initiative (www.afterschool.gov)
Sponsored by the domestic Cabinet secretaries, this initiative supports the federal government in finding ways to better support community youth development and after school programs. The web site includes a data base of over 100 federal grant and loan programs, community success stories, links to guides, reports, and research, and safe, fun, and educational web sites for children and youth.

Connect For Kids (www.connectforkids.com)
Published by the Benton Foundation, this site is dedicated to making communities better places for children and youth. The "Features" area includes a section on Out-of-School Time where school-age staff can find general information and library, sports and recreation, and summer resources. Users can subscribe to weekly and monthly newsletters delivered to their e-mail addresses.

Networking is a way to share ideas and get support.

Networking is spending time with people who perform similar tasks to share ideas, information, and experiences. It is a good way to identify solutions to problems, gain new knowledge, or help colleagues cope with difficult situations. You can network with one other person or with a group. Group networks can include other school-age professionals at the local and state levels. Meetings can be very informal or formal as desired. What is important is that school-age staff have opportunities to meet, share ideas, and get support in coping with the demands of their jobs.

Observe colleagues in action to gain a new perspective.

You can learn a lot by observing a colleague, a supervisor, or someone in another program. Because each person is unique, you can learn new approaches to solving discipline problems, implementing a multi-age activity, or making effective use of shared space. Colleagues and other professionals also may have interesting new ideas for activities and programs.

Participate in training on topics related to your job.

Training is a good way to keep up to date and develop new skills. As you complete each module in this training program, your knowledge of the characteristics of school-age children and how to work effectively with them will grow.

In addition, you can attend courses offered by community groups. Training workshops or conferences may also be available in your area through federal, state, or local funding. Often these training programs are administered by the local or state office of the Department of Social Services, an Office on Child Care Services, a County Extension Office, or other government agencies. In many areas community colleges offer certificate programs for school-age professionals. For example, Concordia College in Moorehead, Minnesota, offers undergraduate and graduate degrees in school-age care. Individual courses at colleges and universities may also be an option.

Planning for Continual Learning

In addition to identifying resources to help you learn more about school-age care, you need to plan how and when to use those resources. When you develop a plan, you clarify what you want to achieve—your goal—and how you will go about achieving it. With a written plan in front of you, you feel like you're already making progress. And you are! Knowing where you're going and how you're going to get there makes it easier to take each step and to recognize your goal when you reach it. As you complete each step and check it off your plan, you know you are moving closer to your goal.

You can continue to improve your skills in the following ways:

- Take advantage of opportunities to attend workshops and training offered by your program or other groups.

- Use other colleagues as resources and offer yourself to them as a resource.

- Consult your supervisor about theoretical issues and practical concerns.

- Seek information from national or regional school-age care, youth development, and recreation groups.

- Review how you manage your time. If you look closely at what you do each day, you may find some time-wasting activities. Doing things faster or better may leave extra time for reading, studying, and reflecting on how the day went.

- Set specific goals for yourself. Try to do something on a regular basis to fulfill them.

Applying Your Knowledge

There are two parts to this learning activity. Begin by reviewing your answers to "Taking a Look at Yourself" in the overview section of this module. Pick one item from your responses to "I would like to be better at" or "I would like to know more about." Consider the sources of assistance available to you: the public library, workshops, professional organizations, your supervisor, and other colleagues. Identify specific resources to help you with the task or topic you selected. List what you find on the chart that follows.

Taking Another Look at Yourself

I want to improve or learn more about:

_____

_____

_____

_____

_____

Resources I can use:

Source	Contact Person
Public library	
Internet	
Professional organizations	
Trainer/colleagues	

The chart you just completed helped you think about resources that are readily available to you. Next, use this information to make short- and long-range plans for professional development, identify possible barriers to reaching your goals, and plan ways to overcome them. For the short term you might focus on areas you think most need improving. For the long term you could build on an area of strength and become even more skilled. Read the example on the following page, and complete the chart that follows.

Plans for Professional Development
(Example)

Short-Range Plan

What would I like to do right away to improve my skills?

Research conflict resolution on the Internet.

Learn more activities children can do outdoors, in addition to sports and games.

Complete Module 7, Creative.

What barriers might hinder me from completing these plans?

It's hard to find time to complete the learning activities and still care for children.

If I'm the only one who knows about conflict resolution, it will be difficult to implement it in our program.

What can I do to overcome these barriers?

I can talk with other staff about trading some responsibilities so we can all have more time to work on the learning activities.

I'll talk to other staff members and try to get them to join me in taking the workshop.

Long-Range Plan

What would I like to be doing a year from now?

Begin work on a degree in child care administration.

Join one professional organization.

Complete the school-age modules.

What barriers might hinder me from completing these plans?

I have no time to attend school.

I can't afford to pay tuition.

What can I do to overcome these barriers?

I can take one or two courses at a time rather than a full load.

I can find out about student loans and scholarships, and I can check with local training agencies about other ways to take for-credit courses.

Plans for Professional Development

Short-Range Plan

What would I like to do right away to improve my skills?

_____

_____

_____

_____

_____

What barriers might hinder me from completing these plans?

_____

_____

_____

_____

_____

What can I do to overcome these barriers?

_____

_____

_____

_____

_____

Long-Range Plan

What would I like to be doing a year from now?

_____
_____
_____
_____
_____

What barriers might hinder me from completing these plans?

_____
_____
_____
_____
_____

What can I do to overcome these barriers?

_____
_____
_____
_____

Discuss your plans with your trainer. What barriers can you overcome? Agree on an overall plan to achieve your short- and long-term goals.

Learning Activity III.
Applying Professional Ethics at All Times

IN THIS ACTIVITY YOU WILL LEARN TO:

- follow the ethics of the school-age profession; and

- identify examples of professional and unprofessional behavior.

Professionals do what is right rather than what is easy.

As discussed in Learning Activities I and II, being a professional involves assessing one's knowledge and skills and continually building on them. But professionalism is more than having expertise. It has to do with how you apply your knowledge and skills daily as you work with parents, children, and staff. It means doing your job to the best of your ability. And it includes your actions in the program setting and in the community.

Ethics are the principals, standards, or guidelines that direct acceptable behavior. Professionals need to follow the ethics of their profession, rather than what is easy. Professionals are committed to doing what is best for all children under their supervision, on every occasion. Here are some examples.

Ethics of School-Age Care	Professional Behavior	Unprofessional Behavior
Maintaining confidentiality about children and their families. Not discussing children with parents other than their own. Restricting conversations to times when children are not present.	Discussing a child's problem confidentially with colleagues or the supervisor, and trying to identify ways to help the child. *"Ms. Kim, sometimes when Tommy loses his temper he's aggressive with the other children. Do you have any suggestions for helping him express his anger in acceptable ways?"*	Talking about a child in front of the child or with a parent other than the child's. *"Did you see what a wild temper Tommy has? I'm glad you're the kind of parent who disciplines her kids at home so they don't act up at the program."*
Being honest, dependable, and reliable in performing duties. Being regular in attendance and performance. Coming to work on time, returning from breaks on time, and performing duties on schedule.	Arriving at work every day on time and prepared to perform assigned duties. *"I'll be ready to go home after I finish wiping these tables."*	Paying more attention to adults than to children. Calling in sick unnecessarily, arriving late, or not doing assigned duties. *"You'll have to watch these kids yourself. I have to call my girlfriend so we can make plans for tonight."*

Ethics of School-Age Care	Professional Behavior	Unprofessional Behavior
Treating parents with respect even during difficult situations.	Talking to a parent who always comes late about the problem this causes and discussing possible solutions. *"Mrs. Lowell, our program closes at 6:30. If you can't get here by then, could someone else pick up Jennifer?"*	Getting angry at a parent who is late and demanding he or she do better. Talking to other parents or acquaintances about parents. *"This is the third time you've been late this week. I need to go home too you know!"*
Treating each child with respect regardless of gender, culture, or background. Treating each child as an individual; avoiding comparisons.	Comforting a child who is hurt or upset. Including activities and materials that reflect the cultures and backgrounds of all children. *"It's okay to cry if you are hurt. Do you want to tell me about it?"*	Teasing children if they cry. Asking one child to behave just like another child. *"You always get in a bad mood when your team doesn't win. Why can't you just smile and forget about it like Jim does?"*
Making sure activities, practices, and routines are developmentally appropriate.	Allowing children to participate in routines according to their personal schedules. *"Randy, I can see you are very involved in your project. Snack is set out on the counter. You can serve yourself when you're ready."*	Making all children do the same activities or routines on a strict schedule. *"I can't help it if you're not ready for snack yet, Sabrina. This is when snack is served. If you don't take some now, you'll have to be hungry later."*
Providing a good model for learning and for language and communication skills. Never using profanities in front of children.	Giving children clear directions that show respect for their activities. *"The interest areas will be ending in about ten minutes. It's time to begin cleaning up now."*	Speaking rudely to children, using harsh words and a negative tone. *"Didn't I say we can only spend 20 minutes on this activity? Get this room cleaned up. Now!"*

Ethics of School-Age Care	Professional Behavior	Unprofessional Behavior
Dressing to do the job. Being conscious of dress, grooming, and hygiene.	Wearing comfortable, clean clothes (ones you can sit on the floor in, bend and lift in, and move quickly in when necessary), so you can play with and care for children. *"I'm most comfortable in wide skirts or slacks that let me sit on the floor easily with the children."*	Wearing clothes that hinder movement and that you have to worry about. *"You'll have to ask Ms. Peterson to help you. I can't walk on the grass in these shoes."*
Recording information appropriately.	Keeping good records to aid in making accurate reports to parents. *"Lori's mother said she really likes our activity check-in system. It helps her find Lori quickly, and it gives her an idea of the kinds of things Lori has done this afternoon."*	Not taking the time to record needed information because it's too much trouble. *"No one ever reads accident reports. I'm just wasting my time filling one out."*
Advocating on behalf of children, families, self, and others. Letting others know the importance of child care work.	Joining a professional organization. *"I'm really glad I joined NSACA. Their newsletter really helps me stay in touch with new ideas in the field."*	Belittling the work of school-age staff as "only babysitting" or denying it is a profession. *"As soon as I can, I'm going to get out of this babysitter job and get a real one."*

Applying Your Knowledge

In this activity you list examples of how your professional behavior conforms to the ethics of high-quality school-age care. Then you read several case studies and write down what a professional would do.

Applying Professional Ethics

Ethics of School-Age Care	Examples of Your Own Professional Behavior
Maintaining confidentiality about children and their families. Refusing to discuss children with parents other than their own. Restricting conversations to times when children are not present.	
Being honest, dependable, and reliable in performing duties. Being regular in attendance and performance. Coming to work on time, returning from breaks on time, and performing duties on schedule.	
Treating parents with respect even during difficult situations.	
Treating each child with respect regardless of gender, culture, or background. Treating each child as an individual; avoiding comparisons.	
Making sure activities, practices, and routines are developmentally appropriate.	

Applying Professional Ethics
(continued)

Ethics of School-Age Care	Examples of Your Own Professional Behavior
Providing a good model for learning and for language and communication skills. Never using profanities in front of children.	
Dressing to do the job. Being conscious of dress, grooming, and hygiene.	
Recording information appropriately.	
Advocating on behalf of children, families, self, and others. Letting others know the importance of child care work.	

Ethics Case Studies[3]

After reading each ethics case study, write down what you think a school-age professional would do. Then plan a time to discuss your responses with your trainer and a group of colleagues. Discussion points are provided at the end of this module. There can be more than one ethical response to each case study.

1. The Abused Child

When 8-year-old Martha arrived at the program this morning, she had a large bruise on the back of her leg. This is the second time you've seen a bruise like this one. Her mother, who seems nervous and tense, says Martha gets bruises because she's going through an awkward stage and is always bumping into things and falling down. Yet you've never seen Martha do this at the program. When Martha comes back after school, she seems very withdrawn. When her father picks her up at the end of the day, he seems impatient and angry. Martha gathers her belongings very quickly and quietly. She and her father do not speak to each other. You are required by law to report suspected cases of child abuse to the appropriate authorities. However, you've heard that when authorities get involved, things often get worse: they don't seem to be able to help the children and families. In fact, one of your friends said some abusers get angry and take it out on the child because they think the child reported their behavior.

What should a school-age professional do?

_____

_____

_____

_____

_____

_____

---

[3] Adapted with permission from Stephanie Feeney, "Ethical Case Studies for NAEYC Reader Response," *Young Children* (Washington, DC: NAEYC, May 1987), pp. 24–25.

2. The Overwhelmed Parent

Ms. Donovan, wants her son Joey to spend his time in your school-age program doing homework. Joey is in fifth grade this year and has a lot of assignments every night. Ms. Donovan is a single parent who works during the day and takes courses at night. She says she has no time to help Joey with homework and wants to be sure it's done before she leaves for class. She is sure he will "goof off" and not complete his work at home with the teenage babysitter. Ms. Donovan is adamant that Joey should begin his work as soon as he arrives at the program—no playing around. If he finishes all his work before she arrives, then he can play, but not before then.

What should a school-age professional do?

_____

_____

_____

_____

_____

3. The Angry Child

Ten-year-old Bobby and his family recently moved to the area. On his first day in the program, he told you and the other kids, "Leave me alone and don't touch my things." Bobby is big for his age, with an athletic build. When children try to play with him or move through "his space," he gets angry very quickly—often hitting people or throwing things at them. You tried a number of positive guidance strategies, discussed the situation with your colleagues, and asked for your director's assistance. Nothing seems to work. You have mentioned the problem to his parents several times, but they think he's just getting used to living in a new place. They refuse to seek counseling for Bobby. A school-age specialist from the Department of Mental Health has observed Bobby, but her recommendations have not helped either. Meanwhile, the other children and parents are starting to complain. You are becoming stressed and tired, and your patience is wearing thin. You and your colleagues spend so much time dealing with Bobby that you worry the other children are not getting the attention they need.

What should a school-age professional do?

_____

_____

_____

_____

_____

4. The Neglectful Colleague

Cathy Johnson has been working with you for about six months. During this time you have become friends and see each other outside of work. Cathy is full of energy and enthusiasm and has lots of skills to share with children. She contributes creative ideas in program planning sessions and has a talent for making even the most ordinary day seem exciting. Today Cathy was responsible for supervising the activities in the gymnasium. Mrs. Juniper arrived early to pick up her son, Thomas, and you directed her to the gymnasium where he was playing volleyball. You reminded Mrs. Juniper to be sure to tell Cathy that Thomas was leaving. Mrs. Juniper came back a few minutes later with Thomas and said, "I looked for Cathy so I could tell her we were leaving, but she wasn't there. Thomas said Cathy went to call her mom." You know the program does not allow staff to leave children unsupervised. You also know Cathy's mom has been very sick, and Cathy's frequent calls cheer her up.

What should a school-age professional do?

_____

_____

_____

_____

_____

5. A Trip to the Bowling Alley

You take a group of children to the bowling alley. After bowling a few games, you run into some older children who are there alone. Ten-year-old Martin, one of the children in the school-age program, sees his older brother Neil and asks if he can go home with him. You don't have the program records with you, so you don't know if Neil is authorized to pick up Martin from the program. Neil insists their mother and father would not mind if Martin came home with him. He says convincingly, "We go places together all the time. My parents leave me in charge of Martin whenever they go out."

What should a school-age professional do?

_____

_____

_____

_____

When you have completed both parts of this activity, plan a time to discuss your responses with your trainer and colleagues. These are difficult situations to handle, and it will help you to discuss your ideas with others.

Learning Activity IV.
Becoming an Advocate for Children and Families

IN THIS ACTIVITY YOU WILL LEARN TO:

- recognize the importance of being an advocate for children and families; and

- become involved in advocacy efforts.

Advocacy is working for change. This often means speaking out on issues that may affect children and families or on issues that affect your own working conditions. Often, decisionmakers aren't aware of the problems and issues related to providing programs for school-age children. Without awareness and understanding, change is not possible. As a school-age professional, you are in a good position to help others appreciate important issues and concerns.

How You Can Become an Advocate[4]

A first step in becoming an advocate is to understand the importance of advocacy. This means recognizing how public and private policies affect children's lives and accepting that children need a strong voice to ensure the programs they attend support their development. Advocates must ask themselves: "What can I do to ensure adequate attention to children's needs by policymakers, elected officials, administrators, schools, businesses, and other groups?" Answering this question requires making a commitment to act.

Advocates try to improve the circumstances of children's lives so they get what they need to grow to their full potential. School-age professionals are well-informed on this issue in terms of both theory and practice. Advocates commit themselves to sharing their knowledge with others. They move beyond good intentions and take action, overcoming the fear of becoming involved. Because they realize the problems faced by children and families are a collective responsibility, they are willing to act on their concerns.

[4] Adapted with permission from Stacie G. Goffin and Joan Lombardi, *Speaking Out: Early Childhood Advocacy* (Washington, DC: National Association for the Education of Young Children, 1988), pp. 2-5.

As a school-age professional, you can become an effective advocate for children and families in at least six ways, as described below.

1. Share Your Knowledge

Your professional beliefs and knowledge are based on understanding all aspects of child development, on experience working with children, and on relationships with parents. Therefore, you can help those who develop policies to understand the developmental needs of children and the characteristics of safe and supportive environments. You can help decisionmakers understand the link between policy and enhancing children's development. As an advocate, you can become a catalyst for change.

2. Share Your Professional Experiences

You work with children and their families daily. You know when a family is under stress. When children and families receive services from community agencies, you can make a judgment as to whether children's needs are being met. As a result, you have the opportunity—and a professional responsibility—to share the personal stories that give meaning to group statistics. Personal experiences help professionals become more persuasive. Without sharing confidential information, school-age professionals can describe how policies affect children and families.

3. Redefine the "Bottom Line" for Children

The debate about programs for children is often tied to other policy issues such as welfare, job training, substance abuse, and teenage pregnancy. Funding for children's programs is often seen as an investment in children's future productivity.

Joining children's issues with broader political issues and social concerns is an effective political technique. It can expand the base of support and help frame children's issues in ways that are consistent with accepted social values.

Your unique perspective on children makes you an effective advocate for children's inherent "worth." You understand that childhood is a crucial time for development. If policies for children and families are devised solely on the basis of "return on investment," children will suffer when investors seek a higher return or decide to pull out of the "market." School-age professionals must remember these strategies are simply means to achieve a desired end. They must not undermine the "bottom line" of advocacy—encouraging policies that promote children's healthy development.

4. Stand Up for Your Profession

School-age care is a growing profession that provides a valuable service to children and their families. Therefore, school-age staff need to speak out on behalf of the profession—and for the special expertise required of a professional who works with children ages 5 through 12.

Many people don't know that providing out-of-school programs for this age group requires a professional knowledge base or that the quality of the program depends on the training and compensation of professionals in the field. School-age staff know how it feels when others view them merely as "babysitters" rather than as professionals. They need to share these stories, too. For example, one school-age staff member took a group of children to a public swimming pool when the pool was open to other patrons. The mother of a child who was not enrolled in the program asked her to "babysit" for her child while she went to the bathroom. The staff member politely responded, "I'd like to help you, but I am not these children's babysitter. We are from a professionally operated and staffed school-age program. I cannot watch your child because that would put me over the maximum number of children I can supervise."

Advocacy efforts on behalf of school-age programs are most effective when professionals emphasize the benefits of their work for children and families. School-age program staff must begin to exercise their own power to speak out on issues that affect their profession.

5. Involve Parents

Your daily interactions with parents provide many opportunities to share common concerns and goals for children's well-being. You are in a unique position to help parents recognize their power as children's primary advocates—for both their own and other people's children.

Parents can be especially effective advocates on behalf of their children. They represent a critical consumer voice. By involving parents, you can dramatically expand the group of people speaking out for children.

School-age professionals may have ongoing relationships with other individuals and agencies that provide services for children and families: public school administrators and teachers, health care providers, religious organizations, youth agencies, child care providers, and professional and volunteer groups. These interactions provide natural opportunities to inform others about the developmental needs of school-age children, appropriate programming for this age group, and the supports that families need.

6. Expand the Constituency for Children

You can choose from many courses of action once you make a commitment to become an advocate for children, their families, and your profession. Here are a few choices:[5]

You can take these advocacy actions.

- Share ideas for appropriate practice with other professionals and parents (instead of just observing disapprovingly).

- Explain to parents why children need time to relax, unwind, and play during school-age programs (instead of complaining parents are too concerned about homework and academics, or giving in and requiring children to spend much of their time studying).

- Help parents recognize that participating in recreational sports and leisure activities may lead to lifelong interests for their children (instead of complaining because parents don't seem interested in their children's activities).

- Exercise your democratic rights by voting for the candidate of your choice (instead of telling yourself that one vote can't make a difference).

- Advocate for local funding and support for school-age programs (rather than accepting that there is "not enough money" to provide children with a high-quality program in a well-stocked, appropriate environment).

- Learn how the legislative process works (instead of thinking you can't make a difference because you don't know how).

- Establish and/or participate in organizations of school-age professionals (instead of feeling frustrated by your isolation and wishing you had colleagues to call or meet with).

- Write a letter to the editor of a newspaper or magazine to respond to an article or letter (instead of just complaining about how other people don't understand the needs of children, their families, or those who work in school-age programs).

[5] Adapted with permission from Stacie G. Goffin and Joan Lombardi, *Speaking Out: Early Childhood Advocacy* (Washington, DC: National Association for the Education of Young Children, 1988), pp. 14-15.

- Meet someone new who is interested in working with school-age children, and ask her or him to join one of the professional groups listed in Learning Activity II (instead of just wondering why that person isn't involved).

- Write to your state or federal legislators about a pending issue and share your experiences as a way to point out needs (rather than just assuming someone else will write).

- Ask a friend to go with you to community meetings where issues of concern to children and families will be discussed (instead of staying home because you don't want to go alone).

- Volunteer to represent your professional group in a coalition to speak out on the educational and recreational needs of school-age children (instead of waiting to be asked or declining because you've never done it before).

- Work and learn with others. For example, join with colleagues at your program to write a position paper on a critical issue, such as why older children still need supervision or how programs like yours can help children develop the self-esteem they need to resist using drugs or alcohol (instead of saying " I don't really know much about this topic").

- Volunteer to speak at a school board meeting about professional standards for school-age programs (instead of resigning yourself to the fact that your school system doesn't understand much about the needs of children in the elementary and intermediate grades).

Applying Your Knowledge

In this activity you consider your own feelings about advocacy and develop a plan for becoming an advocate. Review the suggestions included in this learning activity, then answer the following questions.

Becoming an Advocate

What contributions would you like to make as an advocate for school-age children, families, and your profession?

_____

_____

_____

_____

What obstacles might prevent you from being an advocate, and how can you overcome them?

_____

_____

_____

_____

Describe below an advocacy step you can take this month:

_____

_____

_____

_____

Describe below an advocacy step you can take within six months:

_____

_____

_____

_____

Describe below an advocacy step you can take within a year:

_____

_____

_____

_____

Discuss your responses with your trainer.

Learning Activity V.
Taking Care of Yourself

IN THIS ACTIVITY YOU WILL LEARN TO:

- recognize the importance of taking care of yourself; and

- take care of yourself physically, emotionally, socially, and intellectually.

School-age staff need to be in good health.

Although your first responsibility as a school-age professional is to take care of the needs of children, you also have a responsibility to take care of yourself. All you have to give is yourself—your energy, your ideas, and your commitment. You cannot do this when you are not at your best. To work successfully with school-age children, you need to be in good physical and emotional health. You also need to feel you are appreciated, meaningfully connected to others, intellectually stimulated, and performing a job worth doing. Taking care of yourself means considering your needs and well-being in four areas: physical, emotional, social, and intellectual.

Physical well-being is very important to a person who works with school-age children. Without physical stamina, good health, and a good diet, you are not prepared to work with school-age children every day. Your overall health is influenced by three key factors: eating a healthy diet, getting enough sleep, and exercising regularly.

Your **emotional well-being**—the way you feel about yourself, your work, and the world—affects how you interact with the children and adults around you. The more positive you feel about yourself, the better you will be able to care for children. If you start to feel worried or depressed, it is good to talk with family and friends about your concerns.

Having people to talk to is essential for survival and **social well-being**. A trusted person with whom to share your joys, frustrations, concerns, and ideas, as well as successes can be very important in determining how you feel about yourself as a person and as a professional. The person may be a colleague, spouse, relative, or friend. What is important is that you have someone (at least one, but preferably several people) with whom you can exchange ideas, feelings, resources, and moral support.

Most of us enjoy learning something new and being challenged. Like children, our **intellectual well-being** increases with ongoing exploration, experimentation, and problem solving. The more you learn about working with school-age children, the more satisfying your work will become. This is what professionalism is all about.

In Module 2: Healthy, we discussed how stress affects children and what you and your colleagues can do to reduce children's stress and help them cope in positive ways. Most adults also find that stress—at work and in their personal lives—is a part of their daily routines.

The sources of stress in your life may differ from those of your colleagues. A situation one person finds stressful may not be for another. For example, you may feel very anxious when you get caught in traffic on your way to an appointment; a colleague might sit back, review his plans for the day, and enjoy listening to a new tape. Stress on the job may also affect you and your colleagues. Work-related stress might be due to situations such as:

- disagreeing with a colleague or supervisor;

- running out of materials in the middle of an activity;

- working with children who have many problems in their lives; or

- supporting a parent whose problems are overwhelming.

Some work-related stress can be alleviated through effective communication, improved adult-child ratios, or revised management practices ("From now on, we'll make sure we have sufficient supplies for the activities we plan to offer.") Other stressful situations are "part of the job." Working with school-age children is a challenging job. Even the most qualified and highly-skilled staff experience days when their jobs seem overwhelming.

How we respond to stress can affect our physical, emotional, social, and intellectual well-being. Some examples follow:

- Responses affecting your physical well-being might include:
    increased pulse, racing heart
    increased or decreased appetite
    excitability, hyperactivity
    always feeling tired
    difficulty relaxing, trouble sleeping
    difficulty staying awake

- Responses affecting your emotional well-being might include:
  feelings of inadequacy
  lowered self-esteem
  sadness, mild depression
  fear of losing control

- Responses affecting your social well-being might include:
  clinging to others
  withdrawing from others
  feeling angry with yourself and/or others
  being unusually impatient
  experiencing mood swings

- Responses affecting your intellectual well-being might include:
  having racing thoughts
  forgetting how to solve simple problems
  thinking about performing routine tasks (e.g., getting ready for work in the morning) rather than doing them automatically
  forgetting important events or responsibilities
  being easily distracted

It's almost impossible to eliminate all of the sources of stress in our lives. Instead, we need to cope in healthy ways so the stress does not lead to "burn-out." The responses listed above are "messages" that tell us we need to take better care of ourselves. The suggestions for helping children handle stress that appear in Module 2: Healthy, may also be useful for adults. Many people find eating a healthy diet, getting regular exercise, spending time with friends, and taking time to meet their own needs, can help them manage their stress.

When people don't cope with their stress, these responses may continue for a long time. For example, if a person is forgetful for a few days while handling a difficult situation, there is no cause for alarm. If the forgetfulness continues for weeks or months, the individual may need professional assistance. A mental health counselor can help the individual talk about the situation and learn to cope with stress in healthy, positive, and personal ways.

Applying Your Knowledge

In this learning activity you assess how well you are taking care of yourself. Record your activities for two days. For Day 1 record your activities for today. Then, review your answers, consider areas where you could take better care of yourself, and try to be better to yourself tomorrow. Record your improved activities under Day 2.

Taking Care of Myself

	Day 1		Day 2	
Physical Well-Being	yes	no	yes	no
Did I eat three balanced meals?	☐	☐	☐	☐
Did I get enough sleep?	☐	☐	☐	☐
Did I get any exercise?	☐	☐	☐	☐
Emotional Well-Being				
Did I have a generally positive outlook?	☐	☐	☐	☐
Did I take a few moments to relax after a stressful situation?	☐	☐	☐	☐
Social Well-Being				
Did I spend time with someone I care about?	☐	☐	☐	☐
Did I talk through a day's problem with a friend or colleague?	☐	☐	☐	☐
Intellectual Well-Being				
Did I read anything for information or interest—a book, an article, the newspaper?	☐	☐	☐	☐
Did I learn something new?	☐	☐	☐	☐

Discuss this activity with your trainer and make a commitment to take good care of yourself. Use the space below to note what actions you will take.

I will do the following to take care of myself:

_____

_____

_____

_____

_____

_____

SUMMARIZING YOUR PROGRESS

You have now completed all the learning activities for this module. Whether you are an experienced school-age staff member or a new one, this module has probably helped you maintain or renew a commitment to professionalism. Before you go on, take a few minutes to review your responses to the pre-training assessment for this module. Write a summary of what you learned, and list the skills you developed or improved.

_____

_____

_____

_____

_____

_____

_____

_____

_____

_____

_____

_____

_____

If there are topics you would like to know more about, you will find recommended readings listed in the Orientation in Volume I.

Your final step in this module is to complete the knowledge and competency assessments. Let your trainer know when you are ready to schedule the assessments. After you have successfully completed them, you will be ready to start a new module. Congratulations on your progress so far, and good luck with your next module.

ANSWER SHEETS

Maintaining a Commitment to Professionalism

Continually Assessing Your Own Performance

1. **How did Ms. Chavez assess her own performance?**

   a. She recognized that she lost control and responded to Julie's behavior inappropriately.

   b. She reflected on what might have caused her outburst and what she could do differently in the future.

   c. She wrote down her thoughts and conclusions.

2. **What did she decide to do with the results of her assessment?**

   a. She decided to discuss with her family ways to reorganize their evenings so she could get to bed on time.

   b. She resolved to use positive guidance in the future to help children learn to treat each other with respect.

Continuing to Learn About School-Age Children

1. **How did Mr. Sullivan decide what knowledge and skills he should work to improve?**

   a. He completed a self-assessment.

   b. He talked with Ms. Abrams, his supervisor, to identify areas for improvement.

   c. He set specific goals.

2. **How did Mr. Sullivan plan to expand his existing knowledge and skills?**

   a. He selected a module to review.

   b. He planned to attend in-service training.

   c. He planned an observation and feedback visit from Ms. Abrams.

   d. He scheduled a follow-up meeting with Ms. Abrams.

Applying Professional Ethics at All Times

1. **How did Ms. Johnson maintain professional ethics in talking to Danny's mother?**

   a. She greeted Ms. Perkins politely.

   b. She responded to Ms. Perkins' comments in a positive way.

   c. She maintained confidentiality by not discussing Billy's clothing with another parent.

2. **How did Ms. Johnson interact with Billy in a positive manner?**

   a. She recognized that Billy's feelings might have been hurt.

   b. She commented that Billy really liked what he was wearing and acknowledged it looked nice on him.

Ethics Case Studies: Discussion Questions

1. The Abused Child

Are there signs that indicate Martha might be a victim of child abuse?
If so, what do you think they are?

What should school-age staff do when they suspect a child is being abused?

2. The Overwhelmed Parent

How can you support Joey's need to be actively involved in activities at the school-age program and acknowledge Ms. Donovan's concerns?

How can the staff involve Ms. Donovan in resolving this situation?

3. The Angry Child

What additional information about Bobby might it be helpful to know?

Who should be involved in resolving this situation?

How can the staff address Bobby's needs without taking time and attention from the other children in the program?

4. The Neglectful Colleague

Why is it important to follow the program's rules?

How should staff respond when they think a colleague's actions might put children in jeopardy?

5. A Trip to the Bowling Alley

Is it ever okay to bend the program's rules?

How can staff help children understand the reason why some rules help keep them safe?

GLOSSARY

Competence   A skill or ability to do something well.

Ethics   A set of principles, standards, or guidelines that direct acceptable behavior—what is right or good rather than quickest or easiest.

Job description   An official written statement describing the responsibilities of a job.

Networking   Spending time with people who perform similar tasks to share ideas, information, and experiences.

Professionalism   A commitment to gaining and maintaining knowledge and skills in a particular field, and to using that knowledge and those skills to provide the highest-quality services possible.

Professional behavior   The consistent, thorough application of knowledge, skills, and ethics.

Ethics Case Studies: Discussion Questions

1. The Abused Child

Are there signs that indicate Martha might be a victim of child abuse?
If so, what do you think they are?

What should school-age staff do when they suspect a child is being abused?

2. The Overwhelmed Parent

How can you support Joey's need to be actively involved in activities at the school-age program and acknowledge Ms. Donovan's concerns?

How can the staff involve Ms. Donovan in resolving this situation?

3. The Angry Child

What additional information about Bobby might it be helpful to know?

Who should be involved in resolving this situation?

How can the staff address Bobby's needs without taking time and attention from the other children in the program?

4. The Neglectful Colleague

Why is it important to follow the program's rules?

How should staff respond when they think a colleague's actions might put children in jeopardy?

5. A Trip to the Bowling Alley

Is it ever okay to bend the program's rules?

How can staff help children understand the reason why some rules help keep them safe?

GLOSSARY

Competence

A skill or ability to do something well.

Ethics

A set of principles, standards, or guidelines that direct acceptable behavior—what is right or good rather than quickest or easiest.

Job description

An official written statement describing the responsibilities of a job.

Networking

Spending time with people who perform similar tasks to share ideas, information, and experiences.

Professionalism

A commitment to gaining and maintaining knowledge and skills in a particular field, and to using that knowledge and those skills to provide the highest-quality services possible.

Professional behavior

The consistent, thorough application of knowledge, skills, and ethics.

NOTES

NOTES

NOTES

NOTES

NOTES

NOTES

NOTES

NOTES

NOTES

NOTES